Strategy and Enterprise Value in the Relationship Economy

Strategy and Enterprise Value in the Relationship Economy

Bruce W. Morgan

VAN NOSTRAND REINHOLD
I(T)P® A Division of International Thomson Publishing Inc.

New York • Albany • Bonn • Boston • Detroit • London • Madrid • Melbourne
Mexico City • Paris • San Francisco • Singapore • Tokyo • Toronto

Copyright © 1998 by Van Nostrand Reinhold

I(T)P® International Thomson Publishing Company.
The ITP logo is a registered trademark used herein under license.

The ideas presented in this book are generic and strategic. Their specific application to a particular company must be the responsibility of the management of that company, based on management's understanding of its company's procedures, culture, re-sources, and competitive situation.

Printed in the United States of America

Visit us on the Web   www.vnr.com

For more information contact:

Van Nostrand Reinhold   Chapman & Hall GmbH
115 Fifth Avenue   Pappalallee 3
New York, NY 10003   69469 Weinham
                                         Germany

Chapman & Hall   International Thomson Publishing Asia
2-6 Boundary Row   60 Albert Street #15-01
London SEI 8HN   Albert Complex
United Kingdom   Singapore 189969

Thomas Nelson Australia   International Thomson Publishing Japan
102 Dodds Street   Hirakawa-cho Kyowa Building, 3F
South Melbourne 3205   2-2-1 Hirakawa-cho, Chiyoda-ku
Victoria, Australia   Tokyo 102 Japan

Nelson Canada   International Thomson Editores
1120 Birchmount Road   Seneca, 53
Scarborough, Ontario   Colonia Polanco
M1K 5G4, Canada   11560 Mexico D.F. Mexico

1 2 3 4 5 6 7 8 9 10 QEBFF 01 00 99 98 97

Library of Congress Cataloging-in-Publication Data

Morgan, Bruce W.
    Strategy and enterprise value in the relationship economy / Bruce W. Morgan.
       p.   cm.
    Includes index.
    ISBN 0-442-02625-0 (hc)
    1. Corporations—Valuation. I. Title.
HG4028.V3M66   1997
658.15—dc21   97-34866
                                                         CIP

Contents

Preface

Although it took some time for me to realize it, the origins of this book go back some twenty years. The text draws mainly from my diverse experiences as a financial economist, a university professor, a consultant on public policy, antitrust issues, and mergers and acquisitions, a financial valuation consultant, and a director and member of the audit committee of a public corporation.

The book was born of an unusual request: Could a client claim tax write-offs of a substantial premium it had paid to acquire the deposits of a failed bank? No precedent, in banking or elsewhere, existed. Thus began a long journey of investigation into the intangible sources of value in corporate enterprises. In time, it became clear that:

- Most market transactions involve buyers and sellers who maintain continuing relationships, often over long periods of time.
- The primary objective of competition in the marketplace is not simply to generate transitory transactions but to establish long-term market relationships.
- Once established, market relationships typically have substantial value, representing the future recovery of the investment in their development.
- Tax considerations aside, the very existence of relationship values requires their analysis in mergers and acquisitions.
- Essentially the same relationship principles apply within an enterprise as apply to its external relationships with customers and suppliers.
- A business enterprise seeking maximum shareholder value re-

quires management that fully understands the sources of that
value, including relationship values.

Many of these points first emerged in the context of banking, in major
part because of the large number of acquisitions in banking in the
1970s and 1980s. Clearly, however, these types of relationship values
permeate virtually all economic activity.

The material in this book evolved through a series of articles that
appeared primarily in banking journals. Next came the publication of
my *Foundations of Relationship Banking: Structuring Decisions
to Build Enterprise Value,* in 1994. I am indebted to Lafferty Publications Ltd., Dublin, Ireland, for recognizing the potential importance
of the concept of relationship capital. It has also graciously granted
permission to adapt some of the material in *Foundations* to the present work, for which I am further grateful. *Foundations,* of course,
contains a good deal of material specific to financial services that is of
little interest otherwise.

Publication of a book such as this one represents no more than a
rest stop—it can never really be complete. New ideas persist in bub-
bling to the surface and perspectives keep changing as new facts
emerge. I confess to a certain degree of happenstance in what relevant materials have or have not come to my attention. For whatever I
have overlooked that is important and relevant, I can only apologize.
To pursue each line of inquiry to a point that would satisfy the academic community would be never to complete the book. I also apologize to the extent that the book's many factual generalizations have not
sufficiently recognized that virtually all have important exceptions.

In addition to thanking my wife, friends, and colleagues who have
lent support to this project, I must particularly thank my literary
agent, Ruth Wreschner. Her exceptional perseverance saw this book
through, as she put it, an unusually difficult pregnancy. I am also
grateful to my publisher, John Boyd, and his organization for recognizing the potential significance of the book and for bringing it to
fruition. I also owe an expression of thanks to individuals who made a
point of bringing relevant material to my attention at various times. In
addition to the above, they include Dorsey Baskin of Arthur Andersen
& Co., John Bailey of Wellington Management, Gerry Ballinger of
MMM Direct, and Frank Wickersham of Falcon Group Worldwide and
The Senior Professional Foundation. In addition, my involvement with
The Professional Group, Inc., at George Mason University was helpful
in focusing on internal corporate relationships. I also am indebted to

some financial institutions, which must remain anonymous, for shar-
ing their views of outside management consultants. Finally, I must acknowledge my debt to my late colleague, Joe White, who worked with
me in the early days of developing procedures for valuing relationship
assets.

Introduction:
Trapped Inside the Box

> The ideas which are here expressed so laboriously are extremely simple and should be obvious. The difficulty lies, not in new ideas, but in escaping from the old ones, which ramify, for those brought up as most of us have been, into every corner of our minds.
>
> John Maynard Keynes, *The General Theory of Employment, Interest and Money* (1935)

THE PURSUIT OF PROSPERITY

Consider *prosperity* to be the sense of well-being that society extracts from economic activity. In contrast to instant gratification, it has a future dimension that extends at least through present lifetimes and probably to future generations. A relentless pursuit of prosperity is necessary simply to maintain it. Most societies seek to add to it. Nations seek to increase prosperity, primarily their own, but occasionally that of less advantaged nations as well. Organizations, and particularly business enterprises, pursue prosperity on behalf of their constituents or owners. Households and individuals devote most of their time and effort to that pursuit. Of course, its full achievement is elusive, as aspirations and expectations always exceed its current levels.

How to increase prosperity appeared rather simple a few generations ago, as it seemed to depend on the accumulation of more physical tools of production—transportation systems, factories and other structures for producing and distributing goods and services, machinery, equipment, and housing. In time, however, it became clear that even in the Industrial Age, prosperity requires much more than accumulating physical plant and equipment. Understanding that point has become ever more critical as more manufacturing moves abroad and

1

nonmanufacturing activities assume dominance in the most advanced economies. Yet Industrial Age concepts continue to guide economic policies and business strategies and decisions.

With a broader view of its sources, the pursuit of prosperity still means accumulating more wealth, ultimately in the form of capacity to produce goods and services. The measure of that success is the *value* that society assigns to the productive resources providing that capacity. Achieving prosperity thus means building value, and particularly the value embedded in business enterprises. For a corporation, its value to shareholders represents its capacity to create prosperity.

With the ascendance of nonphysical forms of productive resources, today's economy requires new approaches to pursuing prosperity. However much that pursuit may be a national or international objective, it depends mostly on how private enterprise defines its goals, the strategies it adopts to pursue them, and the criteria guiding business decisions. As becomes clear in exploring this subject, the business principles, conventions, and practices that currently guide most corporate enterprises are flawed. They unconsciously and unnecessarily impede the growth of prosperity by systematically squandering productive resources.

What follows is thus intended for, and indeed dedicated to, all members of society who seek a more prosperous future. In the corporate context, it is for all those members of the business and financial communities who seek ways to do a better job for shareholders.

An Emerging Global Village

The marketplace is shrinking in the sense that time and space impose ever fewer limits on production and distribution. Globalization is but a manifestation of a much more profound trend. Primarily, it is the ascendancy of a relationship economy—an economy representing a symbiosis of services and new information and communications technologies. Today's business environment is in a growing number of respects analogous to a village economy, although on a vastly larger scale.

One would expect economic upheaval such as is now occurring to provide a rich array of new opportunities; it does. It also injects substantial new complexities into the business environment. Communication, and the relationships facilitating it, become horizontal as well as vertical, both internally and between the enterprise and the outside world. The new economic village is not necessarily a cozy place.

Many corporate enterprises have had difficulty coping with the change, mainly due to their inability to comprehend it. Instead of seizing new opportunities, many have become defensive and dysfunctional, with a loss of meaningful strategic direction. A process of disengagement among and across organizational levels has become widespread. Employees no longer pretend to unreciprocated loyalty, nor can they have confidence in or respect for employers displaying no leadership. The consequences include an enormous waste of productive resources—real capital—within the corporate community and by society at large.

Such problems do not arise simply because of unawareness of the importance of economic relationships to a business. Ideas about strengthening customer and employee loyalty, for example, are hardly new. The problems lie, rather, in failing to recognize that traditional criteria for business decisions are inconsistent with the significance of those relationships. The prospects for addressing these shortcomings are not good for the near future. The tools actually are at hand, as the following chapters will demonstrate. What is likely to remain missing is sufficient commitment to address them—a commitment that requires breaking away from a comfortably familiar conceptual *status quo*.

In many respects, the new economic environment poses more challenges for larger enterprises, particularly for those producing and distributing retail goods and services. Correspondingly, the difficulties are probably less apparent for many smaller businesses, particularly for smaller manufacturers in the supply chain. The chief executives of small companies may themselves be the focal point of the entire enterprise communications network, internally and externally. In those cases, perhaps intuition and common sense are adequate substitutes for the more rigorous decision requirements that larger enterprises require.

The Best of Times, the Worst of Times

No matter how seemingly progressive, most corporations remain unconsciously hostage to obsolete business principles and practices. This condition perhaps matters little for the entrepreneurial members of the corporate community, at least for the present, but it can have devastating effects on more mature enterprises. A revolution in the economic order has displaced the environment from which those traditional principles and practices emerged. If they once seemed to work tolerably well, they no longer do so. Today they substantially and systematically subvert the most fundamental and essential corporate objective—the value of a corporate enterprise to its shareholders. They do so by applying short-term criteria to decisions having long-term consequences.

Ways of reversing this pattern to develop corporate enterprise values more fully are not inherently difficult to identify and adopt. With modest adjustments, they become well established and even familiar. Nevertheless, a decision framework to develop shareholder value directly first requires recognizing that many enterprises are performing well below their potential. Most companies are captives of conventions and assumptions that lacked adequate foundation from the outset. Whatever legitimacy those business conventions may once have had is vanishing. Too many corporate directors and chief executives seem to have difficulty comprehending and adjusting to what is, indeed, an economic revolution.

Why do so many leading corporations seem to disappear? According to one account, only about a third of the 500 largest U.S. corporations in 1970 remain in business today.[1] Why are corporate restructurings necessitated by disappointments with previous restructurings? Why do companies persist in engaging management consultants who, in promoting the latest fads in management theory, provide only quick fixes that quickly fail? Among the answers:

- Conventional business principles and practices have shallow roots on muddy hillsides. To endure, they need a solid foundation in fundamental social scientific principles—a true, comprehensive theory of enterprise management.
- Too many of the "solutions" for addressing the new business climate are conceptually shallow, retrogressive, narrowly focused, and out of touch with modern realities. An analogy is looking through the wrong end of a telescope.
- Insufficient accountability to shareholders allows some chief executives to sacrifice shareholders' long-term objectives in favor of their personal, shorter-term goals.

---

[1]John Mickelthwait and Adrian Wooldridge, *The Witch Doctors: Making Sense of the Management Gurus* (New York: Times Business, 1996), p. 7. Further references to this work appear in later chapters.

- A widespread absence of corporate strategic direction results both from an inability to comprehend the new economic environment and from too little focus on long-term objectives.
- Corporate directors and executives are in any event often slow to recognize needs for remedial action, tending to avoid it until too late for it to be effective.

A continual process of rolling out newer and sexier management fads impedes rather than facilitates the alignment of business principles with the changing marketplace. Corporate enterprises instead need a unified framework for pulling together the legitimate elements of disparate theories into something sensible and useful.

Corporate leaders today are off balance because they face an economy very different from that of a generation or two ago. One consequence is fertile ground for charlatanism. Exactly what has changed nevertheless often eludes description. Economic change is at least as much qualitative as quantitative. A historical comparison is the nineteenth-century transformation from an agricultural to an industrial economy. Now, as then, altogether new economic patterns have displaced once familiar ones. *The new economic order is a relationship economy dominated by services in combination with new information and communications technologies.*

Why is it so clear that the present economic transformation is widely misperceived and poorly understood? Consider evidence of failures to adapt:

- Most corporate executives continue to rely on inadequate and increasingly archaic and misleading measures of business condition and performance in formulating business strategies.
- Many corporate restructurings and mergers reportedly fail because of disregard for important *internal* elements of enterprise value, including experience, creativity, and corporate culture.
- Many also may fail because of disregard for important *external* components of enterprise value, particularly customer relationships.
- Many, and perhaps most, corporate mergers and acquisitions seem to yield disappointing results as measured, for example, by subsequent share prices.
- Management consultants are earning enormous fees to undo or

redo recently installed quality management, process reengineering, and other restructuring programs.

- Many corporate directors and chief executives seem unable to articulate any strategic direction for the enterprises they direct and manage, giving the investing public the impression that none exists.
- Many businesses rely for their survival on government corporate welfare and legal protections from competition.
- Persistent and extensive involuntary underemployment and widespread involuntary departures from the workforce indicate substantial wastage of valuable professional skills and experience.
- Public policies toward business and for promoting economic stabilization and growth similarly foster distortions in economic activity by persistently relying on archaic and flawed economic data.

A widespread absence of effective business strategies both reflects and is a cause of many of these problems. That absence is not so much from neglect as due to the impossibility of developing meaningful strategies without full understanding of what truly is a new and still unfamiliar economic environment.

A Relative View of Prosperity

Suggesting that the business community is struggling, too often unsuccessfully, may seem at odds with observed financial and economic performance. Conventional performance measures seem to indicate that the American economy, at least, has continued to grow while containing unemployment and inflation. Stock prices have risen to levels that were scarcely imaginable only a few years ago. By all measures, the American enterprise system is outrunning most of the rest of the world.

Indeed, if one considers the magnitude and pace of the economic transformation now underway, the American enterprise system has proved extraordinarily resilient. That resilience is due in no small part to the relative freedom with which market forces can assert themselves. Whatever its competitive shortcomings, the American marketplace is by far the world's most competitive. Much of the credit for the current level of prosperity is due to an enormous outpouring of entrepreneurship and innovation. In the United States, at least, competition quickly pushes corporate sluggards to the sidelines. Much of the

credit is also due to those many, often unremarked, enterprises that quietly tend to their business without making major mistakes.

Notwithstanding substantial displacements and disruptions, the process of economic change seems on balance to be working to the betterment of society. After all, improvement is normally essential if something new and different is to succeed in a competitive market-place. The mainstream of corporate society seems more on track than off it.

Substantial economic change nevertheless always has a dark side. It is typically ragged around the edges—highly uneven, confusing, poorly understood, and sometimes controversial. Certainly not every-one shares in the benefits, particularly in the short term. Modern ca-sualties arising from the inability and unwillingness to understand and adapt to new circumstances include large and small corporations and their shareholders as well as their employees. The business landscape is littered with the debris left by corporate directors and managers who fell behind. Unemployment and underemployment, especially among older workers, are far higher than any official figures indicate.

Shortcomings in conventional management principles and practices suggest that even those enterprises that currently seem healthy re-main vulnerable. The appropriate issue is therefore not simply whether or not an enterprise or a nation seems to be doing better than its rivals. Relying on such comparative thinking has at least two related pitfalls:

- The apparent advantage is often illusory. Competitive threats often go unnoticed until those undertaking new initiatives are far ahead of their rivals. The factors that launch them into the lead are often internal, and thus hidden from view, as well as external.
- As the pace of change accelerates, timely responses to new competitive conditions become increasingly difficult. The costs of falling behind are escalating, with rising levels of executive anxiety.

American automotive and consumer electronics manufacturers could hardly have been less prepared when the Japanese rose to dominate their markets. The perceived wisdom until much too late was that Japan was incapable of producing high-quality goods. Following a sim-ilar pattern, only IBM's vast resources enabled it to regain ground it lost by failing to perceive the significance of personal computers. Meanwhile, some retailers may never recover from how Wal-Mart burst onto the scene, offering high quality at low prices by adopting revolutionary supply networks. The stealthiness of new competition is perhaps even more of a threat in a relationship marketplace than in an industrial one.

Failure to adapt to economic change leads to enormous waste of economic resources. Too many corporations simply squander much of the capital their shareholders provide. They do so, usually unconsciously, by directing real investment to less rather than more productive uses. This pattern gradually opens the door to more astute, creative, and thus more competitive rivals. An economy tolerating a wastage of productive capacity can only be performing below its potential. That any single enterprise, or an entire nation, exhibits stronger financial or economic performance than others should not be a sufficient source of satisfaction. A more appropriate test is to compare actual with potential performance.

Over time, of course, competition shoves private-sector underperformers aside. Misuse and waste of capital deplete their ability to attract and retain it and thus their ability to remain competitive. They gradually fall further behind. Either they eventually restructure or disappear, or perhaps both. This process may be gradual if only because rivals are victims of the same misdirection, but it can be quite sudden.

In-the-Box Thinking

A common device in business schools and conferences is the concept of thinking *out of the box*. While perhaps it is already familiar, con-

The Box.

sider the following diagram, which consists of three rows and columns of dots evenly spaced horizontally and vertically.

The conceptual exercise is to draw four connected straight lines that connect all the dots. If you are not already familiar with the problem, try it before reading further.

Most people unfamiliar with the exercise will instinctively remain within the boundaries of the box formed by the grid of dots. The only solution, however, is to extend three of the lines beyond those boundaries, as follows.

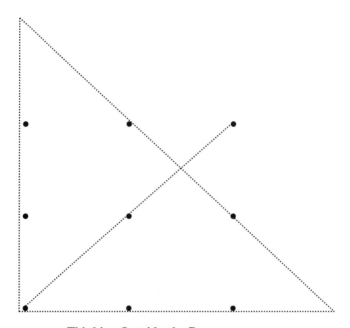

Thinking Outside the Box.

Thinking *inside the box* means being hostage to convention or perceived wisdom. It is to be tied to old, familiar, and perhaps obsolete verities. It therefore signifies clinging to the status quo, avoiding and even rejecting what is new or unfamiliar. It is "establishment" thinking, bounded by rules that are often subconscious. That most people instinctively accept the imaginary boundaries of the box suggests that in-the-box thinking is more natural—an inherent part of the human condition.

If so, it follows that one must force oneself into out-of-the-box thought patterns. Doing so is to become more receptive to possibilities beyond imaginary boundaries. It need not represent imagination and creativity so much as an appreciation of those qualities and a commitment to putting them to use. In the business world, it is the wellspring of competitive initiatives, including innovation in products, services, uses of internal resources, and corporate organization. Breaking loose from the box is what enables an enterprise to break out of the pack, sprint ahead of its rivals, and leave them behind.

One might think that a capacity for out-of-the box thinking is something that a business enterprise should seek to attract and nurture. Alas, the reality is often quite different. A more natural tendency is to hold tightly to sets of principles and practices whose primary qualification is that they worked in the past. Entrapment in the box is typically unconscious. The difficulty is that thinking out of the box means considering possibilities that threaten what is familiar and comfortable.

Encountering a New Economic Order

If a business avoids or resists out-of-the-box thinking, it will miss recognizing and responding to important changes in its environment. Most current business practices developed in the context of an industrial economy—an economy dominated by the manufacture and distribution of physical goods. Today's economic reality is radically different. Somewhat more than two thirds of the *private* (nongovernment) output of the American economy consists of services. In addition, manufacturing and other traditionally nonservice activities are incorporating more service elements. Similar patterns are emerging in the more advanced European and Asian economies.

Part of this transformation arises from manufacturing moving abroad, particularly to locations with lower labor costs. Another cause seems to be that consumers in the advanced economies are approaching satiation with physical goods. They are instead placing more emphasis on the quality of life, including their health and their use of leisure time. They also place more importance on the quality of the goods and services they purchase than on mere quantity, effectively becoming gourmets rather than gourmands. One aspect of this growing emphasis on quality is to attach more importance to the services supporting sales and uses of physical goods. After all, durable goods, in particular, are simply embodiments of services that they will provide over time.

Accompanying this movement toward higher quality and more services is a shift in market balance between sellers and buyers. Consumers, in particular, are sovereign as never before. They demand, and expect, more customizing of goods and services to their individual needs and preferences. Thus, along with the growth in the relative importance of services is growth in the significance of the information and communications technologies enabling that customization. This conjunction of services and technology is the defining element of the emerging relationship economy. Manufacturing, of course, is hardly fading into the sunset, but it will never again be the dominant factor in advanced economies.

Opportunities from Economic Revolution

To appreciate how formidable a task the adjustment to the emerging economic order might be, think of it as representing a transformation every bit as dramatic as the Industrial Revolution of the nineteenth century. The term *revolution* implies the *replacement* of a political, social, or economic order with something radically different. The differences, indeed, are often dramatically at variance with what their perpetrators envisioned or intended. For example, the developers of the early electronic computers hardly foresaw how they would transform society within only a couple of generations. Perhaps today's emphasis on upgrading technological skills will prove tomorrow to have been exaggerated.

One unnerving aspect of economic change is how it has accelerated. Significant economic change seems to have begun when humankind shifted from mere food gathering and hunting to farming and husbandry. This process surely was revolutionary in a local context. Globally, of course, it occurred over many centuries. The next significant step was an occupational shift from agriculture to small-scale manufacturing and trade. Again, however, the process was piecemeal.

Much later, a facilitating factor in the initial stages of the Industrial Revolution was a large supply of labor, made possible first in Britain and later in other European countries, by increasing efficiency in agriculture. Industrialization initially meant new uses of labor resources more than a substitution of machines for labor. The temporary surge in available labor caused by these shifts very likely was the source of the Marxist reserve army of labor theory. Marx argued that capitalism thrives by exploiting labor because it tends to be in excess supply.

The early American experience was nevertheless very different.

Persistent shortages of labor limited American manufactures until well into the nineteenth century. Labor shortages caused by the lure of the frontier led to interchangeable parts manufacturing—a forerunner of the production line—first being developed in American clock and firearms production. Only with large waves of immigration and the closing of the frontier did the United States begin to develop into an industrial powerhouse.

A historical perspective leads to an intriguing question: What would today's economy look like were it not for the emergence of new services and information technologies? The result would surely not reflect preservation of the old order. Rather, it would be a more dramatic transformation of a very different sort, namely, sustained economic depression and stagnation.

A major cause of the Great Depression of the 1930s was public policy, particularly in the form of trade barriers, that constrained the ability of American industry to reach its potential. Today, instead, the economic system, and particularly the American economy, has given rise to extraordinary new opportunities for those able to recognize and seize them. The current vitality of American economic performance relative to its European and Asian rivals is undoubtedly due in major part to more open and vigorous competition. Misguided public policies still inject impediments, but the primary constraints lie within the business community itself.

Another unnerving aspect of economic change, in addition to its long-term acceleration, is that it tends to be anything but smooth and even. Rather, economies have a tendency to lurch from one set of circumstances to another. Indeed, while long-term trends seem to be upward, in the sense of growing output, backsliding often occurs in the short term. Why the process is so uneven is unclear, although the explanations certainly include a good deal more than traditional economics. In part it seems due to the resilience of defunct social institutions that must stretch to a breaking point before giving way.

Responding to Accelerating Change

The following propositions regarding the present economic climate are fundamental and should be incontrovertible:

- The business environment throughout the world is undergoing dramatic, unpredictable, and perhaps discontinuous economic transformation.

- However breathtaking the pace of economic change, it continues to accelerate.
- The accelerating pace of change reflects the accelerating accumulation of knowledge and information.
- Services, broadly defined, are the predominant component of the new economic order.
- Information and communication are essential to the functioning of a service economy.
- New information and communications technologies are therefore fundamental elements in the emerging marketplace.

A common thread in these patterns is the emerging importance of economic relationships, whence the concept of a relationship economy.

Prior to the present century, economic relationships at the household level consisted mainly of direct personal contacts with local retail and service outlets—the village model. Also mostly at a personal level, even if not so localized, were relationships among enterprises engaged in manufacturing, finance, and trade. These economic relationships largely reflected geographical constraints on commercial activity. Still, even in their relatively simple forms, economic relationships substantially increased the efficiency of communication between buyers and sellers. Equally important, they also imparted more certainty to expectations regarding the outcomes of transactions and future dealings.

This pattern began to change with the development of media advertising, which promoted the establishment of *impersonal* relationships with remote sellers. Advertising essentially reflects the impersonal nature of an industrial economy. One might argue that the emergence of an industrial economy was actually a setback to the development of economic relationships. Industrialization connoted mass production to achieve maximum cost economies in competing for mass markets. It usually required centralizing manufacturing in locations having access to energy, labor, and raw material supplies; thus, these were often remote from the business's ultimate customers. Much of the ability to communicate that is essential to economic relationships consequently was lost, awaiting the emergence of new technologies.

Thus, for generations, industrialization meant relatively standardized, homogeneous products, and few alternatives from which to choose. If a particular model became popular, rival manufacturers were more likely to seek to emulate it rather than to differentiate their own offerings. Design engineers sought to shape, rather than to respond to, customer preferences. Exemplifying this product-push mentality, Henry Ford reportedly remarked that his customers could have any color car they wanted as long as it was black.

At some risk of overgeneralization, sellers in that industrial economy tended to know remarkably little about their customers. They had no need to know more. Marketing was above all directed toward selling products, in the sense of pushing them off the shelves. The available production and distribution technologies did not permit much tailoring to differences in needs and preferences.

The primary competitive parameter was pricing, and price competition meant low costs enabled by mass production and product homogeneity. Many goods and services would otherwise have been unaffordable to most consumers. Mass production required mass markets with homogeneous preferences. Indeed, the product-push mentality was not limited to manufactured goods—it extended to many services as well. Even today, markets for consumer financial services remain segmented more according to types of services than to differences among customers.

Further widening the gap between sellers and the marketplace was the evolution of the pyramidal form of corporate organization. The only apparent means of imparting coherent direction to large organizations was the establishment of hierarchical layers of management and administration, with responsibilities becoming narrower and more detailed at successively lower levels. Communication within this traditional form is primarily vertical, extending from each level to immediate subordinates. As eventually became apparent, both internal and external corporate communications tend to bog down as layers of administration proliferate. One by one, many giant corporations became ossified—structurally incapable of responding to economic change without massive restructuring.

Economic relationships supported by new information and communications technologies create entirely new and different business conditions. Later chapters explore in detail why and how this is so and develop a framework for responding effectively to altered conditions. For now, simply consider the present a period of rapid change and information overload. Value thus attaches to mechanisms that allow sellers and buyers, employers and employees, and investors and corporations to understand better and to anticipate one another's needs. Economic relationships have value because they perform this function. The prospect of that value attracts investment in its development. As a result, economic relationships are a substantial and growing component of business capital—real capital in the sense of contributing to production and distribution by adding value and reducing costs. Without economic relationships, the economic corpus would be a body without a nervous system.

The Attractions of Staying Inside the Box

In view of the widespread attention the concept receives, why does much of the business community have so much difficulty with thinking out of the box? The logic of accepting new ideas to address new circumstances will not alone cause a realignment in business principles and practices. Shortcomings in true management skills may be, and probably are, impediments. The primary difficulty, however, lies much deeper.

Consider some common business certitudes:

- The appropriate objective of a business enterprise is to maximize profits.
- Maximizing reported earnings is the same as, or at least a close approximation of, maximizing profits.
- Maximizing profits or earnings promotes the objectives of corporate shareholders.
- Most of the value of a corporate enterprise derives from its physical capital and proprietary technology.

They are familiar, comfortable, and thoroughly institutionalized. They are the beacons that guide business and investment decisions. They are also wrong. Why, then, do they remain so intact and ubiquitous?

Confronting change requires confronting natural human tendencies to resist what is new and unfamiliar. The first level of resistance is to avoid recognizing it.[2] Once recognition becomes unavoidable, the next level is to resist adapting to it, perhaps simply wishing it away. The next step when that fails is to erect defenses around the old order. Eventually, as those defenses break down, threats of dire consequences otherwise *may* induce yet higher levels of recognition and response. Nevertheless, as the urgency of ascending to higher levels increases, casualties tend to rise. Reaching the highest level

---

[2]A helpful discussion of this topic in a business context is Bert Decker's *You've Got to Be Believed to Be Heard* (New York: St. Martin's Press, 1992).

of response, which is to *anticipate* changes in the environment, is rare.

Resistance to change seems to arise from a subliminal perception that anything departing from accumulated experience is potentially threatening and therefore to be avoided. Overcoming this instinctive defense mechanism requires consciously forcing oneself across that visceral barrier so as to process the new inputs through one's cognitive faculties. It requires understanding that rationalizing deferral and avoidance often seems easier and more comforting than confrontation. The threat may indeed be very real, as in many cases of corporate downsizings and restructurings, but the consequences of delaying responses are often much worse.

A classic example of failure to recognize and adapt to new circumstance is how World War I bogged down in trench warfare. Few military commanders comprehended that defensive weaponry, notably the machine gun, had gained overwhelming superiority over offensive weaponry, mainly rifle-carrying infantry. Each side launched one hopeless offensive after another, the only result over many months being enormous casualties. A redress in the balance of weaponry emerged only toward the end of the war, with the introduction of armored vehicles. Even then, however, some military strategists continued to cling tenaciously to outdated concepts. The builders of the Maginot Line obviously had no comprehension of blitzkrieg warfare. Today, how many corporations seem to be building their own Maginot Lines?

Realistically, the process of evading change is rather like the Corps of Engineers continuing to shore up the Mississippi River levees. One way or another, Nature always succeeds eventually in altering the river's course. The greater the resistance to this process, the more dramatic the consequences when the levees finally give way. Count on it. Floods along the Mississippi will become more damaging over time.

Why dwell on this topic? Decision guidelines appropriate to a relationship economy require rethinking and modernizing more than a century's accumulation of perceived wisdom. However familiar many of the components of those new guidelines, the end result is something new, to which the expected if visceral reaction is skepticism. A frequent reaction to suggesting the falseness of the foregoing business certitudes is likely to be to cling to and defend them even more tenaciously. The chapters that follow thus require a *cognitive* reception if the effort is to be worthwhile.

Breaking Out of the Box

Think of a break-out strategy as one breaking out in front of a pack of competitive conventions, leaving it behind altogether. In a business context, such a strategy is a framework for anticipating and controlling events so as to achieve certain corporate objectives. Failure to anticipate is to concede control and fall behind. Rather clearly, break-out business strategies require out-of-the-box thinking. Someone once observed that a major wave of economic change divides the business community into two segments: one builds higher sea walls while the other grabs its surfboards.

The newly emerged relationship economy requires a revised set of business principles bound together in a unified business theory. The reason is the *investment* nature of developing economic relationships. The benefits of this investment normally extend well into the future. As virtually all significant management decisions impact on the development and retention of economic relationships, they automatically become investment decisions. Properly evaluating investment alternatives requires decision criteria representing *value* objectives, not just conventional profit or earnings goals, if it is to recognize the future dimensions of those alternatives.

These considerations require breaking loose from many common surrogates for shareholder value that exist only in the imagination. Confronting the emerging economy successfully—developing and implementing break-out strategies—requires focusing *directly* on shareholder values. Forget substitutes, approximations, and the like. Each management decision must be based on what it contributes to shareholder value. Shareholder values, moreover, must represent the predominant corporate objective. Compromises with shareholder value objectives erode the ability of an enterprise to attract and retain capital. Over time they correspondingly erode its ability to remain competitive.

A growing number of corporations are at least attempting to focus more directly on measuring enterprise performance by estimating changes in shareholder values. Chapter 7 discusses economic value added, or EVA, which seems to be the most popular approach to developing such performance measures. Many of the major management consultancies are promoting it, and some of the largest corporations are adopting it. EVA also is gaining attention among financial analysts. The good news for investors is that more direct attention on shareholder values represents the wave of the future. The bad news is that current methods of estimating these changes are for the most part flawed, often fatally. Their primary weakness is their failure to recognize the significance of economic relationships as invested capital. On balance, the good news outweighs the bad, which in turn is bad news for those who fail to redirect their efforts toward promoting shareholder values, and who consequently will encounter increasing difficulties in obtaining capital.

Objectives and Focus of this Book

An author must simultaneously decide at the outset what, how, and for whom to write. Given the subject matter—in this case, how to compete successfully in a relationship economy—the manner of addressing it depends on for whom it is written. Identifying the intended reader is the most important choice. On yet a higher level, a logical starting point is to address what the subject is all about, and why is it important, and to whom is it most important. Then, if the subject really is important, what issues does it raise, and how are they to be addressed?

Too many business books point to the importance of recognizing and adapting to changes, as in production and distribution techniques or in market conditions, without rigorously addressing how best to respond. Others immerse themselves in how to respond without adequate analysis of the circumstances requiring responses. In both cases, common practice after perhaps forty or so pages is to fall back on examples and anecdotes rather than seek to identify the relevant underlying business principles. One could leaf through any number of such exercises and easily conclude that no unifying principles exist.

To be sure, as new books on the subject keep appearing, it does seem that the significance of customer relationships in marketing is attracting some attention. The same seems true of employee relationships. Also, the financial press suggests that more corporations are discovering, or rediscovering, their shareholders and the importance of attending to shareholder values. Many corporate downsizing and other restructuring programs purportedly reflect this concern, even when the consequences are perverse. Meanwhile, after falling into disrepute, corporate strategic planning is showing signs of reincarnation.

Yet how many corporate executives or their advisors could comfortably answer the following questions, all of which are part of the focus of later discussion?

- What are the business implications of the transformation from an industrial to a relationship (service or information-age) economy? How has this transformation altered the relative positions of various participants in that economy? What does that imply for their own business strategies?
- Why *must* the overriding business objective normally be to maximize shareholder values? What decision criteria assure promoting that objective? What are the legitimate interests of other stakeholders? Does giving overriding priority to shareholder values compromise those interests?
- What is the *economic* significance of market relationships that explains the value attaching to those relationships? What do acquisition premiums, franchise values, and dilution factors in business combinations actually represent? Can one identify and value them directly?
- Why do the value characteristics of economic relationships matter to business strategies and management decision making? What are the underlying sources of value of a business to its shareholders, in terms of assets and liabilities? Can one truly manage a business without a full understanding of those value components?
- Why *must* different concepts and measures of shareholder (enterprise) value, including those in common use by investment bankers and security analysts, ultimately converge with the net market value of underlying tangible and intangible assets and liabilities? What does this convergence imply for business strategies and investment decisions? What does it imply about managing a business to achieve shareholder value objectives?
- Why and how are conventional business decision criteria, as well as common measures of business condition and performance, becoming increasingly meaningless and irrelevant? How does one explain the demonstrable fact that those criteria and measures remain intact even while seriously distorting management and investment decisions and subverting shareholder values?
- What sort of comprehensive strategic and decision-making framework can fully capture the defining elements of the emerging economy in a way that relates decisions *directly* to strategic objectives? What constitutes a workable and relevant synthesis of management theory with the emerging reality?

The focus of the book is therefore on:

- Understanding the key characteristics of today's economy
- Identifying those conventional business criteria that require modification to be responsive to those characteristics
- Developing an integrated, comprehensive decision framework that will enable appropriate and creative responses to economic change
- Implementing strategies for building shareholder value by gaining maximum advantage from this unfamiliar economic environment

One recurring theme is the supremacy of shareholder value objectives and the value contributions of economic relationships as represented by capital. Another is the provision of a comprehensive business theory to guide business strategies and management decisions. The result is essentially a guide to value-based strategies and decision making in a relationship marketplace. Moreover, because of their focus on enterprise values, the resulting business principles should provide new guidance for securities analysts and investors.

Many of the ideas running through the discussion will, and should, seem familiar. Those business principles that are truly fundamental remain intact—it is the manner of their application that requires adjustment. For example, the significance of maximizing shareholder values is certainly a familiar one. What requires revision is the widespread assumption that the seemingly simpler objective of maximizing earnings is a valid substitute. The criteria for business investment decisions concerning relationship development derive directly from long-established and familiar approaches to analyzing plant and equipment investment opportunities. Similarly, many concepts associated with intangibles in the forms of patents, trademarks, and copyrights are likely to be familiar. The same concepts carry over to economic relationships, which are themselves intangible assets of a business.

None of this is to say that implementing a value-based decision framework for a relationship environment will be easy. It certainly will not produce illusions of quick fixes of the sort promised by too many consultants. After all, even the pursuit of earnings goals tends to be full of compromises and approximations. Conflicting goals often intrude and information on which decisions rely is often inadequate. Still, it seems worthwhile to establish a sense of direction and to begin to ask more relevant questions, even if all the answers are not readily at hand.

Who Needs This Book?

Having come this far, a reader might ask what is really new here. Promoting schmoozing with customers (and suppliers) certainly is not new, as a visit to any bookstore with a selection of business books will attest—one need only scan the titles. Similarly, corporate professions of attentiveness to shareholders have recently become so fashionable in the United States that foreigners are beginning to take notice.

All such discourse is incomplete, however. Business principles have too often been a random collection of different and often conflicting ideas and fads. While sometimes lost in the muddle, the requisite building materials are at hand, but without the architectural design. What has been missing, and what this book provides, apparently for the first time, is a comprehensive strategic framework from which to derive practical guideposts for business decisions. Basically, this book is for those who believe in the necessity of instilling more strategic thinking into corporate direction. Correspondingly, it is for those who truly attach significance to shareholder value objectives as the primary goal of corporate strategies.

Who needs this book? *Need* does not mean simply finding the material interesting or entertaining. Rather, *need* means that applying its principles is necessary for long-run competitive survival. Because economic relationships impact virtually every aspect of management, those needing to understand the principles set forth in this book include:

- Corporate directors and senior executives responsible for providing the strategic vision necessary to navigate their organizations through turbulent new waters
- Corporate managers responsible for developing the information and analysis necessary for responsive decision making
- Outside consultants offering advice on developing and implementing business strategies, including consultants on information design, management organization, marketing, and executive compensation
- Financial practitioners concerned with any aspect of enterprise values, including investment bankers, stockbrokers, in-

surance underwriters, and credit analysts, and the investing public at large
- Government officials responsible for business regulation or otherwise monitoring business activity
- Government officials responsible for compiling measures of business activity that serve as the basis for economic stabilization and growth policies
- The financial press, whose commentaries often need closer alignment with economic realities

Also, while directing the book toward a general audience, a dearth of academic treatments of its subject matter suggests adding:

- Business schools, if they are ever to integrate disparate academic disciplines and subject matter into unified sets of business principles
- Economists, many of whom have yet to break loose from now irrelevant nineteenth-century conceptions of enterprise and the marketplace

Ultimately the purpose of this book is to promote the pursuit of prosperity. More proximately, it is to promote better understanding of enterprise resources, and thus more effective resource utilization and investment, which should benefit the entire business community and society at large.

Organization of the Material

Part 1 of the book explores in further detail what a relationship economy represents and implies. Is today's economy really so different from what preceded it? Are revised sets of rules necessary to confront it? Is this emergent economy treacherous for those who fail to understand it? Part 1 concludes by emphasizing the unavoidable need for corporate enterprises to engage seriously in strategic thinking and developing business strategies.

Part 2 addresses various institutional constraints on out-of-the-box thinking. However inadvertently, economists tend to reinforce those constraints, in part by bestowing apparent legitimacy on further constraints imposed by accounting conventions. The resulting misperceptions spill over into financial analysis and investment banking as well as into management theory and consulting.

Part 3 discusses the objective of maximizing shareholder values and the direct linkage of that objective to the underlying value elements of a corporate enterprise. It gives particularly detailed attention to the characteristics of its relationship capital. This discussion lays the basis for part 4, which addresses some practical aspects of developing and implementing a value-oriented strategic program. Part 4 concludes by briefly discussing some recent public policy issues on which misunderstanding of relationship capital has distorted debate.

PART 1

Ascendance of the Relationship Economy

The capital of all the individuals of a nation is increased in the same manner as that of a single individual, by their continually accumulating and adding to it whatever they save out of their income.

Adam Smith, *The Wealth of Nations* (1776)

1

The Invisible Wealth of Nations

A TRANSITIONAL VIEW OF WEALTH AND CAPITAL

Adam Smith, in *The Wealth of Nations,* emphasized that national wealth and prosperity depends on capacities to produce goods and services. For individuals and businesses as well as for nations, enhancement of those capacities requires saving—refraining from consumption—so as to accumulate additional means of production. Although Smith was ahead of his time in recognizing the significance of the organization of production and labor skills, his concern was primarily with investment in trade goods (inventory) and producer goods (plant and equipment).

Smith's inquiry gives rise to two observations. First, in confronting circumstances similar to those now at hand, his work was a direct attack on the prevailing economic thought of his day. Most Europeans thought of national wealth as the accumulation of gold and silver bullion. That view, like today's preoccupation with profits, had a certain amount of historical legitimacy. Up to the early seventeenth century, gold and silver were the currencies by which sovereigns could raise armies and wage wars. Even well after Smith's time, Spain diligently continued to ply the Main with treasure ships, oblivious to an economic stagnation from which it even now has never fully recovered.

Second, Smith pioneered inquiries into why some nations and societies are more prosperous than others, even with similar natural resource endowments. He thus addressed a problem that remains unresolved even today, more than two centuries later. The lamentable fact is that no one, including the economists, truly knows how to launch sustainable economic development programs in Third World countries. Vast amounts of foreign aid have gone to waste simply because no one knows how to use it effectively.

Economists define three types of productive inputs, or factors of production—natural resources (land), labor, and capital. Conceptually, *capital* represents any form of output whose purpose is to increase future output. It therefore represents refraining from consuming some amount of current output. In other words, instead of consuming, or using up, all the current output, some is saved to become investment to increase future output. *Real investment* means additions to a stock of real capital for use in production. Neither *investment* nor *capital* refers only to physical (fixed) capital such as plant, equipment, and inventories. They are simply the most familiar forms of capital. Common discourse and public policy nevertheless often fail to break loose from the restrictive concept of capital as predominantly physical.

Reflecting concerns with potential for economic development, and recognizing the importance of forms of capital in addition to plant and equipment, the World Bank has adopted a broader view. It now measures the resources available to a nation for producing goods and services by defining four categories:

- *Produced capital,* including machinery, factories, roads, water systems, and other physical components of a nation's infrastructure.
- *Natural capital,* consisting of natural resources such as raw land, minerals, timber, water, and other environmental assets.
- *Human resources,* represented by the education levels, experience, and skills of the population.
- A residual category that, like accountants' *goodwill,* reflects value that otherwise remains unexplained but that at least includes social institutions that enhance productive capacity.

The real capital of a business enterprise typically includes most or all of these same components.

An apparent omission, from the standpoint of a nation's wealth, is net credit claims on foreigners. Financial claims simply represent who owns real capital and are not themselves capital in that sense. They do, however, represent opportunities for one nation to obtain additional national resources from others. Similarly, a business may have claims on others that would enable it to add to its real capital, although most businesses are net borrowers.

The first three categories are traditional. Significantly, produced capital, such as plant and equipment, may not be the most important category; the Bank estimates that it typically accounts for only about 20 percent of national wealth, even without inclusion of the amorphous fourth category.

The Bank at least recognizes that the first three categories fall well short of explaining national production capacity. It has yet to develop measures of value for the fourth category, or even to define it fully. It does specifically include social and political institutions, which obviously have major roles to the extent of providing services and stability. The Bank thus perceives the enormous and growing significance of some nonphysical forms of capital, including social overhead.

The Bank does not seem to understand that nonphysical as well as physical capital has substantial private as well as public (or social) counterparts. A specific major shortcoming is failure to recognize the significance of proprietary information and technology, yet at least some forms of such intellectual property, including patents and copyrights, otherwise have a long history of recognition as nonphysical forms of capital. Although developing nations, which are the Bank's primary focus, tend not to be significant repositories of proprietary technologies, they do possess substantial quantities of information important to commercial activity and relationships.

The level of a society's education, including its nonproprietary (as well as proprietary) technology, has enormous impact on the quality of its culture and institutions and on its productive capacity. Much of that value adheres to households and individuals as enhanced income potential. Business investment in training and continuing professional education nevertheless suggests that a significant portion of the resulting value must remain with employers as well. Competition, in other words, often does not raise compensation levels sufficiently to confer the entire value on employees. Some of that value is often so specific to a particular employer that an employee cannot transfer it to a different work environment.

Economic relationships—those linking different participants in the marketplace—also may be private as well as public or social, although only the latter seem thus far to have attracted the Bank's attention. The effectiveness with which its institutions serve a society depends on the extent and quality of relationships among its members. Adam Smith understood more than 200 years ago that the social relationships reflected in a nation's system of government are important determinants of the economic vitality of communities and societies.

The World Bank's classifications, while a step forward in recognizing the variety of forms of productive resources, otherwise provide little clue to the significance of relationship capital to private economic activity. Relationship capital in the business community, and the economic relationships they represent, take a variety of forms:

- Market relationships between actual and potential buyers and sellers. This category includes labor markets as well as markets for products and services.
- Relationships between businesses and governments, both as buyer-seller relationships and for influencing legislation, regulation, and other administrative actions.
- Relationships among business enterprises other than those of buyers with sellers, ranging from legitimate joint ventures and partnerships to collusive arrangements that violate antitrust laws.
- Relationships between suppliers and users of business capital, as between corporations and investment community.
- Horizontal as well as vertical relationships within enterprises that facilitate production and generate new ideas and sources of information.

A neat hypothetical model might differentiate between internal and external business relationships. Internal economic relationships extend vertically from shareholders to the corporate directors, from the directors to the chief executives, and finally through the management ranks to employees. In other words, the shareholders are the ultimate buyers of management and employee services. Internal relationships may also extend horizontally across different layers of responsibility. In addition, a business enterprise is a nexus of various external relationships with customers, suppliers, the financial markets (excluding current shareholders), the labor market, other enterprises with which it might have joint venture or partnership relationships, and government.

Understand, however, that delineations tend to blur in discussing these concepts. They particularly tend to do so with internal relationships. For example, are shareholders truly buyers of corporate chief executives, as the corporate governance ideal prescribes? Alternatively, to what extent do those chief executives essentially buy their corporate directors?

External market relationships between buyers and sellers have legitimate claim to center stage in discussing these concepts, for a number of reasons:

- In major part because of the emerging dominance of services in the economy, external market relationships between buyers and sellers are much the largest component of relationship capital in the private sector.
- The unperceived nature and economic significance of this form of capital are the primary reasons why conventional business principles require reconsideration.
- They are in many respects the least understood of the various forms of relationship and other intangible capital.
- The principles applying to external market relationships apply to the others as well.
- External market relationships also are likely to be of the most widespread interest, impacting directly on competition in product and service markets as well as on business relationships with the investment community.

Of course, no corporate enterprise seeking to come to terms with the new economic climate can overlook its internal relationships. To do so can be fatal. The point, rather, is that the emerging significance of external relationships is the driving force behind the emergence of today's relationship economy.

Real Investment as the Defining Economic Characteristic

Capital, as economists conceive it, is essentially anything that enhances production beyond what is obtainable from natural resources and physical labor. In common usage, however, *capital* often refers to financial claims rather than to productive resources. These seemingly different concepts actually are related, even if their reconciliation is often confusing. That relationship is the stuff of economics; pursuing it here beyond pointing out the distinction serves no purpose.

Real investment is adding to the stock of real capital. The form of investment that is currently dominant in an economy tends to be its defining characteristic. An agricultural economy is one in which agricultural land, equipment, and livestock dominate economic activity. When economic change is at best gradual, real investment tends to be similar to the prevailing capital stock. The American economy was therefore fundamentally agricultural until the present century. Transportation, trade, and, toward the end of the nineteenth century, manufacturing, were certainly significant, but many of those activities were closely linked to agriculture. The transcontinental railroads, for example, were built primarily to settle the agricultural lands of the West and to bring their produce back East to market.

Pinpointing when the Industrial Age displaced the agricultural economy is difficult, in part due to a problem of definition. By 1900 the amount of real, physical capital represented by manufacturing plant and equipment was roughly equal to that in land improvements (but excluding raw land) and equipment in agriculture. Nevertheless, real *investment* in manufacturing was already growing more rapidly. On this basis, it seems that the transformation from an agricultural to an industrial economy was well along before the turn of the century.

Industrialization in the United States seems to have reached its apex by the early 1950s, when the output of services was beginning to grow more rapidly. By that time the achievements of American manufacturing were extraordinary. Consider, for example, how it responded to the challenges of World War II, requiring virtually a complete transition from peacetime to wartime production. Between 1940 and 1945, American factories turned out some 300,000 warplanes, 2 million trucks, 107,000 tanks, nearly 88,000 warships, and nearly 5,500 cargo ships.[1] Wartime production was actually already beginning to wind down and shift back to a peacetime basis by early 1944, well before the war ended. The postwar period then saw an equally impressive outpouring of consumer goods. The wonder of the world in its time, the American industrial model has understandably continued to dominate economic thought as well as business principles and practices ever since.

That era, and the production-line concepts that made it possible, nevertheless left some unfortunate legacies that continue to permeate management thinking and practices. Among them:

---

[1]Data cited in Doris Kearns Goodwin, *No Ordinary Time* (New York: Simon & Schuster, 1994), p. 608.

- A preoccupation with physical means of production.
- A product-push marketing mentality reflecting relatively homogeneous, mass-produced products with little attention to differences in buyer preferences.
- An emphasis on cost containment and pricing as the predominant means of competition.
- A mechanical view of the workforce emphasizing employee costs instead of employee contributions to enterprise capital.
- The supremacy of public accounting conventions that assume reported earnings to be the ultimate test of financial performance.
- A presumption that maximizing earnings as thus reported in turn maximizes the value of a corporation to its shareholders.

The great advantage of mass production is that it minimizes production costs. That advantage is most significant when pricing is the dominant mechanism of competition. Competition on the basis of costs and prices, as well as the mechanics of mass production, leaves little leeway for differentiating products to satisfy varying customer preferences or otherwise distinguishing one product from rivals. The mass-production model, in other words, is incompatible with a marketplace where customers impute significant value to customization and quality of products and services. Most customer feedback in this mass-production marketplace is simply from decisions to purchase or not to purchase.

The industrial model also is incompatible with an economy in which much of the real investment is in forms other than physical capital. Why this is so is an important topic for later discussion. For the moment, suffice it that the accounting model, and the management decision criteria that rely on that model, for the most part do not recognize the investment nature of accumulating capital in nonphysical forms.

Intangible Investment and Capital

The concept of relationship capital is probably unfamiliar. Perhaps more familiar, if only because of its connection with accounting and tax issues, is the concept of intangible assets. These include, but are by no means limited to, economic relationships. In particular, and more familiarly, patents, copyrights, and trademarks also are intangible assets. To establish an appropriate context, consider the assets of a business enterprise as commonly consisting of three components:

- *Physical assets,* such as facilities, furnishings and equipment, and inventories, all of which represent real capital.
- *Financial assets* such as cash, securities, and accounts receivable, which represent, among other things, an ability to acquire physical assets.
- *Intangible assets,* which represent productive capacity—means of generating income—that are neither physical nor financial.

Curiously, intangibility has nothing to do with physical substantiality. In the accountants' lexicon, financial as well as physical assets are tangible. Understanding today's relationship economy requires understanding that intangible assets, including relationship assets, represent economic capital, or producer goods. Their economic attributes are substantively identical to capital in the form of plant and equipment.

The separate classification of intangibles is purely an artificial accounting distinction. Intangible assets represent productive capacity that businesses develop internally rather than purchasing them from others. The outlays for developing these assets are usually difficult and often impossible to identify and substantiate. Compounding the problem, accounting convention normally classifies expenses by types of input (employee compensation, materials, and so on), and not by what those inputs produce. Conventional accounting practice is therefore simply to record those outlays as current expenses, such as for employee compensation and advertising. Most intangible assets consequently never appear on corporate balance sheets.

Although the lines again become blurred, one might consider two broad categories of intangible assets and capital:

- The more familiar is *intellectual property,* as represented by patents, trademarks, and copyrights.
- *Economic relationships,* representing expectations of future transactions between the respective parties.

The underlying economic characteristics, and thus the applicable business principles, are the same for both. Moreover, the financial reporting issues in accounting for each are identical.

An ambiguity arises with respect to intellectual property, for usage of the term often assumes ownership rights under legal protection. An alternative that makes more economic and business sense is to include all forms of proprietary knowledge and information. The term therefore includes a wide variety of customer, credit, and marketing information files. The concepts of intellectual property and relationship capital overlap with the realization that much of that proprietary information is essential to developing and servicing many types of economic relationships.

Further overlap is apparent with the realization that significant elements of proprietary corporate knowledge and information may be embedded in management and employees. They may therefore be important components of a corporation's internal relationships. Thus, *proprietary* simply means knowledge and information that is not easily accessible to outsiders. This point touches on a difficulty that often has no simple resolution: Absent legal protection, who owns this sort of intellectual property? This difficulty is likely to escalate as employees' knowledge and skills become more significant. Similar questions sometimes arise concerning ownership of market relationships.

From the standpoint of common business perceptions, intangible assets usually become visible only as purchase premiums in certain types of corporate acquisitions. Acquisition premiums basically represent intangible assets, even when, as was especially common until the late 1970s, accountants simply record them as goodwill. Stating the point another way, intangible assets give rise to acquisition premiums. Corporate acquirers are hardly likely to pay premiums so consistently unless they represent some type of value. To be sure, acquirers often do pay too much or too little simply because they have not analyzed their acquisitions adequately. For the most part, however, true purchase premiums represent elements of value that were present all along. They simply never achieved accounting recognition prior to their purchase.

Recognition of Relationship Capital

Understanding and confronting a relationship marketplace requires measuring investment results in terms of the values generated by that investment. Whether the investment is simply financial or is outlay on real capital makes no difference in determining results. The appropriate measure of corporate performance thus becomes the value that an enterprise develops for its shareholders. One form of this value is the total value of its various capital components, including its intangible capital. Indeed, understanding its intangible components is absolutely essential for a true understanding of corporate enterprise value. For the most part, however, intangibles continue to be no more than dimly understood. The best one can say on this point is that the present level of understanding is a step ahead of where it was a generation ago.

An intangible asset, as accountants define it for financial reporting and tax purposes, is a nonphysical asset that usually has no identifiable cost basis. As the development of intangibles is substantially internal, linkages between the investment outlays and the resulting assets are difficult to identify. Consider, for example, the difficulty of identifying the outlays from which a current base of magazine subscribers developed. Lacking the sort of identifiable cost basis that arises upon purchasing an asset, they do not appear on the balance sheets of the companies that develop them.

Some intangibles nevertheless *may* subsequently gain balance sheet status as acquisition premiums in certain cases of purchase by another company. The price established by their purchase endows them with the requisite cost basis. Only a small proportion of all intangibles achieves this recognition, however. In contrast, while financial assets also are nonphysical in nature, they are tangible for accounting and tax purposes. Their acquisition is nearly always by purchase, whereby their prices establish a readily identifiable, and verifiable, cost basis.

Recognition of the economic characteristics of intangible assets first emerged in the context of dealing with the tax consequences of corporate acquisitions. Uniquely under U.S. tax law, purchase accounting principles determine the tax treatment of certain types of acquisitions by purchase. Purchase accounting is the process of marking to market all of the purchased assets and liabilities—recording them on the balance sheet of the buyer at their purchase-date market values.

In general, the purchaser of an asset may write off (depreciate a physical asset, or amortize some other asset) its acquisition cost for tax purposes over the remainder of its useful life. These write-offs are expenses deductible from taxable income, giving rise to substantial tax savings. Depreciation of tangible assets for tax purposes must be according to prescribed guidelines. Following revisions in the tax code in 1992, elements of purchase prices that do not represent market values of tangible assets—true purchase premiums—may be written off for tax purposes no more rapidly than on a fifteen-year straight-line schedule. This schedule actually is consistent only with asset lives somewhat longer than commonly observed, reducing the tax benefits.

For tax purposes prior to 1992, purchased intangible assets fell into two different categories:

- Intangibles with identifiable values and attrition (wasting) patterns, which some interpretations of the tax code indicated as qualifying them for tax savings from their amortization.
- A catch-all category typically designated as *goodwill* or *going concern value,* which included whatever remained of a purchase price after assigning values to all tangible assets *and* to all intangibles with identifiable values and lives.

The second of these categories was not eligible for any tax amortization before enactment of the 1992 tax revisions. Taxpayers consequently had substantial monetary incentives to seek tax savings by identifying the values and demonstrating the wasting patterns of purchased intangibles. Without the prospect of tax deductions, most corporations have had little interest in analyzing these assets.

The burden of proof for amortizing intangibles was with the taxpayers, and sustaining that burden usually involved engaging outside valuation consultants. Prolonged controversies nevertheless arose because of the ambiguities surrounding goodwill. The concept of goodwill as simply residuals representing unallocable purchase prices came into dominance in accounting practice by the 1970s. However, an older, generic concept of goodwill, as some sort of ephemeral value associated with continuing but indefinite customer patronage, continued to prevail within the Internal Revenue Service (IRS). One purpose of the 1992 tax law revisions was to put an end to continuing disputes over which intangibles were or were not goodwill, and whether they did or did not qualify for tax amortization. Prior to that legislation, news media referred to intangible assets as among the most arcane topics in tax law. An additional difficulty was an absence of economic substance in much of the debate.

Until the late 1970s taxpayers made few attempts to claim that purchased customer relationships represented intangible assets eligible for tax amortization. The prevalence of the foregoing generic concept of goodwill was one major deterrent. In that view, the periods over which one might expect continuing customer patronage were simply too indefinite to support amortization claims. Reinforcing that view was an absence of techniques for identifying the values and attrition characteristics of these assets.

A further deterrent, which remains prevalent, is that more rapid amortization of intangibles for financial reporting purposes results in higher near-term expenses. The consequence is to reduce near-term reported earnings. In other words, what is advantageous from a tax standpoint may have a negative near-term impact on investors to the extent that they associate current earnings with investment values. Although tax accounting and accounting for public financial statements often diverge, the trend prior to 1992 had been toward bringing the two sets of accounting principles into closer conformity. Still, many taxpayers sacrificed potential tax savings available from amortization in order to avoid the negative impact on reported earnings from conforming the amortization schedules.

A few taxpayers nevertheless were successful even prior to the mid-1970s in claiming tax amortization for customer lists they had purchased. Cases in which taxpayers prevailed in the courts involved newspaper subscribers and renewal lists of property and casualty insurance policies. Their success raised some fundamental questions: Is the difference between information that facilitates attracting a customer and a customer relationship already in place a difference in degree or in kind? How can the former represent an amortizable asset if the latter is merely goodwill? What does attrition in a customer base imply about the appropriateness of amortizing its value, especially if that value is determinable and the attrition pattern is reasonably predictable?

A taxpayer claim arising from a 1976 purchase of bank deposits relied on the argument that the acquired deposit customers represented a valuable asset. A settlement of that claim favorable to the taxpayer opened the door to a deluge of similar claims involving purchased customer-base intangibles—the predominant form of relationship assets. The IRS meanwhile clung to its generic goodwill interpretation until the U.S. Tax Court made clear in several decisions during the 1980s that the expectation of continued customer patronage is not a relevant issue. Ultimately, the underlying economic principles prevailed.

The fundamental economic characteristic of intangible assets, including both customer lists and market relationships, is simply that they arise from investment in their development. Their value reflects the future income necessary to recover that investment with a return. In this respect, intangible capital is substantively identical to physical capital. The only truly legitimate tax issue was not the nature of the asset per se; rather, it was whether it is possible to identify the asset's value and predict its attrition pattern with sufficiently reasonable accuracy to indicate an amortization schedule reflecting its true underlying economic characteristics.

As many accountants recognized by the 1970s, the only analytically substantive definition of goodwill is as representing insufficient value and attrition information. The information may simply not be obtainable, or its absence may simply be because no one wants to incur the effort and expense of its development. In many cases the analytical techniques for determining values and attrition were faulty, which gave the IRS a potentially valid basis for challenging taxpayers' claims. The IRS nevertheless never sought to develop the expertise by which to assess the validity of much of the analysis under its review. Instead, it sought refuge in what became the 1992 tax revisions concerning intangible assets.

The 1992 tax revisions prescribe tax amortization that does not represent the economic lives of most intangible assets. It therefore departs from the financial reporting principle that asset amortization should be according to the true economic lives of the assets. In reality, business enterprises have typically not been very assiduous in applying that principle anyway, and accountants have tended to be somewhat lax in enforcing it. Thus, by removing the tax incentives for separately identifying different intangibles acquired by purchase, most of the incentives for analyzing the characteristics of intangible assets evaporated.

The true economic significance of these invisible assets is so enormous, however, that their tax implications, whatever the tax law, *should* be merely incidental. The reality is that little understanding of these assets has ever developed outside of this now outdated tax context.

The Economic Significance of Relationship Assets

How significant is relationship capital? Just as economic relationships have a growing role in virtually every marketplace, relationship capital is a growing component of the capital base underlying all forms of economic activity. Nevertheless, because of its accounting treatment, quantitative measures of the total stock of relationship capital are, to say the least, elusive. Such measures appear only when investment in their development creates economic values that subsequently emerge in enterprise acquisitions as goodwill (to accountants), or franchise value (to investment bankers and financial analysts). Even then, most of the information is incomplete and unreliable.

Recognizing these difficulties, a very rough guess is that the accumulated corporate investment in economic relationships in the United States approaches a trillion dollars—that is, the total value of relationship capital thus may represent somewhat more than a third of the total market value of U.S. corporate equity. For at least four reasons, even this comparison probably substantially understates the full significance of relationship capital:

- The productivity of much of the physical capital base depends increasingly on joint, or complementary, investment in relationship capital—customer relationships, supplier relationships, cooperatives, and so on. Such complementarities in economic activity can be of enormous importance. Deficiencies in the economic vitality of communities and nations are often attributable to deficiencies in economic and social relationships. Similarly, corporations that improperly manage internal economic relationships often become dysfunctional.

- Much of the investment in new information and communications technologies and data bases is inextricably entwined with attracting, developing, servicing, and retaining customer relationships. Indeed, the huge size of such investments needed to compete in a relationship marketplace is reshaping the corporate landscape. The scale of these requirements is, for example, a major factor in corporate consolidations in financial services and communications.

- Capital representing market relationships tends to erode faster than most plant capacity. The investment necessary simply to maintain a base of relationship capital is correspondingly higher, and therefore a somewhat higher proportion of total private investment, than comparisons of total capital amounts suggest.

- Relationship investment and capital are growing faster than investment in producer goods. As already suggested, investment rates seem to be a factor in defining the characteristics of an economy. One thinks of an industrial economy as emerging in the late nineteenth century, when it became the primary focus of new investment, yet manufacturing continued to account for less than thirty percent of U.S. national income until the 1940s.

The most reliable evidence concerning the quantitative significance of intangible assets comes from an April 1991 U.S. General Accounting Office (GAO) report entitled *Issues and Policy Proposals Regarding Tax Treatment of Intangible Assets.*[2] It contained a compilation of tax claims for purchased intangible assets still pending before the IRS. Its main purpose was to provide information on the amortization schedules for those assets, mostly to ensure that new legislation would cause no loss of tax revenues to the U.S. Treasury. The opening statement of purpose is worth quoting:

> One of the oldest controversies between taxpayers and the Internal Revenue Service (IRS) is the extent to which taxpayers can deduct the price they pay for intangible assets, such as customer or subscription lists. The opportunities for disputes to arise intensified during the 1980's when business acquisition activity increased and led to the growth in the reported values of intangible assets from about $45 billion in 1980 to $262 billion in 1987.

A review of the GAO's analysis must keep in mind that it includes only cases pending before the IRS in 1989. Because many acquisitions never qualified for tax amortization of intangible assets, they in turn involved only certain cases of intangible assets that taxpayers had purchased. The total value represented by all of these cases is less than ten percent of the above-cited $262 billion, the source of which is unclear. Of course, the IRS had settled many claims prior to 1989. In any event, as acquisition activity was significantly more widespread in some industries than in others, the cases remaining for GAO examination were unlikely to be representative of the economy as a whole.

The GAO categorized the different types of intangibles under IRS review, with the taxpayers' total acquisition values, as follows:

- *Customer-* or *market-based assets,* examples of which included pools of deposits held by financial institutions and newspaper and magazine subscribers (valued at $10.5 billion).
- *Contract-based assets,* including assets supported by specific contracts, such as covenants not to compete and leases (valued at $3.7 billion).

---

[2]United States General Accounting Office, Report to the Joint Committee on Taxation, *Tax Policy: Issues and Policy Proposals Regarding Tax Treatment of Intangible Assets* (GAO/GGD-91-88, August 1991).

- *Technology-based assets* such as computer software, drawings, and technical manuals (valued at $2.2 billion).
- *Statutory-based assets* with specific statutorily defined amortization periods that could be elected in lieu of useful lives, consisting primarily of intellectual property—patents and copyrights (valued at $3.5 billion).
- *Workforce-based assets* representing existing workforce and including trained staff and technical expertise (valued at $1.1 billion).
- *Corporate organizational* or *financial assets* representing outlays in acquisitions such as acquisition costs, legal and auditing fees, and favorable financing arrangements (valued at $1.3 billion).
- *Intangible assets* that the IRS was unable to identify for lack of sufficient documentation (valued at $498 million).

The total value of the various assets the GAO examined amounted to $22.8 billion. Overall, this figure is likely to be a substantial understatement even for the acquisitions from which they arose because:

- Taxpayers could claim no more than what they actually paid for intangibles. This not only deterred overstating values but also meant that some assets were undervalued.
- Many taxpayers allocated portions of their purchase prices to goodwill instead of to amortizable intangibles, believing that doing so would add credibility to their tax amortization claims.
- Many taxpayers declined to submit claims for relationship assets, particularly for workforce-based assets (also a type of market-based relationship asset), because of doubts about their admissibility for tax amortization.
- Many claims were simply not worth submitting because the costs of supporting them were high relative to the prospective tax benefits—benefits that taxpayers considered to be in doubt in any event because of IRS opposition.

Distortions also occur among the listed categories. As a specific example, most of the legitimate value of covenants not to compete reflects customer relationships that otherwise might be lost and are therefore essentially but one form of customer-based intangible. Nevertheless, because the IRS normally did not challenge values of such covenants that buyers and sellers specified in purchase contracts, some taxpayers submitted otherwise insupportable claims for amortization of this asset. The consequence is understatement of the value of customer-based assets.

The customer-based assets represent much the largest category of intangibles, even apart from doubts about the GAO classifications. If both customer and supplier relationships buried in other categories are included as well, the total value of market relationships exceeds that of all other categories combined. Notice, too, that the only type of intangible that seems to have widespread public recognition—the statutory-based assets—represents only a bit more than 15 percent of the total value of these intangibles.

Notice the specific mention of bank deposits and newspaper and magazine subscriptions as examples of customer-based intangibles. To be sure, banking and publishing account for substantial volumes of these types of intangibles, and thus for a significant proportion of the economy's relationship capital. Nevertheless, their prominence in the GAO's review also resulted from very high rates of acquisition activity in banking and publishing during the 1980s. A consequence is that whatever their broader significance, much, and possibly most, of the information and analysis that has accumulated with respect to relationship capital has been in the context of banking and publishing. Most of the IRS-initiated court cases on these issues involved bank depositors.

An Alternative Perspective on Intangibles

As disputes over the tax treatment of intangible assets were mounting in the United States, somewhat similar disputes were developing over their financial reporting treatment in the United Kingdom. There, acquiring companies sought revision of what they regarded as unduly onerous requirements for writing off purchased intangibles for financial reporting purposes. A group of such companies commissioned a report prepared by The Economist Intelligence Unit and Arthur Andersen & Company to demonstrate that the values and attrition patterns of intangible assets are indeed identifiable and measurable.[3]

Just as the GAO report was narrowly focused on tax policy, this one, published in January 1992, was narrowly focused on accounting issues. It is of interest mainly because of the examples it provides;

---

[3]Arthur Andersen & Company SC, *The Valuation of Intangible Assets* (London: The Economist Intelligence Unit, Special Report No. P254, January 1992).

otherwise, its perspectives are quite different from those of the GAO report. It classifies intangibles into four broad categories:

- *Brands*
  Consumer goods brand
  Industrial brand
  Service brand
  Trademark, including:
    Name
    Logo
    Device
    Color combination
  Corporate name

- *Publishing rights*
  Magazine
  Book title
  Masthead
  Film library
  Music library
  Photographic library
  TV/radio program listing
  Copyright
  Imprint
  Subscriber/advertiser list
  Trademark
  Exhibition right

- *Intellectual property*
  Patent
  Copyright
  Trademark
  Know-how
  Technology
  Trade secret
  Product design/style
  Database
  Software
  Drawing/blueprint

- *Licenses*
  TV/radio franchise/license

Airline route/slot
Production right
Import quota
Operating license (e.g., transport)
Mineral exploitation
Franchise operation
Distribution right
License of right (e.g., pharmaceutical)
Noncompete agreements

This list is generally less useful than the GAO classifications, focusing mainly on symbolic representations rather than on sources of value. This focus probably explains some of the overlap. More significantly, except for mere name and product recognition, it overlooks most forms of customer relationships. The one possible exception is if "subscriber/advertiser list" refers to an actual base of current subscribers or advertisers rather than to a list of prospects.

These shortcomings may result from differences between the two countries in the types of companies involved in acquisitions. While business combinations in banking and publishing were widespread in the United States, combinations in the United Kingdom were more common among consumer goods manufacturers. More likely, however, the shortcomings reflect two factors: One was an absence of experience with valuing intangible assets in the United Kingdom; the other was failure to draw on U.S. experience, which should have been readily available from Arthur Andersen's large U.S. valuation consulting practice.

A Revised Classification Scheme

A focus on sources of value perhaps leads to a more meaningful categorization than either of the above. It is also simpler:

- *Economic relationships,* including market relationships and relationships between the private and public sectors. Market relationships include predictable continuance of market transactions between parties, as are likely to be associated with brand names, trademarks, company image, or other proprietary identifying characteristics. True goodwill falls into this category even if its value and attrition characteristics defy measurement.
- *Proprietary information,* regardless of how access to that in-

formation is protected. This category includes intellectual property (patents and copyrights), trade secrets, and databases. It also includes proprietary information on market characteristics and actual and potential customers or suppliers, much of which is important to attracting, developing, and retaining market relationships.

- *Going-concern value,* which is an accounting and tax term for the value of bringing together all the separately identifiable assets so as to produce and sell goods and services—values that continue to adhere to an enterprise over some indeterminately long period. It reflects various legal, accounting, and financial advisory services, costs of incorporation and regulatory approvals, and feasibility studies. In substantial part, going-concern value represents start-up investment.

Understanding the Relationship Economy

DIMENSIONS OF MUTUALITY

To define a relationship economy, consider what constitutes an economic relationship. A *relationship* implies some mutual advantage to parties in continuing to have dealings with one another. An *economic relationship* simply applies this concept to economic activities—activities involving the production, distribution, and consumption of goods and services.

Much the most common forms of economic relationships are market relationships between buyers and sellers. Transactions between buyers and sellers are seldom transitory events. Market relationships are primarily a means by which buyers and sellers know what to expect of one another. To the extent that the advantages of a relationship are mutual, customer relationships and supplier relationships typically represent two sides of the same thing. Mutuality does *not* mean that the advantages are equal, which they usually are not.

Market relationships have traditionally tended to be vertical, with buyers and sellers on opposite sides of a marketplace. They therefore represent some coincidence of interests even when their respective interests otherwise diverge. Externally, for example, newspaper publishers have an interest in retaining subscriptions, while subscribers have an interest in being able to expect deliveries on schedule. Publishers would nevertheless prefer to charge higher subscription rates while subscribers prefer lower rates. Internally, whereas employers and employees may have substantial common interests, they typically diverge with respect to the latter's compensation.

External economic relationships also can be horizontal, as in joint ventures, partnerships, and cooperative organizations. Important examples include farm and retailing cooperatives. Horizontal relationships are slowly gaining importance as vertical relationships take on more horizontal elements. Thus, franchise arrangements contain partnership elements rather than being pure buyer-seller relationships. Horizontal relationships nevertheless may be unstable. The mutuality of interest that arose from one set of market conditions may disappear as those conditions change.

Market relationships between shareholders, as suppliers of capital, and corporate managers, as users of capital, imply the former are buying the services of the latter, yet some chief executives probably prefer to view that relationship as horizontal, in the nature of a partnership (or less) with shareholders. Many economic relationships, in practice, are neither purely horizontal nor purely vertical. Indeed, competing successfully in the emerging relationship marketplace requires more cooperative and even collaborative relationships between buyers and sellers. A challenge in each case is to establish the particular balance between the horizontal and vertical that imparts stability to the relationship.

Economic relationships have some role in production and distribution in virtually every marketplace, although their significance varies widely from market to market. They represent a major and often dominant component of the capital base in services, publishing, broadcast media, and other forms of communication, and they obviously are essential in transportation and retail trade. They also are significant components of the capital embedded in agricultural and trade cooperatives.

Even in manufacturing, the significance of economic relationships is growing rapidly. A recent book on the potential advantages of cooperative forms of economic relationships among producers focused mostly on manufacturing enterprises.[1] Buyers of manufactured goods have expanding ranges of alternatives from which they can choose,

---

[1]Kenneth Preiss, Steven L. Goldman, and Roger N. Nagel, *Cooperate to Compete* (New York: Van Nostrand Reinhold, 1996).

shifting the balance of market sovereignty from sellers to buyers. In many cases buyers want more service as part of the product package. As one manifestation of this point, buyers of producer and consumer durables, in particular, are fundamentally interested in the future flows of services and satisfaction such goods provide. As a familiar example, buyers of automobiles consider the maintenance services that come with the services embodied in the cars themselves. A result is opportunities for manufacturers to add value and further secure customer relationships by enhancing those services.

Their potential for reducing inventories provides a good example of the economic value of relationships. A seller of parts to other manufacturers has little obvious concern with customers' inventories of those parts as long as the seller can dispose of its own inventories. Buyers may have similar unconcern with sellers' inventories. Suppose, however, that better anticipation of one another's future needs enables both more stable production flows and lower inventories. The result is an economic gain that, even if not altogether direct and visible, provides benefits to both buyers and sellers. An economic gain gives rise to economic value.

As yet another manifestation, manufacturers in their capacities both as suppliers and customers are also developing new cooperative forms of relationships with a view to making production flows more responsive to market conditions. Benefits of such relationships include reducing inventories and imparting more predictability to supply requirements and production schedules. These types of relationships are often an important element in many cases of outsourcing parts manufacturing.

An understanding of economic relationships provides insights into economic phenomena that otherwise elude explanation. Economic relationships are, of course, as old as commerce. They are traditional elements of personal and business services and retail trade. Even impersonal relationships, such as brand loyalties fostered by mass media, are hardly new. These forms of relationships are elements of a relationship economy but are alone insufficient to define its character.

Information-Age Relationships

Apart from the enormous growth in the relative importance of services, an element further defining a relationship economy is the marriage of sophisticated information technologies with relationships in mass markets. This combination is entirely natural and logical, as services tend to require much higher levels of communication than manufactures. In a growing array of economic activities, many, if not most, employees routinely communicate with actual or potential customers. Service relationships, moreover, tend to require endowing workers with more decision-making responsibility. The era of workers as assembly-line automatons has mostly vanished.

The entire economy, and not just individual markets, is becoming dependent on intricate networks of economic relationships that extend ever further across international borders. These new technologies enable impersonal relationships to assume many of the characteristics of personal relationships. They do so by imparting a degree of affordable customization to the design, marketing, and delivery of goods and services. Buyers assume a new position of market dominance as arrays of market offerings proliferate. Marketing strategies and delivery systems thus assume added significance in a relationship economy.

As a familiar illustration of segmentation of the marketplace according to varied preferences, consider radio broadcasting. A radio station must first determine what sort of listening audience represents the most attractive opportunities, then develop programming to attract and retain that audience. The attractiveness of different audiences depends on size and spending habits, which in turn determine the types of advertisers the station can attract. A substantial amount of detailed demographic and economic information may be necessary to develop an effective marketing approach, particularly if the station is in a densely populated area with substantial competition among broadcasters.

Similarly, to a growing degree successful marketing requires adapting services and products to different buyer preferences in increasingly heterogeneous markets. Customers prefer not to buy goods and services off the shelf if they can be adapted to individual preferences at little additional cost. An analogy is a man's suit that is made to measure rather than off the rack, but not quite custom made. Obviously, adapting to different preferences requires substantially more information about actual and potential customers than off-the-shelf marketing. Compiling and analyzing such information would be impossible in the absence of information-age technologies.

While new information technologies play an important role in a relationship marketplace, they are not necessarily an unmixed blessing. If their applications become too mechanical, they may actually deter relationship development. For example, these technologies may simply make product-push marketing more cost efficient even as a customer-pull approach to the market becomes more effective. Information can become counter-productive if its volume exceeds the ability of the human brain to process it.

Perhaps recent national political campaigns provide some perspective on the possible pitfalls of new information technologies. For much of the public, politics and voting used to be fun. Political conventions and elections were exciting, in part because anyone could easily participate and feel part of the process. Today, much of what volunteers used to do is mechanized and much of the process has become remote. That this trend has actually increased the amount of information available to the electorate seems doubtful. What is certain is that it has vastly increased the costs of the political process, corrupting it further. Is it any wonder that much of the public feels left out of that process, with declining voter turnout?

Values of Economic Relationships

Economic relationships arise from perceived overlapping interests in economic activity. They certainly improve communication, in its broadest sense, within that sphere of mutual interest. The communication is not necessarily direct or personal. It may, for example, be in the form of one party developing a database to track the behavior of another. A seller might then be better able to anticipate buyers' needs. In the inventory example, most of the communication is likely to be by computer linkages.

Information-age technologies also lie at the heart of the relationship economy in a yet very different way. Among their consequences has been an explosion in the sheer quantity of information and misinformation in the marketplace. Information is not simply much more readily available than ever before. Marketers, spin doctors, and other promoters and hucksters thrust it on the rest of society. The result is accelerating information overload, and no end to the growth in volume is in sight.

This phenomenon makes it ever more difficult to process information and even to communicate. It leads to a sound-byte society in which individuals screen out most of what they see and hear. The same primal instinct that treats new ideas and information as potentially threatening creates a threshold that communicators either must cross almost instantaneously or not at all. Notice how carefully advertisers try to craft their messages so as to attract immediate attention.

Of course, sound bytes seldom actually communicate much information. They exist mainly to create or change attitudes—to evoke essentially visceral responses. To understand the point, consider the uninformative, often misleading, nature of much political spot advertising. Similarly, some of the most successful television advertising conveys little or nothing about the quality of the products.

How, then, are businesses and individuals to cope with the enormous expansion both in the range of available products and services and in the amounts of market information and misinformation? Whom or what can they trust? What allays fears of what is unfamiliar? How is one to avoid dire consequences of decisions, particularly when those consequences extend well out into the future? The answer, to growing degree, is to rely on continuing economic relationships with those with whom one has dealt comfortably or successfully in the past. A sense of trust is essential to the ability of societies and markets to function effectively.

One simple and long-familiar example is residential delivery of heating oil. Simply by tracking degree days, distributors know when their customers will require deliveries. This practice relieves customers of having to check oil gauges and of the risks of forgetting to do so. It also keeps distributors abreast of their supply requirements. Moreover, if for no other reason but that it increases the inconvenience to customers of switching distributors, it cements the relationships between sellers and buyers. Finally, by thus reducing the risks of customer loss, distributors incur less risk in investing in storage facilities and delivery equipment.

Market relationships also often provide some assurance to buyers of the quality of what they are buying. Consider Holiday Inn's "no surprises" advertising campaign of a few years ago. It need not have assumed that potential customers were already familiar with Holiday Inn accommodations. Why would anyone advertise in this manner without having some confidence in the quality of the offering?

An example with some additional implications is the recruitment of managerial and professional personnel. Very few openings result from résumés and recruiters. Want ads placed in major newspapers often attract far more responses than most prospective employers want to expend the time and effort on to process fully. Thus, most prefer to hire candidates generated by their own networks of personal contacts even if it risks failing to attract the best applicants. If they must turn elsewhere, they especially avoid overqualified candidates, viewing them as somehow riskier.

Economic relationships consequently serve a dual role by increasing the efficiency of communication *and* by reducing economic risks. As the example suggests, trade-offs often exist between the effectiveness of communication—the extent to which it provides information that will result in the best decisions (whatever the definition of *best*)—and risks. In other words, economic relationships provide a way of limiting risks while avoiding the effort and costs associated with identifying and evaluating significantly better information.

Economic relationships thus enable the respective parties to predict one another's behavior within the sphere of their mutual interests. More predictability means less risk. Human behavior depends on perceptions of risks, not (perhaps unknowable) actual risks. Part of the difference lies in how people process information, about which social scientists still have much to learn.

Less risk ultimately means lower costs of production and distribution. Risk requires that investors receive compensation for assuming that risk. Compensation for taking risks is part of the cost of capital of a business—the returns on investment it must provide to its shareholders and creditors if it is to continue to attract capital. The higher the risks of a business, the more of its income it must ultimately pay to the providers of its capital.

Moreover, as a business seeks to attract more capital for investment, it must attract investors who are increasingly averse to risk. In other words, each additional increment of capital increases the costs of capital, particularly as compensation for assuming risks tends to rise ever more rapidly as investment increases. More predictability correspondingly reduces the need to compensate investors for risks.

A simple diagram illustrates this point.

While purely hypothetical, the upward slope of the line illustrates the higher compensation investors typically require for incurring more risks. Furthermore, its upward curvature indicates that compensation for risk taking normally rises at an increasing rate as risk increases. Reducing risks thus reduces costs of capital and increases the enterprise value accruing to shareholders at an increasing rate.

This increasing aversion to risk, represented by the upward curvature the line in the diagram, appears to be dominant in the capital markets. The reason is that demands for capital tend to exceed the resources of investors who actually like, or are at least neutral, to

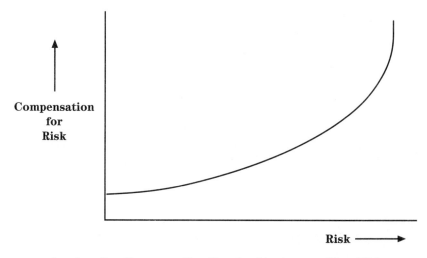

Accelerating Compensation Required to Assume More Risk.

risks. Indeed, the former category is likely to squander its resources in speculation. Thus, *at the margin,* additional capital is obtainable only by extending investment opportunities to risk averters.

Ultimately, aversion to risk means that investors attach more value to market mechanisms, whatever they may be, that reduce risks. Economic relationships are thus sources of economic value in at least four fundamental ways:

- *They increase the efficiency* of communicating information by enabling communication of any given amount of information at lower costs.
- *They increase the effectiveness* of communication by enabling communication of more information at any level of cost.
- *They reduce the amount of capital required* for facilities and inventory by increasing the predictability of customer requirements.
- *They reduce the costs of economic activity,* including business costs, by reducing the risks attached to information on which decisions must rely.

Consider the significance of relationships in reducing risks in confronting revolutionary change in the economic order. The obvious implication is that even apart from the changing output mix and new technologies, change alone imparts more value to anything that reduces the risks it represents.

Anything that adds economic value must itself represent value. Thus, the more complex the economy and the more the uncertainty to which that complexity gives rise, the greater the value represented by economic relationships. Economic value, in turn, represents a price that something can command in the marketplace. If economic relationships have value, it means that anyone seeking such relationships has to pay for them. That means buying them from others who possess them, or it means incurring the effort and outlays necessary to develop them.

Earlier discussion emphasized that economic relationships represent capital in the same substantive sense as plant and equipment. The final step in considering their economic value comes from recognizing that, virtually by definition, their benefits to the respective parties extend into future time, often many years. From a business standpoint, they generate future as well as current income. Outlays to develop economic relationships therefore represent *investment* outlays and the accumulation of real capital. Business decisions concerning economic relationships are therefore *investment* decisions requiring the application of investment principles. It becomes clear upon considering the significance and pervasiveness of economic relationships, and specifically of market relationships, that most management decisions are effectively investment decisions.

Buyer-Seller Relationships

Some of the foregoing points come into better focus when one looks more closely at relationships between vendors and their customers. Transactions with customers are no longer likely to represent the transitory events of textbook economics. Today's customers are highly likely to be tomorrow's customers as well. Potential benefits of these continuing relationships—the ways in which they add value to transactions—include:

- Vendors can more readily determine buyers' preferences, accelerating responses to changing needs and tastes, while buyers can more precisely identify what is for sale, and on what terms.
- Drawing on new information technologies, vendors can often adapt goods and services to specific customer needs or preferences.

- Information flows reduce sellers' investment and market risks
  both by directly imparting more predictability to buyers' behavior and by indicating how to retain customer relationships
  for longer periods by serving them better.
- For both consumers and businesses, information flows similarly reduce buyers' uncertainties about the availability of
  goods and services at the expected times and places.

Market relationships are economic goods representing value in the
marketplace not just because they add value but also because they
are themselves in limited supply. When one vendor develops a relationship with a customer, a direct rival can obtain that relationship
only by competing it away. Customer relationships often exhibit a
good deal of inertia. Absent good cause, buyers may be reluctant to
switch from what is familiar to something less familiar, particularly if
they view the new choice as a long-term commitment. Switching may
be inconvenient. Inconvenience is itself a form of cost, as people are
typically willing to pay a price to avoid inconvenience. In some cases,
switching suppliers may also involve direct costs. For example, banks
traditionally have been more willing to lend to their established customers than to newcomers.

Most types of business activity simply are not worth undertaking
unless they involve continuing relationships in some form. How, for
example, could a daily newspaper exist without a dependable base of
readers, whether regular newsstand buyers or subscribers? How
could banks make loans without confidence that depositors will continue to provide funds with which to fund those loans? How, indeed,
could a cereal manufacturer stay in business without customers having some form of brand identification?

Competitive survival in a relationship economy means making
fewer mistakes in capital commitments than one's rivals. It therefore
requires the information relationships generate. Feedback from customers often provides the only reliable information about such matters as quality and design, particularly as service relationships tend
otherwise to be invisible.

To a growing degree, too, competitive survival requires recognizing
the significance of information flows to the efficiency of production
and distribution processes. Suppose, for example, that one seller is
able to achieve substantial reductions in inventories by establishing
better information and communication flows with suppliers (or customers), thereby reducing costs. If that seller puts this advantage to

use by offering better terms to customers, how are rival sellers to respond? Either they will develop similar arrangements or their higher costs will gradually push them out of the market.

Market relationships develop from sellers and buyers providing services to one another, even if the services consist only of communicating preferences. In most markets, and particularly in markets for consumer goods and services, the onus of competition is on sellers, and competition increasingly involves differentiating one's products with services. While the trend toward differentiation has radically altered traditional services, even more radical changes may be emerging in manufacturing. Better serving customers means integrating customers into sellers' design, production, and distribution processes. This trend is most pronounced in markets for industrial products, such as between manufacturers of parts and finished goods manufacturers, but it is also permeating consumer markets.

One widely publicized consumer goods example is the Levi Strauss "Personal Pair" program whereby, through computer linkages from stores to the manufacturers, customers can order custom-fitted jeans for just $10 above the off-the-shelf price. An even more extreme example is a program offered by Textile and Clothing Technology Corporation whereby women can custom design as well as fit their own garments by means of computerized manufacturing and communications technologies.

Such arrangements may not be entirely cooperative, however. Relationships normally require some degree of compromise. Retailers, for example, want to develop and retain their own relationships with customers rather than cede them to manufacturers. Thus, Nordstrom, Wal-Mart, and Home Depot, to name a few familiar examples, also recognize that something more than just price competitiveness is necessary to develop their own repeat customers. This may lead to a complicated question of just who owns which relationships. As more manufacturing moves abroad, perhaps customers will tend to identify more with distributors than with producers.

Competing successfully in relationship development, essential to competitive survival in a relationship economy, thus involves a good deal more than just competing for sales. Success in selling today implies expectations of future sales as well. Failure correspondingly reduces future as well as current sales prospects. Competition assures that the relationship investment expands as long as each additional dollar invested yields value in excess of that amount. In other words, the additional value each dollar contributes to the enterprise should exceed the investment outlay (that dollar) necessary to obtain it.

Investment in Market Relationships

The mutuality of market relationships suggests that there is no clear distinction between buyer and seller relationships, as the benefits flow both ways. Do not assume, however, that the benefits are equal for both parties. The usual, although not invariable, pattern is for sellers to receive the major portion of the benefits. An absence of quantitative evidence supporting this proposition requires relying on logic. Because customers usually have alternative sellers among which to choose, the loss of a relationship with any one supplier may be no more than a minor inconvenience. Sellers normally incur the most market risks, and they must compete for buyers. Moreover, they usually are in a position to obtain the largest reductions in direct costs from integrating production and distribution processes.

Vendor purchases of customer relationships from other vendors therefore usually include premiums, and often substantial premiums, above the tangible assets and liabilities they acquire. The value those premiums represent is mostly the value of the sellers' customer relationships. The acquirers are willing to pay the premiums as an alternative to investing at least as much in soliciting customer prospects and developing customer relationships for themselves. Customers, on the other hand, normally do not pay premiums to switch sellers with whom they deal. Indeed, they are more likely to receive premiums for switching, such as cash offers from long-distance telecommunications carriers.

Exceptions to that pattern sometimes occur when assurances of supply availability are critically important. An industrial customer might therefore provide financial or research and development assistance to a supplier to facilitate its entry or expansion into a particular line of business. Supplies of parts and materials to finished goods manufacturers provide examples. An example at the consumer level is how poor credit risks sometimes pay a price in the form of deposits with issuers to obtain credit card accounts.

Bank credit cards otherwise illustrate the fierce competition among sellers in a relationship environment. Cardholders, of course, receive significant benefits from having convenient access to the payment mechanism as well as to credit. Nevertheless, they surely need not compete with one another to obtain credit cards—creditworthy prospects tend to be overwhelmed with preapproval solicitations. They may invest some effort in comparing card programs before selecting among competing providers, but few actually are likely to conduct extensive comparisons or even pay attention to all of the features of their accounts.

If the benefits of market relationships were in limitless supply and freely available, they would have no market value. They would be as likely to command a price in the market as ocean water at the beach. Of course, the availability of market relationships to buyers is not entirely unrestricted, but competition among sellers usually assures that alternatives are readily, and almost freely, available.

Summarizing, market relationships are not simply windfalls, particularly from the standpoint of sellers. As objects of competition, they are obtainable only from internal investment in their development or, much less commonly, by paying premiums to other sellers who previously developed them. Market relationships must be objects of business decision making to the extent they tend to be economic goods, meaning simply that they are not freely available. This point in turn means that that they must be a factor, if not the primary factor, in evaluating decision alternatives.

Types of Market Relationships

One might envision different types of market relationships as distributed along a spectrum representing relationship strength (for lack of a better term), as follows:

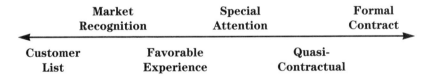

Spectrum of Vertical Customer Relationships.

At one end of the spectrum are relationships consisting of no more than customer lists representing proprietary information. Such lists tend to have more value the more they are proprietary and the more they include important marketing information about prospective customers. In other words, their value arises from providing their possessors with advantages over rivals in soliciting customers.

Some early instances of valuing market relationships pertained to purchases of customer lists. An example was insurance agency information on forthcoming expirations of property and casualty insurance policies, when they would require renewal—information normally available only to the agency that had sold those policies. Common practice used to be that agencies would solicit renewals shortly before policies were due to expire. Policyholders typically took the more convenient course, renewing rather than shopping among alternatives. Renewal therefore was much the lowest-cost method of selling these types of insurance. Some of the earliest tax cases involving customer-based intangibles involved claims of expense deductions by amortizing purchase premiums for policyholder lists.

The idea underlying those tax cases was that renewals would decline as policyholders went elsewhere, perhaps because of changes in their own circumstances. An example is cancellation of homeowners' insurance with sale of a home; the value of the list would decline accordingly. Today, automatic policy renewals are much more common, moving these relationships along the spectrum to something more binding than mere solicitation advantages.

Moving a step rightward along the spectrum is mere recognition of products and vendors by prospective buyers. Brand names, company logograms, and other distinctive identifiers illustrate the significance of the recognition factor. Recognition is therefore the main objective of many advertising programs. Unless some opprobrium attaches to it, recognition typically increases the likelihood of patronage. Indeed, brand names sometimes command substantial premiums in corporate acquisitions. The British sponsors of the 1992 Economist Intelligence Unit study of intangibles, discussed in Chapter 1, were primarily concerned with obtaining balance sheet recognition of premiums they had paid to acquire brand names.

Another rightward step along the spectrum leads to relationships arising from favorable experience with a seller or product. Unlike the foregoing cases, these normally require prior purchase, although it may have been by someone referring the customer. They typically represent some degree of customer loyalty whereby a buyer chooses one option over some other that has equal recognition. Holiday Inn's "no surprises" advertising campaign undoubtedly assumed customer satisfaction as well as familiarity.

Next along the spectrum are situations when sellers themselves somehow display recognition that a buyer is a loyal customer, perhaps calling for preferred treatment. A familiar example is a restaurant patron whom the maître d' addresses by name. Even if the consequence is not preferred seating, this special attention leaves a favorable impression. Most people like to stand out from the crowd. In particular, they like attentiveness to their needs and preferences. Modern technologies increasingly enable vendors to provide this sort of personalized attention even without the personal contact inherent in the restaurant example.

Quasicontractual relationships are those involving agreements about the respective obligations of the parties. They are less than full contracts in the sense that they are terminable at any time by one or both parties. A common example is a bank deposit. A bank agrees to make payments at the depositor's direction to the extent the account has sufficient funds. The depositor nevertheless has the right to close the account at any time. Similarly, a credit card issuer must extend credit on an account up to the specified limit as long as the cardholder is not delinquent in making payments. However, a cardholder can close an account at any time upon paying the balance due in full.

Many relationships internal to a business have quasicontractual elements. At least in theory, corporate directors assume fiduciary responsibilities for representing the interests of shareholders. Employers incur certain obligations to employees as long as they perform their duties. Indeed, some of those obligations are legally enforceable—a form of blanket contract coverage—even without formal agreements with individual employees.

Finally, some market relationships involve firm contracts of specified duration. Fully contractual relationships seem to be most common between businesses. For example, a supplier may need the security of a contract in order to commit sufficient resources to provide a good or service, particularly if it is specialized to the needs of that buyer. Relationships between businesses may entail a variety of commitments. Thus, suppliers to major retailers are often subject to numerous requirements governing packaging, shipping, and labeling. Whether these requirements are fully contractual or simply terms of sale, outlays by suppliers for maintaining these sorts of relationships may extend over the life of the relationship.

Some internal relationships also involve formal contracts. Employment contracts between companies and senior executives are common examples. Perhaps, too, agreements with officers and employees not to compete upon severance of employment fall into this general category. Not all internal contracts create or preserve relationships, at least directly. Labor union contracts with employers may impact on relationships only indirectly by specifying terms of employment. On the other hand, they may assume a relationship flavor to the extent they restrict the basis for employment termination.

Market relationships generally seem to endure longer and have more value the more there exists some mutual understanding or agreement between the parties. In other words, values of relationships tend to increase toward the right-hand side of the spectrum. Observed instances of staunch brand loyalties nevertheless suggest many possible exceptions.

Who Owns Relationships?

Situations often arise in which the loyalty of a customer is actually or potentially divided. One type of situation is when both manufacturers and retailers vie for primacy in their relationships with customers. One has the advantage of direct contact, whereas the other has the advantage of product identity. An element in determining the balance is the amount of service each provides to add value to the product.

Consider a common dilemma confronting many businesses in a relationship marketplace. Customer relationships may adhere more to individuals rather than to the businesses that employ them. These situations are more likely to arise when:

- Delivery of a product or service includes services provided by direct personal contact between sellers' representatives and customers.
- The relationships involve a number of different transactions, each of which the customer could take elsewhere.
- The compensation for servicing relationships depends significantly on the business volume the sellers' representatives generate.

An instructive example of relationships adhering to individuals arises in mortgage banking. The thrust of competition is in originating the mortgages, which often means obtaining mortgage referrals from real-estate brokers and developers. Many mortgage originators are commission sales representatives of mortgage companies. The mortgage companies in turn provide the initial mortgage financing until they can sell the new mortgages to permanent lenders. The mortgage companies may retain or sell the right to service the mortgages, which represents significant value due to future servicing fees and other income.

As a result of this division of roles, relationship values in mortgage banking consist of two major components. One is the relationship value developed by individual originators, which often stays with them if they change their mortgage company affiliations. The second component arises from the servicing of the mortgages once they are in place, which adheres to the mortgage companies' right to the servicing income. Servicing rights themselves are valuable institutionalized relationship intangibles.

Individuals need not always be the point of contact with customers. Many sellers are represented locally by small local and independent companies rather than just by individuals. Thus, an independent insurance agency may develop customer relationships that are not tied to any one individual but that also are not accessible by the underwriting companies.

Whereas the major issues of relationship ownership arise as a consequence of compensation incentives, this topic would not be complete without some mention of corporate culture. The knowledge and skills of employees are in substantial part portable—an employee can take them along in moving among employers. Nevertheless, some value does attach to a common sense of direction and how to do things that often distinguishes one enterprise from another. It can facilitate communication in ways that make production and distribution more efficient and responsive, and it can encourage new ideas and innovation. Essentially by definition, that value is transferable only by large numbers of employees moving as a group. At least one source of disappointment in acquisitions and corporate restructuring has been mindless destruction of this asset resulting from management failure to comprehend its value.

Summarizing, the ownership of a set of market relationships is not always obvious, in which case the entity with claim to their value may be unclear. Clarity on this point nevertheless must govern business strategies and decisions. Many companies invest in developing customer relationships that adhere to individual representatives rather than to themselves. As such relationships may be transportable, the investment may be unrecoverable. Consequently, investing in market relationship development often requires special care that the outlays will be recoverable.

Hybridization of Market Relationships

Earlier discussion distinguished between vertical and horizontal market relationships, and, from the standpoint of an individual corporate enterprise, between internal and external. It nevertheless suggested that these distinctions may be rather blurred. Indeed, in many cases, they may be becoming increasingly so.

Most of the previous discussion focused on vertical relationships, which commonly contain significant adversarial as well as cooperative elements, as the respective parties are on opposite sides of the marketplace. Beyond the range of mutual advantage, the more one party obtains from it, the less is available to the other. Mutual interests are more likely to predominate in horizontal relationships, the parties often being on the same side of the marketplace.

A very common example of horizontal relationships, although perhaps unfamiliar to much of the urban population, is the agricultural cooperative. In some cases the cooperative is a supplier. In many farming communities the grain elevator and feed mill are cooperatively owned and operated by the local farmers. Electrification of many rural areas might never have taken place without electrical cooperatives. Rural telephone systems developed in the same manner. More visible and familiar are some of the marketing cooperatives among sellers, although many consumers probably are unaware of their cooperative form. A few, including Land O'Lakes (dairy products), Sunkist (citrus fruit products), and Ocean Spray (cranberry products) are common household names.

Horizontal economic relationships spread across a spectrum in much the same way as vertical relationships, depending on relationship strength or intensity. Many involve only private enterprise, but many others represent cooperative or partnership arrangements between government and the private sector. Government involvement in weapons systems design, housing, and home finance provides numerous examples. Additional examples are cases of government favoring certain firms or industries with subsidies, protection from competition, or other forms of corporate welfare.

Without attempting to be comprehensive, which is scarcely possible in any event, a depiction of the intensities of different types of horizontal relationships might be as follows:

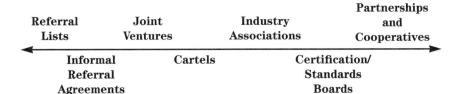

Spectrum of Horizontal Business Relationships.

The general idea behind the diagram is to rank horizontal relationships according to both their enforceability and their potential longevity. Partnerships and cooperatives normally rely on binding agreements to be maintained. Constructing and operating a grain elevator, for example, require long-term commitments. On the other hand, customer referrals such as among sellers of different products and services may be rather transitory. Joint ventures are inserted slightly to the left of the center of the diagram simply because they may be temporary. One example is two manufacturers of military aircraft agreeing to jointly design and produce a particular new model. Another is a now defunct international joint venture to build a super-jumbo passenger aircraft.

Cartels as arrangements governing the pricing practices of their members are more common abroad than in the United States, where they are for the most part illegal. They may arise from informal agreements that tend to be short-lived or, particularly where public policy encourages them, they may endure indefinitely governed by firm agreements. Thus, some cartels belong somewhere near the center of the diagram while others belong toward the right. This point touches on the difficulty of attempting to rank these types of relationships.

Many types of cartels with objectives other than colluding on prices, such as industry-standard and certification bodies, are legal in the United States because they increase efficiency in production and distribution. They may set design or professional standards but must avoid all forms of involvement in setting prices or otherwise engaging in anticompetitive behavior. They therefore affect or control only certain elements of the business practices of their members, but the arrangements they represent tend to be rather permanent.

Distinguishing horizontal from vertical relationships may nevertheless overstate matters. Interests of different participants in the marketplace overlap, diverge, and conflict in different degrees. In particular, the growing complexity of economic activity has caused areas of mutual interest to expand while the adversarial elements shrink. Cooperation and even collaboration along the supply chain appear to be increasingly common, particularly in manufacturing. Cooperative relationships may extend up the supply chain to a supplier's suppliers and down the chain to a customer's customers:

Alternative Supply Chain Relationships.

Thus, even traditionally vertical forms of relationships are tilting toward the horizontal:

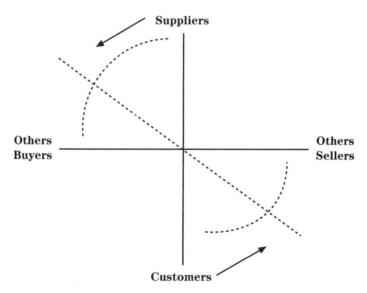

Expanding Horizontal Characteristics of Market Relationships.

Examples are suppliers who assume responsibility for keeping track of their customers' parts inventories and the Levi Strauss custom-fitting program. Notice how the latter involves cooperation between the customer, the retailer, and the manufacturer. The customer gets a better product, paying for value added, while both the manufacturer and the retailer reduce their inventory requirements.

Similarly, if perhaps to a lesser degree, a melding process seems to be taking place between internal and external market relationships. A common example is widespread outsourcing of parts supplies and services that managers regard as outside the core competencies of their business. To be effective, outsourcing requires close relationships with suppliers. While the overall trend seems to be toward more outsourcing, instances of a reverse pattern are not uncommon. Cooperative relationships still are likely to contain divergent interests as well, often causing them to be unstable.

Government Economic Relationships

This discussion would be incomplete without commenting briefly on government participation in economic relationships. Governments are, of course, major buyers of goods and service as well as direct sellers of services. They also coventure with private enterprise in areas such as military hardware, education, and, more recently, welfare. In these respects governments are partners with the private sector in a wide variety of market relationships.

Clearly, the impact of government is far more pervasive than mere statement of this point suggests. Apart from its role in providing the infrastructure essential to orderly economic activity, political relationships are inextricably intertwined with economic ones. Within broad limits, public policy is for sale. The high costs of political campaigns assure as much. In some cases the result may be special favors; more often, though, what is for sale is inaction, not action. Under normal conditions government is primarily an instrument of establishment interests in preserving the status quo. Political gridlock occurs not so much because of opposing interests as because of enormous pressures to do nothing. Major exceptions occur mainly in times of crisis. The Great Depression enabled enactment of Social Security and securities regulation. The manpower needs of World War II resulted in the first steps by government in promoting civil rights.

Government, indeed, often acts to constrain private initiative. In some instances the applicable statutes and regulatory structures once had some justification that eroded with time. The Interstate Commerce Commission's original role was to prevent monopoly pricing when railroad franchises hauled most of the nation's freight. In time it became an agent for deterring competition by preventing competitive pricing. Legislation that for years prevented geographic and product expansion by banks had a more dubious origin. The problems confronting banking in the early 1930s were at least as much an excuse as a reason. Meanwhile, pressures for foreign trade protection never go away. One often-used section of the trade statutes, commonly called the *escape clause,* purportedly is to protect an industry and its workers from competition due to new circumstances until they have had time to adjust. The adjustments somehow rarely reach the point of rescinding the protection.

The lesson from this brief review is simply again to underscore the powerful constituencies underlying common convention and the status quo. One need only to look at government for models of reactionaryism even more extreme than those afflicting much of corporate society.

Conclusions on Relationship Capital

The objective thus far has been to demonstrate the growing significance of market relationships in today's economy. Business management and decisions must recognize that significance or go awry. In particular, they must recognize that such relationships both permeate virtually all economic activity within organizations as well as with the outside world. Furthermore, those relationships normally have consequences extending well into future time, in which case management decisions inescapably become investment decisions.

Remaining ahead is an examination of how to incorporate these concepts into a workable business decision-making framework. That effort nevertheless requires first dispelling various institutionalized misconceptions underlying management theory and business principles and practices.

CHAPTER 3

Seizing Opportunity from Economic Revolution

BUSINESS STRATEGIES AND DECISIONS

The June 1944 Allied invasion of Normandy implemented an enormously complex and ambitious strategy resulting from many months of analysis and planning. Its ultimate objective, of course, was to defeat the Axis powers, particularly Nazi Germany. That objective was beyond all compromise, and any other objectives had to be consistent with it. For example, an earlier attempt might have reduced civilian casualties in Europe and the Soviet Union. On the other hand, an earlier invasion, enabling less preparation, would have had a higher risk of failure, with little possibility of any foreseeable further attempt. As it was, the priority given to victory in Europe entailed a lower priority to near-term victory in the Pacific.

Military operations such as the Normandy invasion are instructive on a number of points, not least of which is the military origin of *strategic* and *strategy*. In modern usage a strategy is a careful plan or method by which to achieve some goal. Perhaps, however, the earlier military context has special relevance. Business strategies are means of achieving objectives in what the strategists regard as a threatening or hostile environment.

Upon determining a strategic objective, the first step in achieving it is to determine how to accomplish it. Germany's defeat required obtaining substantial Allied military superiority on the Continent. That first required removing the threat of the Luftwaffe to Allied troop and supply ships. Nazi land defenses along and behind the beaches required quick and effective attack by both sea and landing forces. Finally, the landings had to be where the Nazi defenders were least prepared, yet within manageable distances for a continuing flow of supplies and air cover.

The planners thus had to decide what to do, how and when to do it, and even who should do it. What to do (the Normandy invasion) depended on how and when, which depended in turn on the logistical availability of sufficient equipment, supplies, and manpower. Manpower availability particularly depended on the buildup of American personnel, which depended in turn on events in the Italian and Pacific theaters. Because of the interdependence of these decisions, they essentially had to be simultaneous.

Even at the highest level of planning, the invasion strategy required continuing adaptation to changing circumstances and new information. Thus, when weather conditions precluded adequate air cover on the first date selected, the invasion was postponed a day, but was again contingent on weather conditions. A still later date would have been contingent both on weather and on tidal conditions.

Finally, implementing the strategy required a hierarchical decision process. Once the invasion was underway, events would unfold in ways that were not, and often could not have been, fully foreseen. Decisions passed from the Allied supreme command to the commanders on the beaches, and as circumstances became more localized, they passed down through the ranks to the noncommissioned officers and common soldiers in the field.

Business strategies are similar to military strategies, and equally important to achieving objectives. Just what constitutes a strategy in a business context has nevertheless been an object of much obfuscation and dispute. Contemporary business "theorists," consultants, and the like too often promote ideas as strategies that surely are nothing of the sort. One all-too-familiar example is process reengineering, which is too incomplete by itself to be strategic. The same difficulty arises with visioning—imagining all sorts of future possibilities and what they might mean for a business.

An absence of a comprehensive framework built on fundamental business principles has led some corporations to flip-flop from one management fad to another. Without unifying principles and a firm understanding of the economic environment, a true sense of strategic definition and direction becomes an impossibility. The faddish flip-flops, seemingly most common in corporations that are already slipping behind, may thus be no more than stopgaps to placate an anxious investment community. In any event, an apparent disarray in defining business strategies necessitates briefly reviewing certain key points.

A business enterprise must first determine its objectives: *Why* does it exist? *Should* it exist at all? It should exist only to the extent that it identifies opportunities whereby its shareholders are better off with than without its continuing existence.

Assuming it justifies its existence, the business enterprise must then *simultaneously* address three basic questions. They are essentially the same as those that an economic society must address and to which the answers mostly arise from competing in the marketplace:

- *What* goods and services should it produce?
- *How* should it produce and distribute those goods and services?
- *For whom* should it produce and distribute those goods and services?

Finally, to complete the litany as it applies to an individual enterprise, one might add:

- *When* should it produce and distribute those goods and services?

What to produce in a relationship economy may extend beyond simply a physical product or a service. Customers are increasingly interested in the services that physical goods provide, whether they are producer goods or consumer durables. They furthermore are increasingly interested in services that may enhance those direct services, such as through maintenance, servicing, upgrading, or providing useful information.

For whom to produce similarly involves new considerations in today's environment. A relationship marketplace both reduces response times and increases the variety of options. Focusing on one's mainstream customers is temptingly easy but may miss fringe developments that will prove more significant over the longer term. A major potential pitfall of a relationship marketplace is that it can easily give rise to its own status quo.

Determining *when* requires recognition of the constraints imposed by external circumstances, including the market position, that face the enterprise and its internal resources and capabilities. Timing is an essential element of strategy. A strategy may permit at some future time what is not possible today. Substantially more capital may be necessary to develop some perceived opportunity. The financial markets, however, may provide it only with more demonstration of its potential. Leapfrogging into some altogether new market may be beyond the enterprise's current resources, yet entry may be achievable if undertaken by gradual expansion.

A true, viable corporate strategy therefore should have at least three attributes:

- It must be a comprehensive, unified framework for addressing *all* of the foregoing questions simultaneously.
- It must extend through future time at least as far as the outcomes of adopting any of today's options extend.
- It therefore must be *the* basis for *all* corporate policies and management decisions.

A business program failing to address all of these issues simultaneously therefore cannot be a complete strategy. A strategy must also be incomplete if it overlooks alternatives by focusing on too short a time horizon. Marketing, acquisition, and corporate restructuring strategies therefore are generally not by themselves genuinely strategic. Rather, properly conceived, they should represent extensions of more comprehensive strategies.

Many currently popular management ideas and "theories" focus almost entirely on the *how* of production and distribution. Visioning—speculating on future possibilities—is an exception, yet it may be too abstract to reach any of these questions. Nevertheless, any of these various exercises, whether for reorganizing production and distribution or for trying to predict the future, may well be entirely legitimate if properly applied to appropriate circumstances as elements of more comprehensive strategic frameworks. To apply them as strategies in and of themselves, however, guarantees disappointment or worse.

The apparent attractiveness of many so-called strategies that are fundamentally nonstrategic is a symptom of some deep-rooted problems:

- *Corporate misdirection:* Many enterprises exhibit strategic confusion by pursuing inappropriate and often incompatible

business objectives, unaware of or insensitive to the inconsistencies.
- *Misperception of the environment:* Failure to understand the relationship economy and underlying sources of enterprise value acts to erode linkages between business strategies and enterprise objectives.
- *Corporate myopia:* In cases when competitive momentum erodes, companies may cast about for what seem to be the quickest and easiest remedies that at least will provide the investment community with some appearance of redress.

Might one sense the potential for tragedy, in the true sense of the word? Tragedy is when the central figure (a CEO) misperceives the surrounding reality. Perhaps he is blinded by hubris, as in Greek tragedy, or simply uncomprehending of the effects of his actions, as in Shakespearean tragedy. The true reality ultimately emerges, but only too late for the hero to save himself (or the enterprise in his charge).

The Necessity of Strategies

Every business requires a strategy. Actually, every business *has* some sort of strategy, even if it is only implicit and simply by default. Even avoiding all initiative—doing nothing—is a form of strategy. Of course, following a strategy, however passively or reactively, need not mean systematic pursuit of defined objectives. Some strategy must exist if only because many business decisions have consequences extending well into the future. Strategies ultimately represent selecting among long-term commitments—a process that ultimately is unavoidable.

The issue is therefore not just having a strategy; it is having a strategy that uniformly directs an organization toward its defined objectives. As decision outcomes extend to future circumstances that are not fully foreseeable, a strategy must further recognize the uncertainties and be adaptable. Developing an effective business strategy is a continuing, never-ending process.

The Supremacy of Shareholder Value Objectives

The overriding strategic objective of a corporation must be to maximize the value of the enterprise to its shareholders. Understanding the uncompromisable supremacy of the shareholder, or enterprise, value objective does not preclude adopting additional objectives. It only requires that other objectives be consistent with it. Too often, however, additional objectives intentionally or unintentionally undermine achievement of the primary objective.

A corporation is above all else a financial entity. It is an instrument for funding business activity. Shareholders provide it with the financing necessary for it to exist and to compete in the marketplace. More specifically, they provide it with equity capital, representing ownership. Equity capital in turn enables the corporation both to acquire income-producing assets unencumbered by debt and, by providing that protection, to incur debt so as to acquire yet more income-producing assets. What corporate managers can or cannot do ultimately depends on the willingness of shareholders to continue to provide capital.

The objective of the shareholders themselves is to obtain the highest possible return on, and eventual recovery of, their equity investment. Investment returns and recovery necessarily occur over future time. The only means of recognizing the element of time, and the manner in which the marketplace does so, is to translate the future returns and recovery into current, or present, values. These reflect the fact that a dollar today is worth more than that same dollar sometime in the future. Moreover, that future dollar is worth less with increasing risk of receiving something less than that dollar.

Without risk, that dollar a year from now might have a value of, say, 95 cents. The difference between today's value of 95 cents and the future value, $1.00, represents the time value of money—compensation for letting someone else use the 95 cents for the next year. It may be that the individual possessor of the 95 cents simply will have no need for it over the next year. For society as a whole, however, surrendering the use of funds to others means deferring one's own consumption—immediate enjoyment of those funds—to some future time. If doubt exists about repayment of those funds, providers require additional compensation for that risk. Thus, with some risk, one might pay only, say, 80 cents for the (uncertain) prospect of receiving that dollar. Of the difference, 5 cents is the time value of money, and 15 cents covers the risk.

Shareholders as a class ultimately receive returns and recover their investment from a corporation only as dividends, which consist of all forms of cash payment by the corporation to its shareholders. In addition to periodic dividends in the conventional sense, dividends also include any proceeds from future sale or liquidation of part or all of the enterprise. Here, a sale includes sales of just some assets, and even distributions of assets, including cash, in exchange for some of its outstanding shares (stock buybacks). In other words, by definition, shareholders collectively receive nothing back on their investment other than dividends.

The value of corporate equity must therefore be the present value of all expected future dividend payments. To be sure, shareholders normally expect to sell their shares sometime before sale or liquidation of the corporation. Future share prices nevertheless still must be consistent with long-term dividend expectations. Share prices may deviate in the short term from long-term dividend values, but such deviations are necessarily temporary. Of course, the expectations governing those values are likely to be changing constantly. Keep in mind, too, that this conceptual view of equity values requires some qualification due to the double taxation of most dividend income, first as corporate earnings and again as personal income.

Corporate directors have a fiduciary responsibility to shareholders to maximize the value of their investment; acting on behalf of those shareholders, directors presumably hire chief executives to pursue that objective. For whatever reason, directors and managers who fail to pursue shareholder value objectives unavoidably undermine a corporation's ability to continue to attract capital and to compete effectively. In the first instance, such failure impairs the ability of the enterprise to obtain new capital. If the corporate governance operates according to theory and fiduciary responsibilities, continuing failure induces the shareholders to demand higher dividends, thereby reducing capital. The end result might be sale of the enterprise.

Corporate governance issues do seem endemic, however. Shareholders often have little say in the selection of directors, and senior executives often have some latitude to pursue their personal, more immediate objectives to excess. One ploy is to overinvest earnings in the business—reinvest beyond the point of obtaining returns at least equal to what the shareholders require—and claim additional compensation because of the "growth" in sales, earnings, and share prices. Still, however attractive such management practices may seem in the short run, the long-term effect of such corporate evisceration must be a gradual erosion in dividends *and* share prices. Management may simply have postponed the day of reckoning, albeit perhaps to its own advantage.

Apart from possible disregard, shareholder value objectives tend also to be compromised by other objectives. Especially pernicious is the idea, promoted by some management theorists, that various other "stakeholders" have legitimate claims on a corporate enterprise. Actually, those other stakeholders often represent entities with which economic relationships are shared, as with customers and employees. Maximizing the relationship components of the underlying enterprise value will both meet those claims to the extent they are legitimate, *and* maximize the value of the enterprise to shareholders. Beyond this coincidence of interests, attending to such stakeholder interests merely depletes corporate resources and competitiveness.

These concepts of converging values and interests represent fundamental principles requiring further attention. Later chapters will return to them in more detail.

The Responsiveness Spectrum

Competing effectively to pursue shareholder value objectives requires understanding the emerging marketplace. It further requires determining how to deal with the process of rapid economic transformation. Simple logic suggests that new circumstances require new response mechanisms, which in turn require new types of information and new ways of understanding and analyzing that information.

Part of the difficulty in adapting to the emerging relationship economy is the constantly accelerating pace of change—a pattern that seems to have been present throughout human history. An additional difficulty in a relationship environment is that important changes, including new forms of competition, are often less visible, at least in their earlier stages of development. Keeping pace with economic change consequently requires ever faster response times, whatever the level of response. Consider responses as along a spectrum extending from no response at one end to anticipation at the other end, like so:

No Response ⟶ Reaction ⟶ Creative Response ⟶ Anticipation

Spectrum of Responsiveness to Market Changes.

Moving from left to right along the spectrum indicates more resilience to change. Failure to respond, perhaps due to failure to recognize and understand what is happening, invites extinction. The Romans, for example, never really comprehended the corruption and lassitude that ultimately undermined their empire. Simple reaction to change is a relatively passive form of response, such as by following the responses of others.

Many cases of corporate restructuring seem to be reactive responses in that sense, however dramatic some may seem otherwise. Prior failures to respond adequately may have caused a loss of competitiveness. Upon becoming aware of the problem, corporate managers tend first to seek quick remedies. The difficulty with this type of reaction is that it may actually put the corporation on a course contrary to any viable long-term strategy. In too many cases it seems rather like trying to stem a hemorrhage with a Band-Aid. Meanwhile, do the quick fixes solve the management problems that required remedy in the first place?

Creative responses may still follow rather than lead the change process, yet do things differently or better than rivals that are leading that process. Creative responses therefore tend to be innovative. Finally, anticipation means being ahead of changing circumstances and thus being prepared to meet them head-on as they emerge. It, too, implies innovation in some form. Success does not necessarily require being the most creative or innovative, however. On the contrary, the most successful innovators are often those who are prepared to move most quickly to improve on the pioneering, and perhaps unsuccessful, efforts of others. Anticipating change successfully implies some ability to predict it. It usually implies as well a willingness to assume the risks of wrong predictions.

As the change process accelerates, confronting it in the same old ways results in shifting to the left along the spectrum of response. For example, as the time necessary to develop a creative response gets shorter, what may once have been a creative mechanism for responding may drift into being merely reactive. Failure to recognize the obsolescence of response mechanisms is one reason corporate giants often ossify, shrivel, and perhaps disappear altogether, yet passive acceptance of this shift is often unnecessary and self-inflicted. Later chapters explore those strategies and decisions necessary to reverse this process and thereby become more, not less, creatively responsive and anticipatory.

Responsiveness does not always mean initiating action, even if anticipatory. Rather, it represents management's degree of understanding of the changes in its environment. Fully understanding those changes may indicate adopting a wait-and-see posture. That implication nevertheless is probably much the exception, and may be dangerous.

Strategic Options

Previous chapters considered the major characteristics of a relationship economy. Now consider what those imply about choosing among strategic options. Fundamentally, alternative approaches to the marketplace reduce to choosing between lower prices and better quality. Define *quality* to encompass a number of elements that represent how well a product or service meets a customer's needs, preferences, and expectations. Qualitative factors might thus include:

- *Availability:* Upon recognizing a want or need, how quickly and conveniently can a customer obtain the goods or services that meet that need?
- *Flexibility:* How much choice is available to customers in meeting particular wants or needs?
- *Customization:* To what extent will a seller adapt a good or service to the needs or preferences of different buyers?
- *Reliability:* Will the good or service provide the satisfaction that the seller has led a buyer to expect?
- *Durability:* Particularly in cases of durable goods, how long will the expected services continue to be available?

Notice the variety of possibilities suggested by these qualitative characteristics, understanding that the list is probably incomplete.

Availability (or accessibility) includes nonprice elements of the cost of obtaining a good or service. Thus, if something is available only at some distant location, a buyer might choose among the inconvenience of fetching it, the cost of having the seller ship it, and simply not purchasing it. Meanwhile, flexibility and customization may partly overlap, as may also reliability and durability. For present purposes, consider *customization* as a continuum with increasing customization meaning adaptation to ever smaller market segments. It is much more likely to reach its limit at the individual customer level when sales are to business customers rather than to consumers, yet full customization is slowly becoming more common even in consumer markets.

Most industrial-age consumers had very little choice between price and quality. Beyond quite basic levels achievable with mass production, adding more quality meant sharply higher production costs, with prices that would be unacceptable to most buyers. Competitive pricing thus required homogenization of output to allow substantial cost economies from large-scale production. Observe that just as the options available to buyers were restricted, so too were the strategic options available to sellers. Apart from boutique enterprises catering to the rich, cost economies drove business strategies.

Today, nonetheless, modern technologies have made quality in all of its dimensions substantially more affordable to much of the marketplace:

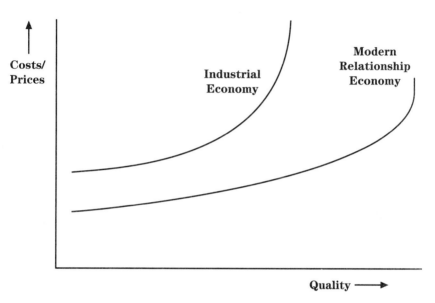

Quality Gains from Customer Relationships.

One consequence is expansion in the number of dimensions in which a business must compete. As each competitor upgrades or proliferates its own offerings to attract customers, its rivals must either do likewise or develop new ways to reduce costs and prices.

The significance of this shift is the opening up of new dimensions for business strategies. Strategic options are now likely to include:

- *Output specialization versus more flexibility:* Internally, given the size of an enterprise, the declining significance of cost economies from large-scale production allows more variation in outputs for any particular market.
- *Output homogenization versus customization:* Although the significance of scale and resulting cost economies has de-

clined, it has by no means disappeared altogether. Externally, while more consumers can afford some customization, prices remain the primary concern of many producers and much of the consuming public.

- *Output accessibility versus centralization:* The tradeoffs here are between different types of distribution channels. In the consumer marketplace, for example, is distribution through community outlets or centralized warehouse discounters? Among industrial buyers and sellers, to what extent should a supplier integrate its production with the needs of individual buyers?
- *Core concentration versus conglomeration:* To what extent, if at all, should an enterprise diversify into a number of essentially unrelated businesses? In at least some instances the same factors that reduce the importance of specialization within product and service markets are likely to reduce it among altogether different markets.

Credit cards provide a good as well as familiar example of strategic options and how they can change with the emergence of new technologies. Credit cards emerged as a significant payment and credit instrument in the late 1960s. Their early growth was a result of local banks issuing them to their own deposit customers, enabling important cost economies in card marketing. Cardholder solicitation was mainly by take-one application forms available in bank lobbies or bank statement-stuffer promotions. Both within card programs and among different issuers, credit cards were an essentially homogeneous product.

By the early 1980s, a number of developments were evident. First, credit card administration is predominantly a data-processing function, which by that time offered enormous cost economies from large scale. Second, the prospects of those cost economies led some of the largest banks to reach well beyond their traditional markets in soliciting new cardholders. In many instances they also acquired portfolios from other banks. In others they used information from automated credit files to solicit otherwise unknown and remote cardholder prospects while controlling their credit risks. Depositor relationships with banks, meanwhile, became much less significant to credit card marketing. Many smaller bank issuers dropped out of this business altogether. Finally, new data-processing technologies allowed issuers to offer new card products, such as "gold" cards with higher credit limits, as well as standard cards.

Still different trends were apparent by the end of that decade. Marketing assumed new significance as card prospects became inundated with solicitations. Opportunities for competing purely on pricing (annual fees and credit terms) were disappearing. Issuers instead sought new ways to differentiate their card products. One approach was affinity cards linked to various nonbank products, services, and associations (airlines, automobiles, and alumni associations, for example). Another approach was market segmentation, which uses large databases to distinguish among different types of cardholder prospects, customizing offerings according to the preferences their different characteristics suggest.

Marketing programs by this time were becoming national in scope, with larger shares of the market falling into the hands of predominantly nonbank corporations (AT&T, Advanta, and Discover, for example). How was it that many banks let this business, which most observers perceive as enormously attractive, simply slip away? In the first instance, most apparently lacked the necessary marketing skills. That shortcoming reflected an absence of workable strategies for retaining this business. Many banks gave little, if any, thought to how credit cards might strengthen other dimensions of their relationships with banking customers.

Enterprise Specialization or Diversification?

Enterprise specialization, particularly as concentrating on core competencies, has gained momentum over the past few years. It essentially represents a retreat from diversification. Is that retreat strategic, or is it a sign of desperation? To be sure, the more extreme versions of conglomerates, as pioneered by ITT, lost their allure some time ago, but some degree of internal corporate diversification has never entirely disappeared.

The case against significant internal diversification rests on perhaps two arguments. One is that a multiplicity of businesses can easily become unmanageable. Even variations within product lines may challenge management capabilities. More complexity at top management levels may detract from the agility with which an enterprise is capable of adapting to rapidly changing market conditions. This disability probably is particularly acute for those who have already slipped behind in their competitive responses.

Once deterioration sets in, what was once manageable may become less so. For an enterprise in this situation, however, more urgency may attach to corporate shrinkage to preserve what capital and other resources remain. At least some cases of emphasizing core competencies seem to fit this description.

A second argument against internal corporate diversification is that investors attach no value to it. Theoretically, they can achieve virtually any level of diversification they might choose by diversifying their stock portfolios. Actually, this argument is related to the previous one, as the issue is not entirely one of investor risk. Diversification also has some importance in an operating sense. In theory, a corporation should achieve fuller utilization of at least some of its resources diversifying its output and markets. With a decline in demand in one market, perhaps rising demand in others will absorb a larger share of the overhead—elements of costs that are difficult to reduce in the short run without adverse long-term consequences.

These possibilities have a new significance in a relationship environment. At issue are levels of utilization of capital in the forms of customer relationships, management skills, employee relationships, and corporate culture. Many companies have difficulty recouping prior losses of relationship capital, which tends to be more susceptible to loss in the short run than plant and equipment. Capital, whatever its form, is scarce. A corporation must pay for it regardless of its level of utilization. Investors therefore have legitimate concern with its use quite apart from financial diversification.

Constraints on Strategic Options

Various constraints limit the strategic options actually available to an enterprise. A necessary step in developing a strategy is to take inventory of its available resources. Its options depend in the first instance on its physical capital, the capabilities of its directors and management, the skills of its employees, its corporate culture, and its external relationships with customers, partners, and suppliers.

These limiting factors all ultimately represent the capital resources already in place. Indeed, the ultimate strategic constraint is on the availability of capital, first in the form of financial capital and then as the production capacity it can use that financial capital to acquire. Expansion into new markets, whether as a shift in market focus or as an overall expansion program, normally requires commitments of additional capital. The more extensively or rapidly an enterprise expands, the more capital it requires.

The need for more capital is more obvious when expanding into new markets without abandoning old ones. An issue in cases of abandonment is how much capital is transferable from one use or market to another. Capital in the form of plant and equipment may be transferable at least in part if new products require only modest modifications. A steel mill, on the other hand, has little alternative use if customers turn to foreign suppliers or substitute aluminum for steel. Counterparts to such situations arise with relationship capital. Abandoning a market may mean sacrificing some customer relationships while investing in developing others in new markets. A shift in strategic focus may similarly require investing in internal accumulation of new skills while others become obsolete.

The availability of capital—the ability to invest in developing new opportunities—depends on the rate as well as the scale of investment and expansion. Logically, the more rapid the investment, the faster the enterprise is likely to venture from the known to the unknown. Rapid changes of direction and expansion thus signify more risks to investors. The higher those risks, the higher the returns investors require.

The availability and costs of capital to an enterprise thus accentuate the significance of the dimension of time in formulating business strategies. A simple diagram illustrates this point:

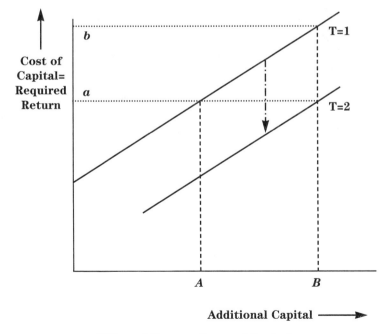

Effect of Time on Costs of Capital.

Suppose that an amount of capital A in the diagram is available today at a cost of capital a. If the corporation tries to raise an amount B *today*, its cost of capital will rise to b. The same amount of capital, B, nevertheless may be available at cost a if sought over a longer period of time. The strategic issue is how to use amount A—with or without a view to eventually obtaining B. An analogy is whether to construct a small building now with the possibility of an addition later; a larger, better-designed building now at a much higher cost of capital; or delay the latter until a more modest cost of capital is available.

Some of the most attractive alternatives may require capital accumulation and repositioning over long periods. They may also require sacrificing near-term opportunities that are not as attractive over the long term. Again, failure to extend strategic horizons to the limits of opportunity is to risk eventual relapse into a reactive posture.

Strategies as a Form of Capital

A discussion of business strategies is incomplete without observing that their successful development is itself an investment process requiring significant commitment of internal resources. Again, keep in mind that implicitly, if not explicitly, every business has a strategy. The analogy is that decision alternatives usually include the option of doing nothing. The issue is therefore the effectiveness of a strategy in achieving appropriate objectives.

The responsibility for developing effective strategies ultimately falls on a corporation's chief executive and the directors. They, in turn, must first commit however much of their own time as is necessary to exercise that responsibility. Instead, directors often are not fully drawn into the process and chief executives are too distracted by administrative details or other pursuits to give it the attention and exercise the leadership it deserves.

Secondly, resources must be made available to assemble and absorb strategic inputs—the creative ideas, insights, and information that the process requires. In reality, corporate managers often have too little information about customers and markets to provide adequate inputs. They also look too often to mainstream thinking for insights and ideas, partly because it is the most conveniently available and partly because unconventional, out-of-the-box thinking is discomforting.

Establishing Strategic Control

Consider the purpose of a business strategy as being to establish control over one's business environment. At some risk of repetition, if it is to be effective, a strategy must be a comprehensive framework that governs all corporate policies and decisions. This requirement means that:

- Every decision must have a *direct*, identifiable linkage to the strategy.
- The criteria governing decisions must therefore tie *directly* to corporate objectives.
- The overriding corporate objective, maximizing the value of the enterprise to its shareholders, requires formulating decision criteria in terms of *direct* contributions to that value.

Strategies, even when explicit and seemingly well intended, often fail for a variety of related reasons:

- Tentativeness, reflecting failure to commit sufficient resources.
- Inconsistencies among objectives.
- Preoccupation with the near term, often reflecting urgency in redressing past failures.
- Incompleteness due to failure to consider fully long-term possibilities and opportunities.
- Incompleteness due to failure to address all of the key strategic issues—*what, how, for whom,* and *when.*
- Tunnel vision due to failure to consider, and perhaps avoiding, unconventional and possibly contrary ideas and insights.
- Retrogression, by relying on past economic patterns and apparent certitudes.
- Insufficient commitments, whereby strategy formulation becomes a mechanical process with little senior management and director involvement.
- Insufficient information due to inadequate investment in developing relevant information.

These lapses in attentiveness and commitment are not alone in causing strategy failures. They may not even be the major causes. In addition, strategy failure will remain all too common as long as the business and financial communities continue to adhere to outdated and increasingly subversive business principles and practices.

PART 2

The Four Sides of the Box

The primary focus of financial reporting is information about earnings and its components.

Financial Accounting Standards Board, *Statement of Financial Accounting Concepts No. 1: Objectives of Financial Reporting* (1978)

4

The Timeless World of the Economists

THE FOUR-SIDED BOX

Four different major types of boundaries impede out-of-the-box business thinking, thus deterring questioning of, and thereby preserving, outdated principles and assumptions:

- The practice of economics as a social science, which, often for simplification, relies on incomplete and inadequate concepts of economic theory. One result is apparent endorsement of inappropriate business principles and measures of performance. Another is improper measurement of economic variables by economists in their own research.
- The principles governing public financial reporting, particularly as a basis for internal business decision making. Conventional measures of corporate condition and performance unavoidably misstate, often seriously, the economic realities. Particularly in a relationship environment, using those measures as a basis for business decisions systematically undermines achieving essential corporate objectives.
- Financial analysis and advisory services that, while relying on inadequate information, exert pressures on corporate enter-

prises to pursue inappropriate objectives. Some tend further to exaggerate misinterpretations of enterprise performance and condition, in large part to promote their own objectives.

- Management "theorists" and consultants, who similarly exaggerate the decision-making significance of public financial information. Some add further to corporate misdirection by promoting false and inadequate remedial programs that have little or no strategic content and no comprehensive foundation in business principles.

One should not necessarily assume that the box has no more than four sides. Furthermore, a close look suggests boxes within boxes. An example is lack of communication among different members of the same professions. Even academic departments within universities, to say nothing of the schools and departments themselves, are often conglomerations of independent groups and individuals. Communications within many business organizations are similarly compartmentalized. The above four sides of the box nevertheless seem to be those with special significance to obtaining an understanding the relationship economy.

Elements of Strategy

Simultaneously determining the *what, how, for whom,* and *when* of production and distribution requires a comprehensive framework for evaluating and selecting among alternatives. Developing that framework involves at least the following steps, each of which will receive further attention:

1. General recognition that conventional, profit-oriented principles tend to be contrary to shareholder interests, impairing the long-term ability of a corporation to attract and retain capital and thus jeopardizing its long-term competitive survival.

2. Corresponding abandonment of profit objectives in favor of enterprise value objectives, which in turn requires information whereby management can base individual decisions directly on how they will contribute directly to enterprise value.

3. Corresponding adoption of value-based decision criteria, in turn requiring that corporate directors and chief executives

fully understand the underlying sources of value of the corporation.

4. Recognition that management's fundamental understanding of its business is impossible without fully understanding and attending to those underlying value elements.

5. Understanding that the true capital and value of the enterprise include identifiable intangible assets, among which are its continuing economic relationships with customers and employees as well as its proprietary knowledge and information.

6. Recognition that the absence of such a framework results in leeway for pursuing inconsistent and potentially deleterious objectives.

The most difficult task ahead is to make a convincing case for replacing profit conventions with value criteria. Making that case first requires exploring the following questions in some detail, exercising the patience necessary to recognize the obvious in what may initially seem obscure simply because it is unconventional.

- What do the different definitions and measures of *profit* and *earnings* really represent? In what ways are they a deficient basis for corporate objectives? Why do economists, financial professionals, and the business community attach so much significance to them, even when aware of their flaws?

- As profit concepts and measures have indeed become so deficient and distorted as to require their discard for internal decision making, why are value measures and criteria any better? With growing recognition that value criteria are more meaningful and relevant, what impedes their adoption?

Presupposing satisfactory answers to these questions, a value-based decision framework falls into place rather straightforwardly.

The process of assembling that framework yields basic insight into economic behavior. One comes to appreciate the extraordinary tenacity with which economic decisions adhere to common suppositions that preclude contrary objective judgments. The typical economic man tempers his pursuit of material satisfaction with aversion to risks. Avoiding risk by avoiding the unknown guides much of economic activity. That means widespread implicit adherence to familiar, well-understood, institutionalized objectives.

The supremacy of shareholder value objectives is by no means a new idea. Indeed, imparting a value orientation to management decisions is gaining currency in some quarters. A book emphasizing these points within the context of an industrial model (and thus not within a relationship context), written by management consultants from a leading consultancy, is now in its second edition.[1] The problem is not so much the unavailability of new and better ideas as it is widespread resistance to adopting them. That resistance has powerful roots.

A logical starting point is with the economists. Many of today's misconceptions date back to their efforts to develop a theoretical framework for analyzing the then-emerging industrial economy.

The Economists' Perspective

If common textbook principles of economics fall short of providing guidance for addressing contemporary business reality, it is not so much that the economics is wrong; rather, those principles derive from theoretical abstractions whose purpose is normally something different from practical business concerns. The primary concern of microeconomics is to explain market behavior, perhaps but certainly not always with a view toward public policy. Most economists fall into one of three categories:

- *Academicians,* whose inquiries tend to be very narrowly focused.
- *Public policy specialists,* who rely mainly on factual inquiry.
- *Business economists,* who are primarily business forecasters.

Academicians, economists among them, seem no less susceptible to in-the-box entrapment than the rest of society. They also are risk averters, reluctant to venture radically new ideas that might draw scorn from their peers. Moreover, most teachers of economics are quick—arguably too quick—to distinguish their subject matter from business subjects.

Economics nevertheless has not always been so removed and arcane. As Alfred Marshall, a patriarch of contemporary microeconomics, admonished almost a century ago:

---

[1]Tom Copeland, Tim Koller, and Jack Murrin, *Valuation: Measuring and Managing the Value of Companies,* 2d ed. (New York: John Wiley & Sons, 1996). Further references to this work appear in later chapters.

The study of theory must go hand in hand with that of facts: and for dealing with most modern problems it is modern facts that are of greatest use. . . . Economics has then as its purpose firstly to acquire knowledge for its own sake, and secondly to throw light on practical issues.[2]

Marshall was especially concerned with developing insights into the economic revolution of his time—the displacement of agriculture by industrialization. His interest nonetheless extended beyond mere explanation to how to respond to the new economic climate.

The immediate difficulty in applying conventional economics to a relationship marketplace arises from the concept of economic profit. How commonplace is the idea that business is the pursuit of profit, which dates back at least to Adam Smith? Economists routinely develop their inquiries on the assumption that profit maximization is the primary motive of private enterprise. Logically, or so it would appear, business executives, accountants, financial analysts, and management theorists adopt profit as the primary measure of enterprise performance.

This preoccupation with profits creates several difficulties:

- The economists' definition of profit—*economic* profit—is fundamentally different from the profit measures in common use in the business and financial communities.
- Economics actually does recognize that economic profit is imperfect as an enterprise objective or performance measure; rather, it uses the concept as a simplifying assumption while understanding that it lacks a time dimension.
- Many economists therefore understand that the truly appropriate enterprise objective is to maximize its *value* rather than profits, even if they perhaps are derelict in communicating that understanding to noneconomists.
- The widespread lack of concern among economists with the deficiencies of profit maximization results in part from merely assuming that it approximates value maximization—never quite correct in an industrial economy and seriously incorrect in a relationship economy.
- Economists are nevertheless themselves guilty of perpetuating

---

[2] Alfred Marshall, *Principles of Economics,* 6th ed. (New York: The MacMillan Company, 1948), p. 39.

misunderstanding on these points, commonly using conventional but often badly misleading accounting measures of enterprise condition and performance in their own empirical inquiries.
- More broadly, as few economists have much understanding of accounting theory and conventions, they commonly use accounting measures without understanding its deficiencies for those uses.

One major example of such misunderstanding among economists is the compilation of national income and output data, which are important inputs for government economic stabilization policy. Those data come mainly from corporate public financial statements that, as becomes clearer in subsequent chapters, often seriously misstate actual corporate condition and financial performance. In particular, recording outlays on intangible forms of capital as current expenses has generally resulted in substantial understatement of saving and investment rates. The widespread impression that private saving rates in the United States are somehow too low is at least partly illusory.

Measures of corporate performance obviously should be relevant to its objectives. Understanding the meaning of different measures is particularly important to understanding economic relationships. Fortunately, the modifications the conventional economic treatments require are modest and easy to understand without invoking a lot of theory. From an economist's perspective, at least, a value-based decision framework flows directly from its profit-based predecessor.

The Deficiencies of a Profit Objective

How supportable is the proposition that profit criteria and measures are fundamentally faulty to the point of being pernicious? Why abandon what is comfortably familiar for something unfamiliar, especially when it is likely to entail additional costs? In addressing such questions, understand that the alleged deficiencies mainly apply to *practical* uses of profit objectives in a business context. Economic theories relying on profit assumptions retain some important lessons.

The difficulty with any profit measure of financial performance, whatever its definition, is that it cannot itself provide a sufficient basis for comparing and selecting among competing investment opportunities. Management decisions in a relationship context tend inescapably to be investment decisions, as their outcomes usually extend well into

the future. Profit measures have no time dimension. They are therefore incapable of providing appropriate criteria for decision making.
Some simple examples illustrate the problem.

First, consider two different investment alternatives, *A* and *B*:

End of	Profit Received	
Year	*A*	*B*
0 (now)	$60	$50
1	0	50

Alternative *A* provides the investor with an immediate profit (cash
return) of $60, but nothing thereafter. Alternative *B* pays out $50 immediately and another $50 at the end of the following year. Applying a
profit criterion that ignores the future results in choosing alternative
A. Also, the investor might choose *A* in any event due to assigning an
exceptionally high time value of money in making the choice, such as
by having an urgent immediate need for the cash.

Suppose, however, that the marketplace (perhaps measuring the
time value of money differently), requires an investment with *B*'s risks
to yield 20 percent per year. In other words, it is willing to invest in *B*
if it yields at least 20 percent annually. It would then discount the
profits in alternative *B* at 20 percent per year, for a present value of
$91.67. In this case the investor with an immediate need for cash
could simply sell this investment claim, obtaining the $60 otherwise
obtainable from alternative *A, and* have an additional $31.67 for fur-
ther investment or some other purpose.

Before drawing conclusions from this illustration, consider what the
discounting procedure represents:

- An investor in *B* receives $50 immediately.
- To determine how much the $50 at the end of Year 1 is worth
  today, an investor would calculate how much to invest today at
  20 percent to have $50 one year later. The calculated amount
  is approximately $41.67. In other words, in one year an in-
  vestor would receive $41.67 plus 20 percent of that amount, or
  $8.33, for a total of $50.

Thus, of the $50 the investor receives at the end of Year 1, $8.33 is
compensation for waiting one full year to receive it. That amount is
therefore a cost of deferring its receipt, which is a simple version of
the cost-of-capital concept of financial analysis. Net of this cost, the

value of the investment receipts is $50 + $41.67 = $91.67, which is the maximum amount the investor would pay today for this opportunity.

A more conventional method of calculating this present value is to divide the future amount by what $1 would accumulate to over the period (here, one year) at the required rate of return (here, 20 percent), which would in this case be $1.20. Thus:

$$\frac{\$50.00}{\$1.20} = \$41.67$$

This approach, which yields the same result more directly, expresses the cost of capital as a discount factor. (Common practice actually is to omit the dollar sign in a discount factor, which becomes simply 1.2 as a multiple of $1.00 instead of $1.20.)

However simplistic and unrealistic the foregoing illustration may appear, it demonstrates a fundamental proposition: Value-based decision criteria always include *and must supersede* profit criteria. Even when decisions have no future outcomes, value criteria will always lead to selecting those alternatives that best meet value objectives while also maximizing profits.

Only a modest extension of the foregoing example is necessary to demonstrate further that variations in timing of profits undermine their significance as decision criteria. Consider choosing one from among three competing investment opportunities:

End of	Profit Received		
Year	A	B	C
0 (now)	$100	$50	$ 0
1	50	50	50
2	0	50	100

These alternatives are a simplified version of the alternative profit streams depicted in the following diagram. In both of these cases the average profit over time is the same for all three alternatives.

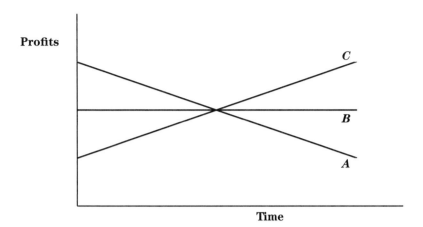

Different Patterns with Identical Average Net Cash Flows.

Again, how can one even define a single profit measure by which to describe and distinguish the three alternatives? Even an average is insufficient. Returning to the table, the average profit in each case is $50, but the values should differ. To the extent of any time value of money—if the present value discount factor is anything above zero—alternative *A* has the highest value. For the same reason, alternative *C* has the lowest value. Investors therefore cannot be indifferent among the three alternatives. Only value measures provide a rational basis for distinguishing among them. This example bears on two important propositions:

- Profit objectives bear the burden of proof that they are at least as relevant to investor preferences as value objectives—a burden they normally cannot sustain. They can never be more relevant than value objectives.
- Relationships and other intangible assets typically have patterns of future investment recovery and returns that are various combinations of the patterns in the above example. Consequently, *only* value criteria provide appropriate decision criteria for those assets.

In particular, the income flows from relationship assets virtually never approach even an approximation of the constant flow of alternative *A*. The second proposition is therefore in contrast to the conventional model of fixed asset investment, as in plant and equipment. The fixed investment model assumes a substantial initial outlay followed by a relatively constant flow of receipts, as in *A*. In contrast, the productive capacity of most intangible assets declines with age rather than remaining even approximately constant.

A diagram comparing future cash flow patterns for a new credit card program, which approximates those of actual cases, with projected cash flows from new machinery may help in understanding this point:

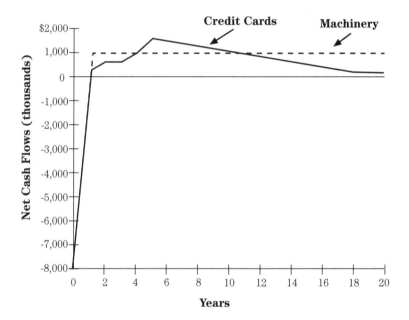

Net Cash Flows from Investments in Machinery and Credit Card Issuance.

The future net cash flows (cash receipts minus cash outlays) represent the source of investment recovery with an investment return. Capital is to be invested either in a new credit card program or in some (hypothetical) form of machinery. The initial outlay, at Time 0, is $8 million in each case. The net cash flows are after expenses necessary to maintain the capital. To be sure, those net cash flows for the machinery probably would decline gradually as maintenance costs increase and efficiency declines, but the assumed pattern is not too unrealistic. Meanwhile, the diagram assumes that the credit card program would generate a positive net cash flow in the first year after its initiation. Subsequently maintaining no more than that amount could never justify the investment, however.

Subtracting straight-line depreciation from the net cash flows generated by the machinery provides a measure of earnings, which in turn might be a reasonable measure of returns on the investment. That measure would at least allow comparison of this investment with other alternatives exhibiting similar patterns of net cash flows (other machines, for example). For that comparison to be legitimate, however, the durations of the cash flows (the useful lives of the various machines in the comparison) must be similar. The longer the life of the assets with the posited pattern, the greater will be the value.

On the other hand, no measure of cash flows—profits, returns on investment, earnings, or whatever—can begin to describe the much more complex patterns associated with the credit card investment. The net cash flows in each year are different from those in any other year. Cash inflows tend to be modest until cardholders build up interest-paying credit balances. High credit losses, common among new cardholders, reduce cash inflows for a few more years. From that point, the net cash flows peak in about the fifth year, then decline continuously as cardholders sever their cardholder relationships. Historically, a few cardholders have maintained such relationships for thirty years or more, although only about five percent have remained as long as twenty years.

Profits and Costs of Capital

An obscure element of the textbook theory of the firm is the treatment of capital outlays and of the required returns on those outlays. Costs in economics represent uses of resources in production. The costs associated with real capital normally consist of two components:

- The using up of that capital in the production process, essentially representing real depreciation.
- The required return on the unrecovered portion of that capital.

To understand the idea of using up capital, think of a machine as having the capacity to produce x total units of product over its lifetime. With time and use in production, less and less of x remains until none is left, at which time the machine is fully depreciated in real terms. If the life of the machine is 10 years and production is at a constant rate, the annual real depreciation is simply $x/10$.

Obviously, the revenues resulting from a capital outlay must be sufficient both to compensate for what is used up and to provide the necessary return for committing resources to future use. The latter component is the economist's time value of money adjusted for inflation and risks. Revenues above these required amounts—above these costs—are economic profits, whenever they occur.

As a rule, investment outlays tend to precede cash inflows, although they may overlap to some extent. Cash receipts essentially consist of three components:

- Recovery of all outlays for both investment and current expenses.
- The required return on unrecovered investment (cost of capital).
- Excess returns, representing economic profit (positive or negative).

Consider, for example, an outlay of $100 on a piece of equipment that will last one year, with no subsequent salvage value. Assume that the required rate of return is 15 percent annually. Revenues of $125 received at the end of the year would break down as follows:

$$
\begin{array}{lr}
\text{Costs: Recovery of capital} & \$100 \\
\text{Required return at 15\%} & \underline{15} \\
& \$115
\end{array}
$$

Economic profit = $125 – $110 = $10

In addition to including the cost concept of required returns on investment, this example further illustrates the idea of using up of capital and its recovery as reflected, if imperfectly, in accounting for depreciation. Thus, the economist's view of how to determine whether some capital outlay was or was not warranted is not by itself a source of difficulty. The difficulties arise in selecting alternatives from arrays of competing opportunities.

Many businesses use the concept of *internal rate of return* (IRR) in evaluating capital outlays. An internal rate of return is the discount factor at which the net present value of a set of expected cash outlays and inflows equals zero. It is therefore an average rate of return on investment, but with no time dimension other than whatever happens to be the life of a particular investment opportunity. It may, superficially, seem to be a measure of profit. Actually, it is a combination of the cost component of a return on investment—the required rate of return, or cost of capital—and economic profit, which may be positive or negative. An internal rate of return exceeding the required rate indicates a prospect for profit.

To conclude, a relationship environment involves patterns of investment outlays and returns that defy summary profit measures. Relying on profits to choose among alternatives in a manner consistent with enterprise value objectives is simply not possible for intangible forms of investment and capital.

Defining Economic Profit

The traditional economics presentation of profit concepts is in terms of *marginal revenues* and *marginal costs*. To maximize profit, production and sales should expand as long as the revenue from selling one more unit (marginal revenue) exceeds the cost of producing and selling that one more unit (marginal cost). The excess simply represents a positive amount of additional profit resulting from that sale (marginal profit). An equivalent proposition is that an enterprise should expand its sales as long as the marginal profit is above zero. Sales at any negative marginal profit reduce total profit.

The economics textbooks assume that revenues and costs are fully distinguishable from one another. That assumption relies on the further assumption that competition revolves solely around a clearly identifiable price. As competitive parameters multiply, some may entail reductions in revenue rather than higher costs; the distinction blurs and loses its usefulness. Thus, decisions even in this timeless world must focus increasingly (and more simply) on marginal profits. The same difficulties arise in adding a time dimension, in which case decision criteria must be in terms of *marginal net present values.*

The following diagrams show the relationships between the concepts of total and marginal profit. Total profit reaches its maximum at sales of 10 units, at which point the difference between total revenues and total costs is largest. This sales level is exactly where marginal profit reaches zero.

Revenues increase with sales at a declining rate because higher

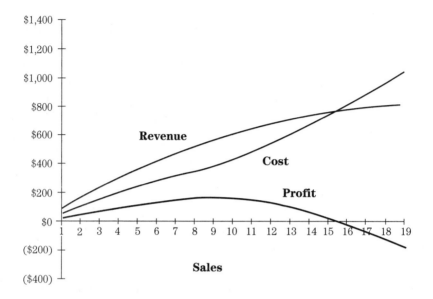

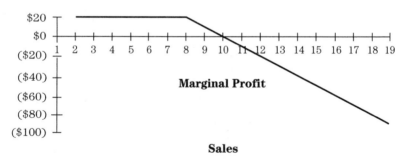

Marginal Profit as Derived from Total Revenue, Cost, and Profit.

sales require reducing prices. Costs tend to rise with sales at an increasing rate because of heavier use of limited production capacity—a specific application of the law of diminishing returns. The main point to notice is that marginal profit goes from positive to negative at exactly that sales level where profit is at a maximum. A profit-maximizing business would increase output and sales in the short run, and increase investment in the business in the long run to the extent that the resulting marginal profit is positive, but would extend its sales and investment no further.

Measures of sales and profits require specifying the amount of time over which they occur. Extending that time has several consequences:

- More time allows for more competition, reducing such control as a seller may have over prices.
- More time allows for expansion or contraction of plant, equipment, and other inputs that are initially fixed in amount.

The effects include:

- The total cost schedule loses some of its curvature as the law of diminishing returns loses significance with more inputs becoming variable rather than fixed in amount.
- The total revenue and total cost schedules collapse toward each other as competition pushes down prices and, very possibly, pushes up input costs.

These pressures mean that:

- Marginal profit tends to disappear altogether, although it may reemerge in either positive or negative form as a consequence of external market developments or with innovation.

To repeat, profit in this context is *economic* profit, which is what remains after recovering prior investment with an adequate return. In the short run it arises either as a windfall gain or a loss due to an external, presumably unanticipated, market change, or as a reward or penalty arising from a seller's own successful or unsuccessful innovation. Except in special cases of monopoly—artificial protection from competition, usually with government collaboration—competition undermines the forces that give rise to profits.

Economic profit always tends to disappear in the long run. It is a short-term phenomenon that sows the seeds of its own destruction by inviting more competition. A continuing pattern of profitability in the economic sense represents a sequence of short-term profits obtainable only by continuing to run ahead of competitors. It requires continuing to innovate successfully or staying ahead of rivals in anticipating changes in the marketplace and technology.

Economists define a short run as any period of time when an enterprise cannot fully change the available amounts of some inputs—the fixed factors of production (such as plant and equipment). The long run refers not only to periods when all inputs become variable but also when additional capital and competition can respond fully to changed circumstances, eliminating profits. In the long run those fixed factors become variable for rivals as well. Insofar as profit potential remains, it attracts expansion and entry by others. Generally, then, profit is a short-run phenomenon.

The easier it is to emulate products and services, the more rapid are likely to be the competitive responses and the shorter will be the economists' short run. Nevertheless, in the real world of imperfect information, constant change, and market frictions, the economic long run never actually comes into being. It is a pure abstraction—real economic life is simply a sequence of short runs. New circumstances tend to develop before adjustment to their predecessors is complete.

Ease of emulation does not necessarily assure this result, however. In some cases potential competitors wait to observe the results of another's innovation before following suit. Those results may become apparent slowly. Of course, response times are much longer when responses require heavy investment in capital equipment or new technologies. Responses requiring development of new market relationships may also be a gradual process.

Notice that the economists' distinction between short and long runs is not really a temporal concept at all; it has no relation to the periods of calendar time over which decisions result in future cash outlays and inflows, and it is therefore useless as a device for comparing profits or investment opportunities. This point requires clarification because of an apparently widespread perception that a long-term measure of profitability exists.

An additional aspect of the economist's long run is that opportunities may exist to change its temporal characteristics. An enterprise might, for example, be able to install equipment that is more adjustable to changing circumstances such as shifts in buyer preferences. At least some of the shift in manufacturing toward robotics is to obtain more flexibility. Obtaining that flexibility normally requires additional investment, but new technologies are increasing their feasibility in many applications. The same principles of built-in flexibility apply as well to relationship investment with respect both to relationship management and to supporting databases.

An important lesson from economics is therefore that a recurrent pattern of true profit is usually very difficult to sustain. If such a pattern is due to a correspondingly recurrent pattern of external market change it becomes more predictable and competition tends to eliminate it merely by anticipating it. If it is due to internal advantages, competition will develop for the sources of those advantages. For example, if management is particularly astute at identifying and developing opportunities for innovation, competition should assure eventual absorption of the profits as commensurate management compensation. If the advantage is from technology, information, or market relationships, competitors will seek to emulate or improve on that edge.

Finally, consider that these concepts of short and long run and capital flexibility probably apply to nations as well as to business enterprises. A more competitive marketplace probably gives rise to more economic flexibility, with adjustment to changing circumstances requiring less time. A major example of an absence of these attributes is the former Soviet Union, which emphasized heavy industry and military hardware. Much of the Russian Republic's adjustment problem today involves overcoming that legacy. A similar problem, perhaps to a lesser degree, exists in Japan. The Japanese postwar economic miracle involved emphasizing certain types of production, particularly of products for export. This emphasis probably still affects the mindset of Japan's economic bureaucracy. Speculating, expect both Eastern Europe and Japan to have inordinate difficulty adjusting to an international relationship economy.

Adapting to Value Principles

What, then, is one to make of the economic models of profit maximization? To the extent that it involves comparisons among alternatives, economic analysis typically assumes tight constraints on the terms of those comparisons—*ceteris paribus,* or everything else being equal. Profit comparisons are often instructive within such constraints. In the real world, however, everything else is anything but the same. Different investment opportunities are likely to have widely varying cash inflow and outflow patterns. They also typically involve different amounts of financing.

If economic theories are to come into closer correspondence with realistic and useful business principles, compromises are necessary. The reasonable course is for economics to recognize the different requirements that a relationship economy imposes by giving more public attention to value principles. To do so is merely a process of adaptation rather than substantial revision. The most fundamental economic principles remain intact.

Failure to adapt in this manner already is resulting in fatuous analysis. Thus, a judgment that a market is uncompetitive may rely on the most visible price variable while overlooking other terms on which a good or service is available to buyers. Similarly, a price may seem uncompetitive because it substantially exceeds production costs, whereas the difference may be necessary to recover prior investment in bringing a good or service to market. Moreover, rates of return on capital will be misleading to the extent of improper definitions of what that capital represents.

Such pitfalls are not imaginary. A familiar example involving intangible assets is the pricing of prescription pharmaceutical products. Allegations of extortionate pharmaceutical pricing were commonplace a generation ago and still recur from time to time. What they often overlook is that most of the outlay in bringing these products to market is prior investment in research and development.

A less excusable example comes from an article, published a few years ago in a major economics journal, that asserted that credit card issuance in the United States was highly uncompetitive.[3] The article attracted an inordinate amount of attention as its publication coincided with congressional deliberations on legislation that would have imposed limits on the interest rates issuers could charge on balances. It argued that finance charges on credit card balances had failed to decline with interest rates because of insufficient competition among card issuers. In doing so it simply overlooked other changes in the cost and pricing characteristics of credit cards, and failed altogether to explain how issuing credit cards could be uncompetitive with some 4,000 U.S. issuers.

To demonstrate this alleged lack of competitiveness further, the article indicated that rates of return on issuing credit cards were at least some three to five times greater than normal. By measuring returns using conventional earnings measures, it failed to recognize the potential for temporal distortions. Worse, it measured the invested capital—the denominator in the rate-of-return calculation—as book equity, estimated at 6 percent of the balances due on cardholder accounts (6 percent representing the ratio of book capital to assets that

---

[3]Lawrence M. Ausubel, "The Failure of Competition in the Credit Card Market," *American Economic Review* 81 (March 1991).

bank regulatory agencies required). Both the earnings and the assets, and hence the capital, thus represented measures according to conventional accounting standards. For a sample of credit card issuers, the calculated average after-tax rates of return on equity over the period 1983 to 1988 ranged from an astonishing 62 to 87 percent!

These comparisons were nonsensical because they failed to recognize that the true equity in credit card issuance, including the capital embedded in cardholder relationships, is typically some 15 to 20 percent or more of the assets. What the article missed underlies the patterns in the credit card example earlier in this chapter. Much of what it measured as profit was nothing more than recovery of prior investment.

This episode also illustrates the apparent difficulty among many economists in recognizing the multidimensional nature of competition in many markets—again, particularly in a relationship marketplace. Credit cards have no single price. Indeed, the different terms on which they are available—annual fees, late-payment charges, over-limit penalties, grace periods without finance charges, minimum payments, credit limits, and so on—vary widely. One significant factor during the 1980s was simply making credit cards available to higher-risk cardholders. Higher finance charges were necessary simply to absorb the costs of higher credit losses.

Innovation, Competition, and Competitiveness

One purpose of this venture into the world of economists is to induce a shift from a profit to a value focus. A second is to emphasize further the perils of complacency in today's rapidly changing business climate.

With regard to this second objective, consider further the process of innovation. An enterprise seeking to remain profitable in the pure economic sense must be an innovator. Simply rolling with the punches of economic change is at best to accept the negative with the positive and hope for luck. Innovation also can have negative as well as positive results. It probably is profitable on balance. The prospect of receiving some positive profit more often than not would seem to be a necessary inducement to innovate. As many innovations do fail, even innovation is by no means an assured path to true profitability. An enterprise that merely succeeds in earning its cost of capital may actually be performing rather well.

Some enterprises approach innovation, usually as new products resulting from their research and development, as virtually itself a form of output. Prescription pharmaceutical manufacturers again provide a familiar example. While some of their research and development (R&D) effort is to develop altogether new therapies, much of it is to improve on existing drugs, particularly those developed and marketed successfully by rivals. Competition thus tends to eliminate the economic profit from R&D investment, although the rates of return on that investment may nevertheless remain relatively high due to relatively high risks. A likely consequence of these sorts of competitive risks is high volatility in prices of technology stocks.

Profits nevertheless do emerge, often in different forms, when competition is weak. The classic economic textbook case is monopoly, whereby one seller (or cartel), having a market to itself, can thwart the forces of competition. Antitrust laws prohibit restrictions on competition in the United States except with government collaboration, often for obsolete or misguided purposes of public policy. Monopoly practices seem more pervasive in many foreign countries.

Consider, however, that while generally more competitive than elsewhere in the world, much of the American marketplace is less than fully competitive. A few years ago a large financial enterprise undertook a major cost reduction program. Its previous earnings record seems to have been reasonably good, and it had been expanding rapidly. Nevertheless, it recognized that a lot of fat had accumulated in the organization over the years. At the time, the chief executive expressed wonderment that the company had been able to remain competitive. According to the economists, competition should have put that sort of company on the ropes years earlier.

How have companies such as this, of which there are many, managed not just to survive competitively but even to prosper? Competition, to be sure, normally takes time to do its work, but that is only part of the answer. The economic models of markets and profit generally begin with an assumption of perfect competition, beyond which they vary the assumptions underlying that model to examine their market effects. The perfect competition model assumes a market with many buyers and many sellers and competition among sellers focusing on pricing. It further assumes that the product offered by those sellers is fundamentally homogeneous and that information about pricing and product offerings is freely available throughout the marketplace.

A counterpart to the economists' competition model is the legal concept of fair market value, which assumes willing buyers and sellers with no compulsion to buy or to sell. It further assumes that buyers and sellers are fully informed. A traditional concern of economists is the effects of buyers having access to relatively few sellers. A more recent concern is the effects of imperfect information in the marketplace.

How can competition work fully if information about a rival's competitive behavior is not readily obtainable? How can it work if buyers have imperfect knowledge about what sellers are offering? More significantly, what happens if the information on which business enterprises depend for developing strategies and making decisions is simply wrong and misleading? Because of insufficient and misleading information, widespread lapses in competitiveness are altogether consistent with market participants perceiving themselves as vigorously competitive.

Suppose, in particular, that every seller in a market pursues goals that are significantly at variance with shareholder value objectives. Indeed, this behavior is commonplace in today's relationship marketplace. A consequence is that each seller wastes resources in developing opportunities that add little if any value while missing others that would add more value. Such waste deters investment in these lines of activity, raising the costs of capital. Competition, such as it is, leads to suboptimal behavior and results.

Where, then, are the profits of these enterprises? They emerge not as profits in the usual economic sense but rather as their ability to waste capital and other resources. In the case of the cost reduction program cited above, "profitability" seems to have been in the form of supporting excess personnel and other unnecessary expenses rather than being something available for distribution to shareholders. The lesson here, however, is not simply that pursuing misguided, distorted objectives thwarts competition; it is also that enterprises engaged in such behavior may count too much on its continuation, remaining trapped in the box. In time, some rival will break out of the box. More effective competition will chew away at those profits and shareholders will become disgruntled.

Indeed, competitive distortions are an inevitable consequence of reliance on distorted performance measures and decision criteria. As the next chapter demonstrates in more detail, these distortions arise from the standards required for public financial reporting. Of course, particularly in looking abroad, deficient information is not the only cause of competitive lapses. Japan perhaps provides the leading example of where convention and custom foster uncompetitiveness, even without intervention by standards-setting bodies or government. Beyond certain social limits, the Japanese have tended to frown on competitive behavior. That attitude has begun to come apart, however, as more Japanese have come to realize that it is costing them dearly in higher prices and fewer options.

Converting to Value-Based Decision Criteria

Converting from the economists' profit concepts to a value-based decision framework requires two fundamental adaptations. One is to recognize forms of capital, particularly relationship capital, in addition to traditional producer goods; the other is to recognize the investment nature of most business decisions and hence reformulate enterprise objectives in terms of present values—in particular, it is to focus specifically on marginal net present values expressed in terms of the amount of investment that a decision entails. The concept of a marginal net present value is essentially an extension of the marginal profit concept presented earlier in this chapter.

The *marginal net present value of investment* is the additional net present value resulting from one additional dollar of investment outlay. *Net* present value is the present value of all cash flows, netting outlays against cash receipts (inflows). Notice, however, an important difference between this formulation and how economists would typically measure marginal profits. The economists' profit model is to determine the amount of some output or sales. The net present value model is to determine inputs, not outputs, in the form of how much to invest. Diagrammatically, the basic decision framework is simply:

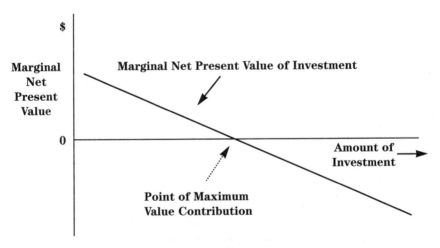

Marginal Net Present Value Contributions from Investment Outlays.

With this construction, achieving the maximum contribution to enterprise value means extending investment to the point at which the marginal net present value falls to zero, and no further. If *every decision* follows this rule, the result is to maximize the total value of the enterprise to its shareholders. Marginal net present values tend to decline with more investment if only because one presumably first selects the most attractive opportunities, then extends the investment stepwise to increasingly less attractive opportunities.

Of course, matters are not quite so simple. Additional guidelines are necessary for selecting among competing alternatives when selecting one excludes others. Additional guidelines also are necessary when expanding investment increases the applicable costs of capital—the discount factors determining present values—for each investment.

CHAPTER 5

Conflicting Objectives of Public Financial Reporting

MEASURING FINANCIAL CONDITION AND PERFORMANCE

Establishing decision criteria in a business context requires *metrics* —measures by which to gauge whether the criteria are met. Obviously, both those criteria and the associated measures must derive from, and pertain to, appropriate business objectives. In practice, corporate directors and managers as well as the financial community rely on public financial reports for decisions.

The financial community uses public financial reports to decide where and how much to lend or invest. Government economic policy relies on aggregations of this information to track corporate profits, saving and investment activity, and national income and output. With certain modifications, these reports also become a basis for corporate and individual taxes. Corporations set their business objectives primarily on the basis of how their decisions will affect those financial statements. One might therefore suppose, as many apparently believe, that standards for public financial reporting are responsive to these sorts of decision requirements.

To suppose as much is to be terribly misled. The problem is too many conflicts among the different legitimate objectives of users of public financial information. Accounting standards governing public financial reporting simply cannot meet all those objectives simultaneously. A single set of accounting standards thus requires assigning priorities to varying objectives. The inconsistencies may have been, or at least seemed, minor during the earlier development of those standards, perhaps causing little concern. They nevertheless have grown enormously with changing economic realities. In particular, they have grown with the expanding significance of intangible assets such as market relationships.

Compromises that seemed reasonably acceptable in an industrial context have thus become major conflicts. Consequently, continuing to meet traditional priorities has meant divorcing financial reporting standards from those realities. While the extent to which this should cause concern is debatable, public financial statements have increasingly serious shortcomings as decision-making tools. Remedies that would satisfy everyone are probably unachievable.

Standards for Financial Reporting

If the ultimate objective of a corporate enterprise must be to maximize its value to shareholders, working toward that objective requires:

- Measuring the condition of the enterprise in terms relevant to its value.
- Measuring enterprise performance in terms of changes in its value.

Conventional measures of the financial condition and performance of public corporations rely on accounting standards prepared according to generally accepted accounting principles, commonly referred to as "GAAP." The primary responsibility for establishing the GAAP standards normally lies with the Financial Accounting Standards Board (FASB), an industry standards-setting body. The role of the Securities and Exchange Commission (SEC) in setting accounting standards is normally limited to oversight and review, although it occasionally intervenes directly.

The FASB has primary responsibility for setting standards for *public* financial reporting—the financial statements corporations issue to the public. A public corporation *must* issue public financial statements according to GAAP standards as audited by independent public accountants. The corporation *may* elect to provide additional financial information, but this must be clearly distinguished from the audited statements. Whether and to what extent the auditors should review any such additional information remains an open question.

Because public financial reports are the predominant source of information available to investors, the financial community is unavoidably reliant on GAAP. If that information is misleading—if it fails to reflect the true condition (value) and performance (changes in value) of a corporation—the inevitable result must be bad financial decisions. Internally, corporate management is free to develop and use whatever financial information it wishes. Nevertheless, as with outside investors, deficiencies in the available information lead to bad decisions.

Here, then, is the crux of a problem: Both internal management decisions and external investment decisions rely almost universally on financial information prepared according to GAAP, whose relevance to enterprise value is eroding. While corporations may elect to develop additional financial information for internal management use, to do so is costly. As is, many large corporations have expended substantial effort to allocate costs among different product lines, define profit centers, and allocate capital according to different levels of risk. Nevertheless, they have for the most part not broken away from the mainstream of GAAP principles even for internal decision making.

Internal applications of GAAP accounting encounter the following realities:

- The relevance of GAAP to enterprise value has deteriorated rapidly with the displacement of the industrial economy by a relationship economy.
- While at least some accounting professionals perceive this problem, perhaps without entirely understanding its source, addressing it fully would require enormous levels of investment over many years.
- The FASB, which traditionally moves cautiously in any event, seems to be institutionally limited to a piecemeal solution approach while the problems accumulate at an accelerating rate.
- Although these problems apparently defy easy solutions, the accounting profession generally has not been altogether forthcoming with the public on their importance.
- Few corporate executives other than accounting professionals

have sufficient understanding of, or interest in, accounting issues to have much concern with GAAP's shortcomings as a
basis for management decisions.
- Although accountants and others at least have some concern
  with the economic relevance of financial information, few
  economists have sufficient understanding of, or even interest
  in, accounting to contribute to ensuring that relevance.

In considering such criticisms, understand that the U.S. standards for
public financial reporting are the world's most rigorous. This probably
both contributes to and results from the fact that U.S. financial markets are the most sophisticated and competitive as well as the largest
in the world. Indeed, the thoroughness with which this accounting
framework evolved, and the fact that it achieves its chosen objectives
so well, is arguably part of the problem. It is too substantial to disas-
semble without sacrificing many positive attributes as well as incurring enormous costs. Thus, at least in the short run, suffice it simply
to alert management decision makers to the nature of the measurement difficulties.

A curious sidelight on the present situation is that large public accounting firms are in many ways more familiar with the characteristics of a relationship marketplace than most types of business.
Building long-term relationships with clients has obvious importance.
In addition, these firms have for some years invested heavily in training their professionals, understanding full well that most will depart
from audit practice. In this process, however, they develop strong
bases of loyal alumni who further strengthen the client relationships.
Thirdly, these firms have also been on the forefront in developing
much of the new information technology that is important to a relationship marketplace. None of this suggests, though, that they have
focused directly on how to analyze relationship investment, nor that
they have given attention to applying the principles governing their
own businesses to other forms of enterprise.

Profits and Earnings

The main potential pitfall in corporate direction is the significance
that managers, directors, and the financial community attach to earnings as measured according to GAAP—a significance the FASB seems
to endorse. Consider, first, that net earnings as they appear on corporate income statements do not purport to be measures of economic

profit. Thus, such virtues as economic profit may have as financial performance measures do not carry over to GAAP earnings.

The traditional reason is that net earnings *include* required returns on capital, which are, as a practical matter, difficult to identify separately. In contrast, economic profit is net of those required returns, which it counts as a cost of production and distribution. An obvious implication of this difference is that reported net earnings can be positive, and perhaps growing, even as true profits are negative. In other words, positive earnings may represent a positive yet insufficient rate of return on investment. An example is earnings at 10 percent of invested capital when the return investors require—the cost of capital—is 15 percent. This sort of discrepancy clearly indicates misjudgment in some prior investments.

A second and increasingly important reason for discrepancies between true profits and net earnings is the accounting treatment of investment recovery. The concept behind depreciation, depletion, and amortization of investment is to reflect recovery of investment, which does not represent profit, as the capital is used up or wastes. Chapter 4 suggested the idea of true depreciation as representing the loss over time of the remaining productive capacity of plant and equipment. Nevertheless, depreciation as reported in corporate financial statements often has little correspondence with actual wasting patterns.

The considerations determining how depreciation appears in those financial statements can be complex. On one hand, temptations often exist to depreciate assets as slowly and over as long a period of time as possible. Corporate managers tend to favor the *appearance* of higher near-term earnings. Thus, to the extent that accounting standards and auditors allow, they tend to stretch depreciation of existing plant and equipment further into the future. The near-term result is to reduce depreciation expense and correspondingly increase reported earnings. Of course, this treatment simply defers some of those reported depreciation expenses to later years. Such manipulations obviously are not directly related to true income and expenses nor to cash flows. Nevertheless, to the extent corporate managers and investors rely on the resulting financial reports for decisions, distortions can occur that ultimately do detract from underlying profitability and enterprise values.

A contrary temptation is to depreciate assets as rapidly as possible to obtain near-term reductions in net income subject to income taxes. This tax treatment can indeed have a significant positive impact on cash flows, values, and profits. Although the effect is simply to defer those taxes to later years, it meanwhile provides interest-free funds as temporarily untaxed cash flows—a true, not illusory, source of value. Many businesses seek maximum reported earnings while reducing tax liabilities simply by keeping two sets of books, issuing one set of accounting statements for financial reporting purposes and preparing another for tax reporting. Auditors and tax authorities do impose limits on the extent of acceleration or deceleration of depreciation, but a good deal of leeway remains.

Intangible forms of investment—investment in information and relationship development—represent extreme cases of discrepancies between reported and actual investment recovery. The convention of reporting the outlays on intangibles as current expenses implies immediate recovery of these forms of outlays, although actual recovery often occurs only over many years. The immediate effect is substantial understatement of returns on investment and true profit, followed by substantial overstatement of returns and profits in subsequent years. Thus, as intangible components of real capital become more significant, investment and earnings become increasingly distorted.

These patterns provide some insight into the sources of the corporate evisceration resulting from many cost restructuring programs. Achieving their objective of increasing reported earnings requires only reducing reported expenses. All too often, the quickest and easiest way to achieve that result is to cut back on intangible forms of investment. Research and development are likely targets, but cutbacks in investment in customer relationship development seem to be particularly common.

The adverse consequences of reducing investment in intangibles—the erosion in enterprise capital from failure to maintain and replenish it—are slow to become apparent. In the meantime, the higher earnings may result in handsomer executive compensation and retirement packages. Indeed, a dismaying practice is to tie compensation of senior executives to reported earnings, sometimes offered as an inducement for recruiting new chief executives to turn around faltering enterprises. Creating a false illusion of improved financial performance by increasing earnings may be all too easy. Executives adopting this course are often long gone with their rewards by the time the sham becomes evident. Perhaps by then other excuses for weak financial performance will emerge.

To conclude, instead of measuring profits in any true sense, net earnings reported according to accounting convention normally do not measure *any* truly relevant economic variable. They are at best no more than crude approximations of other variables that actually determine the value of an enterprise to its equity holders or owners. Such significance as GAAP earnings measures have for economic decisions arises more from common perception—indeed, a conventional wisdom or economic myth—than from any reality.

Further Evidence of Financial Reporting Shortcomings

The financial performance of a corporate enterprise over some period is the change in its financial condition over that same period before any distributions to shareholders. True financial performance is its contribution to shareholder value. It therefore is the change in the true underlying value of the enterprise from the beginning to the end of some period, plus any dividends it pays to the shareholders during that period.

From the standpoint of accounting convention, the value of the enterprise after dividend disbursements is simply the excess of the assets on its balance sheet over the liabilities—its shareholders' equity or book net worth. Do those accounting measures of enterprise value actually bear any correspondence to the equity value reflected in share prices? Those share prices represent what the financial marketplace believes the share ownership to be worth and are thus a market measure of net enterprise (equity) value. To be sure, some discounting of share prices occurs because most stocks are not traded very actively. Even so, substantial discrepancies are commonplace, while approximations of book net worth to share values are usually only coincidental. Hardly anyone expects balance sheet data to measure values in any market sense. Balance sheet data, rather, are a special sort of fiction governed by their own peculiar set of rules.

A similar demonstration of the distorted nature of many public financial statements, with direct bearing on intangible assets and capital, comes from observing corporate acquisitions. Time and again, the acquisition terms include substantial premiums reflecting, in Wall Street parlance, franchise values. Premiums in this sense are acquisition prices well in excess of any balance sheet values. The initial recognition of relationship intangibles developed from efforts to identify the underlying sources of value those premiums represent. In cases of acquiring service and publishing enterprises, for example, the premiums were too substantial and persistent not to represent some form of underlying value.

One measure of a premium is *book premium*—the excess of an acquisition price over the book net worth measured according to accounting convention. The book net worth is what a balance sheet shows as the excess of the book value of the assets over that of the liabilities. A more meaningful measure is the *true premium*—the excess purchase price after restating the balance sheet at the market rather than the book values of the listed assets and liabilities. Many corporate acquisitions exhibit large premiums applying both these measures.

To illustrate, the amount a publisher pays to acquire a newspaper is typically far above the net worth shown on its books. The excess is a book premium. To account for a corporate acquisition by purchase, however, accountants revise the book values of the individual assets and liabilities it acquires to their market values at the time of their purchase. For the purchase of a newspaper, this process first would involve revaluing the assets, including computer equipment, printing presses, and delivery vehicles. Both accounting and tax rules require revaluing those tangible assets before assigning what remains to the intangibles. To that extent, the revaluation essentially corrects for valuation errors arising from depreciation rules.

The excess purchase price or premium remaining after the revaluations is the true premium. The accounting and tax rules require assigning this excess amount, but no more or less, to the various intangible assets. The amount is recorded as one or more assets in the buyer's financial statements. It is typically a substantial component of the total acquisition price for a newspaper, mostly representing market relationships with subscribers and advertisers.

True premium values as they emerge in acquisitions are more likely than other measures to represent underlying values. However, they are usually taken for granted rather than explained or understood. They are, indeed, commonly misunderstood, particularly in cases of corporate combinations as exchanges of stock, as in poolings of interest. They usually are fully measurable only in certain special cases of acquiring corporations as cash purchases. In those cases, unlike in acquisitions for stock, a premium applies only to the entity being acquired. An acquisition then simply appears on the books of the acquirer as the purchase of a collection of various assets and liabilities.

Substantial premiums are especially common in acquisitions of businesses with one or both of two characteristics: One is a substantial base of proprietary technology or information; the other is a substantial base of customers from which it is reasonable to expect future patronage. These characteristics may, indeed, reinforce one another with a substantial database of customer information. In general, large acquisition premiums emerge when intangible capital is a substantial component of the capital base.

Acquisition prices in banking, for example, range up to, and occasionally exceed, twice the values represented on their balance sheets. Acquisition prices in publishing and broadcasting often bear even much higher ratios to balance sheet net worth. Newspapers and magazines are examples of two complementary sets of customers, namely, subscribers and advertisers. Both are likely to be essential to the viability of the business.

Another measure of a premium that also reflects values of underlying intangible assets is the excess of the total value of a corporate stock over its market or book net worth. This form of premium tends to be lower than acquisition premiums for reasons unrelated to the intangibles. Among them, the information available to stock market investors is generally a good deal less than what a prospective acquirer can obtain.

Still, extreme cases of these types of premiums do arise, perhaps particularly among technology companies. An example was the initial public stock offering (IPO) by Netscape Communications Corporation, a software and communications company. With little recorded net worth and no earnings during its 15-month life prior to the IPO, its total stock value quickly soared to more than $2 billion. Restating just the balance sheet assets and liabilities to what they might be worth in the marketplace, as by adjusting values of securities portfolios and physical plant, has little effect on these patterns. Thus, an opinion on Netscape's actual value is hardly necessary to see that something is going on that eludes the financial statements.

The Basic Accounting Model

The very term *public accounting* implies that financial reporting has responsibilities extending beyond the reporting enterprises themselves. The development of accounting principles and standards has been primarily for, and directed to, public financial statements. Most users of that information have little or no control over its form and content. The concerns of these users—primarily financial analysts, actual and potential shareholders and creditors, tax authorities, and government regulators—presumably include, but are by no means limited to, current enterprise values.

Financial reports derive from records of transactions with outside parties. They record income and expenses whether they represent immediate or deferred cash receipts or outlays. Balance sheet net worth changes by the amounts of net income not paid out as dividends plus any receipts or payments representing sale or redemption of stock (equity). For the most part, the original purchase price of assets determines the basis of their reporting over their subsequent lives. If an asset is expected to be productive for a number of accounting periods (years), normal practice is to write it off—depreciate or amortize it—according either to some standard schedule or on the basis of its expected loss of productive capacity.

One point in this brief summary has particular significance in interpreting and using public financial reports in a relationship economy. It is the significance of transactions with outside parties in determining a cost basis for accounting treatment. Arm's-length transactions provide the basis of historical-cost or, as some critics put it, once-upon-a-time accounting. Audit considerations are a significant factor in determining its conventions. Accounting audits are mainly to verify and attest to the proper recording of transactions as of when they occurred. Improper recording of transactions may mean loss or theft of assets, or it may simply represent carelessness. In either event, improper recording undermines the integrity of the resulting financial reports.

Changes in balance sheet values of assets must reflect recorded transactions or write-offs. An immediate difficulty is that some additions to assets result instead from internal investment. If that internal investment is in tangible assets such as facilities or equipment, the accounting rules call for recording and capitalizing all the outlays on construction or production. The result is to treat the investment as if it represented purchases from outside parties. In the case of investment in intangible assets, however, the common assumption is that those outlays are too difficult to identify and verify, as is indeed often the case. According to the accounting rules, recording an addition to assets absolutely requires a basis for verification. The accounting treatment otherwise is to record outlays as current expenses. To do so denies them balance sheet recognition, however much they represent real investment.

Changes in the underlying values of assets and liabilities that do not appear on corporate balance sheets can occur for a number of reasons. Changes in interest rates, for example, can change the market values of financial assets. Producer goods may lose their productive capacity more rapidly or slowly than is reflected in depreciation schedules. Market values of plant, equipment, and real property also may increase simply due to inflation, which receives no recognition in their accounting treatment.

Nevertheless, much the most severe distortions in public financial reporting normally arise from applying historical-cost accounting principles to intangible assets, particularly to market relationships. These assets usually result from internal production rather than outside purchase, typically leaving an insufficient record of transactions to allow the verification necessary to record them as assets. Except in special cases of their purchase from other enterprises, accountants usually cannot distinguish outlays for these assets from other types of outlays. They therefore record them as current expenses, which denies them any form of balance sheet recognition. Most intangibles consequently represent invisible investment and capital. To accountants, something more than a third of the capital embedded in U.S. corporations—perhaps a trillion dollars' worth—simply does not exist.

Some critics argue that it actually is possible to identify and capitalize certain outlays on developing economic relationships. Indeed, proposals periodically emerge for capitalizing and amortizing outlays on advertising. A difficulty is identification of the linkage between a particular outlay and the relationship value it produces. New relationships may develop as a consequence of promotional programs extending over a number of years. In many cases they result from combinations of different marketing devices. Consider, for example, that many financial services outlets, such as brokerage and insurance agency offices and bank branches, exist both to service existing customers and to attract new ones. Thus, part of the operating cost of this sort of facility actually represents relationship investment. The linkage of investment to resulting customer relationship values becomes even more tenuous when the facility continues to attract new customers well into the future.

Objectives of Public Financial Reporting

Understanding the problems with public financial reports and why they may be intractable requires understanding the objectives determining accounting standards. No one can seriously question that public financial statements must conform to strict rules. The alternative would be anarchy in financial information, whereby it surely would become self-serving and otherwise nearly useless. Establishing rules that best serve diverse users is nevertheless enormously difficult.

Compounding the difficulty, constant updating is necessary if the rules are to keep pace with a changing economy. It is also difficult because of conflicts among different financial reporting objectives.

The economic relevance of the financial information provided to public users—its relevance to enterprise value objectives—is but one of a number of criteria by which to judge the sufficiency of financial reporting. Another objective, to which accountants give substantially more weight, is reliability, which requires public financial reporting to reflect each of the following qualities:

- *Verifiability,* whereby reported results can be substantially duplicated by independent measurers using the same measurement standards and methods.
- *Neutrality,* by which the reported information does not itself bias decisions of the users of that information.
- *Objectivity,* in the sense that there is no manipulation of the reported information by its providers to their own ends.

Neutrality and objectivity are similar but not identical concepts. Neutrality concerns whether the standards themselves contain any bias. As an example of bias, the historical-cost accounting convention encourages earnings manipulation by recognizing realized capital gains while ignoring unrealized losses. Current accounting standards therefore do not fully meet the neutrality objective.

Objectivity pertains not to the standards themselves but rather is concerned with the potential for management manipulation because of insufficient definition and enforcement of the accounting standards. One example is the occasional practice of misclassifying purchased intangibles as goodwill qualifying for 40-year book amortization, thus minimizing its adverse impact on reported earnings. GAAP formally requires separately identifying intangibles, assigning their market values as of the time of their purchase, and writing them off (recording amortization expenses) according to their economic lives—the periods over which they are expected to generate income. Misclassification of purchased intangibles to reduce near-term amortization expenses has declined in recent years, but it has by no means disappeared.

A related example of objectivity coming into question arises from a device for avoiding recording and thus writing off goodwill altogether. A loophole in accounting conventions for corporate acquisitions is to allow immediate write-off of purchased research and development as a direct deduction from equity.[1] These components of purchase price consequently never pass through the acquiring corporations' income statements as expenses, thus insulating earnings. Why treat purchased R&D differently than other intangibles? More fundamentally, just what is purchased R&D? Whatever it is, it seems to have become much more common over the past few years.

A further reporting objective is consistency in financial statements. Proper interpretation of financial statements requires a common frame of reference. In particular, it should be possible to compare the financial performance of an enterprise both over time and with the performance of other enterprises. For example, two corporations with the same assets and liabilities and the same income and expenses should issue much the same financial reports. Financial analysis thrives on these sorts of comparisons. The pursuit of consistency nevertheless is sometimes set aside in favor of other objectives.

Intelligibility and conciseness also belong among the desirable attributes of financial reporting. Neither of these objectives lends itself to a precise definition, however. Providing information that no one can interpret and use is obviously pointless. Still, is the body of eligible users to be only a small handful of financial specialists, or does it encompass a much broader investing public?

The capacity of the user public to absorb and analyze financial information has its limits, and thus information content and focus may be more important to effective communication than its volume. A current trend is toward substantially expanding the amount of disclosure information contained in footnotes to financial statements. Indeed, some accountants seem to suggest that this is the only available method of improving the meaning and relevance of financial statements. Perhaps the rapid growth in disclosures is at least one way to avoid direct confrontation with the deficiencies in current accounting conventions. Too much information, however, may actually obfuscate rather than elucidate salient facts. The provision of large volumes of information could even become a deliberate method of obscuring material facts.

Conflicts among Accounting Objectives

Under conditions of price and interest rate stability, with assets being primarily physical and tangible, perhaps historical-cost accounting

---

[1] "More Firms Write Off Acquisition Costs," *Wall Street Journal*, December 2, 1996, A2.

could accommodate a variety of accounting objectives. Compared to alternatives, it also has advantages in its degree of objectivity and simplicity. The basic rules governing the preparation of public financial reports are for the most part commonly understood among accountants, whatever their true information content. Yet, as the real world moves away from this simple pattern, conflicts develop among objectives, and financial reports relying on the historical-cost model lose much of their economic meaning and relevance. Certainly not least among the resulting deficiencies is the invisibility of most intangible assets.

Standards relying on historical-cost accounting best meet the test of verifiability and tie most closely with audit functions and responsibilities. They achieve verifiability by applying an elaborately complex set of rigid rules and procedural standards. Historical costs nevertheless fall well short in meeting the tests of neutrality and objectivity. With respect to neutrality, for example, accounting rules unrelated to underlying economics often play a major role in determining the structuring of mergers and acquisitions and the recognition of capital gains and losses.

An example of such problems occurred not long ago as two large financial services corporations competed for the acquisition of a third. One prospective acquirer argued (erroneously, as it turned out) that its offer was better because it could treat the acquisition as a "pooling of interest," whereas its rival could not. A pooling essentially melds the respective balance sheets without recognizing the intangible assets involved in the acquisition. As a consequence, there would be no purchased intangible assets requiring amortization, thus avoiding substantial amortization expenses with correspondingly lower reported earnings. Yet, this accounting treatment would have been entirely cosmetic, with absolutely no effect on cash flows or true profits. Its significance would have arisen solely from widespread and uninformed perceptions among the investing public.

Similarly, although new rules may be closing some loopholes, the 1980s savings and loan debacle provided numerous examples of both legitimate (if often misleading) and illegitimate management manipulation of balance sheets and reported earnings. In particular, accountants developed increasingly ingenious methods whereby thrift institutions could record earnings well before actually receiving the corresponding income. They even recorded income, in some instances, without certainty that it would ever be forthcoming. They similarly developed ways to defer recognition of current expenses to later years. With the concurrence of government regulators, some thrift institutions stretched out the amortization of premiums paid in deposit acquisitions to as much as 40 years—well beyond the true useful lives of the underlying assets. The consequence of such abuses was that many of these institutions appeared much healthier than they actually were; some failed shortly thereafter. However closely their financial reports conformed to accounting conventions, they could hardly have been less reliable.

Accounting conventions certainly fare no better when judged on the basis of consistency. Because historical costs can pertain to quite different times and circumstances, two different enterprises can have absolutely identical balance sheets and yet have entirely different financial performance characteristics and prospects. Similarly, an enterprise such as a financial institution can restructure its balance sheet irrespective of actual change in its financial performance or in its underlying economic or value attributes. The absence of consistency, particularly as it undermines the relevance of financial statements, certainly is one of the most widespread shortcomings of historical-cost accounting. Of course, the shortcomings in relevance, reliability, and consistency all act to reduce intelligibility.

These shortcomings are accentuated with higher inflation rates and less stability in economic activity, inflation patterns, and interest rates. Fundamentally, though, the main problem with historical-cost accounting is that it pertains to no particular economic or market context—it represents a financial never-never land. Inescapably devoid of value or economic significance, it becomes an Indian rope trick without the rope.

With no direct basis in relevant values, the timing of income and expense recognition assumes excessive significance while it simultaneously becomes more ambiguous. A consequence is to undermine the linkage between balance sheets and income statements while increasing opportunities for manipulation. Simply attempting to contain these problems, even as they ultimately elude solution, has required a rapidly growing body of ever more elaborate and complex accounting standards. Examples include the enormous amount of accounting attention given to such matters as reserves, accruals and deferrals, capitalization of income and expense, amortization and depreciation, and valuations of financial instruments. The eventual and increasingly worrisome result may be that this process actually will undermine the achievement of all of public accounting's various objectives. The eventual outcome may well be, if it is not already, financial bedlam.

Meeting one financial reporting objective seems unavoidably to mean detracting from meeting others. For better or worse, whether conscious and deliberate or otherwise, verifiability normally receives priority above all other objectives. In other words, irrespective of the quality and significance of the information conveyed, two independent sets of accountants using the same enterprise transaction data should produce similar financial statements.

Correspondingly, of the different legitimate and often competing objectives of public financial reporting, the relevance of financial statements to true enterprise value—the actual value of an enterprise to its shareholders—normally ranks lowest in priority. This ranking is exactly opposite to what is necessary for internal decision making as well as to what is most relevant to outside investors.

To identify these difficulties should not imply supporting a major revision in accounting standards, nor is that the intention. Merely pointing them out does not mean that any easy solution is at hand. Rather, identifying the problems provides a warning, particularly to corporate officers and directors: They are on very thin ice in relying on financial statement standards for management decision criteria.

A further warning is that accounting practices normally do not extend much beyond what the standards require. Audits focus only on reported assets, reviewing them carefully to ensure no impairment, while ignoring most intangible assets altogether. Much of the economy's embedded capital consequently falls outside the scope of audit requirements, standards, and review. The fact that financial statements are audited, with independent accountants attesting to their accuracy, represents nothing about true enterprise value. Moreover, even when values are of primary concern, due diligence investigations, as for issuing securities and for acquisitions and mergers, tend to follow the audit model. They, too, are therefore prone to ignore important components of assets and capital.

Economic Relevance and Business Practices

Few corporate directors and executives give much thought to the widespread exclusion of intangible assets from their balance sheets. Rather, most display little awareness of the incompatibility of conventional accounting standards with the widespread prevalence and significance of relationship capital. The intricacies of accounting are a mystery that many would as soon avoid. Much of the business and investment community is surprisingly naive concerning accounting theory, displaying little interest in, and often resisting, efforts toward making accounting data more meaningful and useful. Ambivalence toward accounting and accountants seems, indeed, to be widespread in corporate executive suites, reflecting helpless dependence on and misgivings about accounting information.

Economic relevance means providing meaningful measures of, and direction to, economic activity. In a corporate context, it requires measures of enterprise values and their components and of changes in those values. Without value relevance, financial statements provide poor guidance for corporate management. Corporate directors and officers as well as financial analysts therefore need to understand better, and to acknowledge, what current accounting conventions and measures do and do not mean. Thus, they need to recognize that:

- A *value* is the price at which something can or does exchange in a market as of some particular time. It is only in that context that it can have any economic relevance. Corporate balance sheet data instead reflect original purchase prices of assets at many different times in the past. A net balance sheet value—shareholder's equity or net worth—is therefore a conglomeration of different historical values at different times and under different price conditions.
- *Earnings,* which seem to reflect current activity, are nevertheless not substantially more meaningful. Even in an industrial environment, asset depreciation may bear little correspondence to the changing values of underlying assets and therefore to the true value of the enterprise. Misstatement of investment outlays on relationship assets and other intangibles simply exacerbates long-standing problems.

In the abstract, at least, corporate managers could simply ignore conventional accounting information for internal decision making. They might instead develop the sort of value information that imparts economic relevance to their decisions. For a variety of reasons they actually tend to do so directly, if at all, only to the extent that they apply capital budgeting principles to plant and equipment investment decisions. Capital budgeting, stripped of details, estimates present values of the future cash flows representing different investment opportunities. Although its present range of application tends to be narrow, it actually provides an appropriate framework for virtually all management decision making.

Cost is one impediment to developing financial information containing more economic relevance, whether for internal or external use. While more meaningful data begin with the same underlying transactions, they are organized, configured, and updated differently. In a similar vein, many corporate executives have publicly cited cost concerns in vigorously opposing proposals for reporting financial data according to their different lines of business. How they can manage their businesses without this sort of basic information is a mystery. In any event, the benefits of potentially more meaningful information, and how those benefits weigh against its costs, deserve more attention.

Many chief executives are, indeed, quite content with current accounting requirements, however much they generate ambiguous, if not equivocal and misleading, public information. Some seem to regard clarity as disadvantageous, contending, for example, that more accurate and precise information benefits market rivals. Of course, as any benefits from requiring more relevance would be reciprocal, such concerns seem dubious.

Perhaps a more basic concern is that more meaningful information could reflect unfavorably on management. Notice the descriptive, as opposed to normative, content of the FASB's position that "[e]arnings information is commonly the focus for assessing management's stewardship or accountability."[2] Thus, accounting professionals could well argue that in emphasizing reported earnings, whatever they may or may not mean, they are simply responding (passively) to the needs of users of financial statements.

Obfuscation may provide a corporation with opportunities to promote its share price. A firm can easily take advantage of the myopic perceptions and short horizons of much of the investment community. Such devices may actually pay off in the short run as preludes to new stock issues or to acquisitions, or by enhancing executive compensation. They tend, however, to substitute for, and detract from, long-run strategies for developing intrinsic values.

Prospects for More Relevant Financial Information

Public accounting professionals exhibit little inclination toward significant revision in financial reporting standards, whatever their faults. A

---

[2]Financial Accounting Standards Board, *Statement of Financial Accounting Concepts No. 1: Objectives of Financial Reporting,* November 1978, Paragraph 58.

change in reporting priorities to emphasize relevance to enterprise values would require a massive overhaul of existing standards. The present structure is a result of years of painstaking effort that would be enormously difficult to dismantle and replace. In particular, to substitute true value-based measures of enterprise condition and performance would require valuation concepts and methods very different from present accounting concepts and methods.

At least as significantly, replacing the present set of standards would almost surely compromise important and altogether valid objectives of the present financial reporting model. Thus, a switch to a true value framework would probably undermine the reliability of financial reports. The FASB certainly understands the dangers and appropriately promulgates new accounting standards with substantial caution—it moves slowly and deliberately for good reason. Such caution also means that new standards are normally incremental changes in or, more often, additions to the present framework.

The FASB also certainly understands as well as anyone the deterioration in the relevance of reports issued in accordance with the current framework. Indeed, it has taken the initiative in increasing the amount of market value reporting in financial services and in at least exploring possibilities of reporting customer-based intangibles. Institutional constraints nevertheless probably put any but incremental changes beyond the FASB's reach. Any major overhaul of standards for public financial reporting would require a broad consensus as to its necessity—a consensus that is not currently on the horizon.

A possible but costly resolution of such problems might be multiple sets of statements, each conforming to a different set of rules. A reluctance among accounting professionals to tinker with priorities is therefore understandable and, to a substantial degree, defensible. By understanding these difficulties, however, accountants assume a special responsibility to exercise care not to claim far too much for what they provide.

The business and financial community seemingly has no option but to confront continuing dependence on financial information that is often, and usually unavoidably, distorted and misleading because an inevitable consequence of relying on faulty information is perverse management as well as investment decisions. Although public financial statements fall short of relevance for some valid reasons, the extent of current reliance on them for internal corporate decision making is another matter. Corporate strategies and decisions relying on that information must consistently and systematically subvert long-term shareholder interests, squander scarce capital, and undermine economic prosperity. Unfortunately for investors, the adverse consequences are often not readily perceptible in the short term.

To summarize, management information relying on accounting conventions impairs shareholder value in two fundamental ways:

- Directly, it results in decisions that are adverse to, and thus subvert, achievement of shareholder value objectives.
- Indirectly, regardless of distortions, it obscures the linkages between decisions and their outcomes, resulting in higher investor risks.

Still, taking a more positive view, however much deficiencies in the American accounting model may detract from national prosperity, other nations presumably are worse off in this respect.

CHAPTER *6*

The Unavoidable Myopia
of Wall Street

WHAT DO FINANCIAL ANALYSTS PRODUCE?

If accounting professionals sometimes claim too much for the services they provide, much of the Wall Street financial community outclasses them in this respect. The primary business of investment bankers, stockbrokers, and sell-side financial analysts is to generate financial transactions. The fundamental fact of life for many, and perhaps most financial professionals is that their income derives from the fees and commissions that transactions generate. This fact, in conjunction with limitations on the information available to them, induces a short-sighted view of possibilities and opportunities. To the extent such myopia is pervasive in the financial community, it is reinforced among the ultimate providers and users of capital.

A corporate enterprise is unavoidably dependent on the financial community for its lifeblood. Recall that the ultimate constraint on business opportunities is the ability to attract and retain capital. Thus, if financial professionals pronounce x to be so, and most investors therefore accept x as so, then a corporation depending on those investors must behave as if x is truly so. Its directors and chief executive might well regard what they otherwise believe as having little relevance.

Do not interpret this point as suggesting that questioning the skills and professionalism of the financial community is especially common. Rather, the Wall Street mindset constitutes but one of four sides of the box. It, too, emerged from the industrial era and the capital markets that emerged with it. Many financial professionals themselves adhere to an in-the-box mentality. In much the same manner as politicians, they tend to reflect the audience to which they play.

Generalization on this point clearly risks overstating the case, as different financial professionals have different objectives and employ different techniques. Yet, just how informed is the advice and direction emanating from the financial community? After all, it frequently holds itself out as the ultimate arbiter of how corporations *should* behave. Many corporations therefore have dutifully undertaken major restructuring and downsizing programs simply because investment bankers and financial analysts promoted them. Many business combinations occur for the same reason. Notice how often corporations engage investment bankers to counsel them on their strategic options. What is the likelihood that participation in a business combination will not be at the top of the list?

For the most part, the financial community persists in relying on, and attributing too much significance to, information that is often highly imperfect and distorted. Its record is not always encouraging:

- Many, and some critics would say most, efforts to reduce costs through restructuring and downsizing are unsuccessful when measured by subsequent stock price performance.
- Many mergers and acquisitions reportedly fail to produce the synergies, such as cost reductions or new products and services, that motivated them.
- The investment returns of some 85 percent of stock mutual funds reportedly lag behind those obtainable from investing in the Standard and Poor's 500 stocks. To be sure, some operating expense and cash reserve is unavoidable, but those factors do not fully explain the shortfall.

One suggestion as to why many business combinations fail is that neither the partners themselves nor their financial advisors have a true understanding of the respective enterprise values, and especially of the underlying components of those values. More specifically, they tend especially to overlook the internal components of relationship value—the capital embedded in employees and corporate culture. What often happens as a consequence is that the acquirers simply let those acquired values disintegrate, totally oblivious of any loss.

More broadly, many financial analysts have alarmingly little understanding of enterprise values. They tend particularly to have little understanding of, and to give little attention to, underlying sources of enterprise value. At least three reasons account for these shortcomings. First, what the investing public and the rest of the corporate society may not fully understand is that financial analysis is often not really what analysts and investment bankers are selling. Rather, their stock in trade is to promote securities transactions to generate fees and commissions, to promote securities issuance and to support underwritings by attracting buyer interest, and to promote mergers and acquisitions for the fees they generate. Observe, for example, the preponderance of *buy* over *sell* recommendations and the pressures on younger stockbrokers to oversell their wares.

Second, the concepts and valuation techniques for intangible assets, particularly for relationship assets, developed from tax considerations as a specialty of a few business valuation consultants altogether outside the Wall Street orbit. Rather than paying attention to the broader implications of these value concepts, Wall Streeters have been content simply to dismiss them. Instead, they refer vaguely but sagely to some amorphous notion of franchise values.

Probably the most important, as well as certainly the most defensible, reason is the severe limitations on the available inputs for financial analysis. Analysts have no choice but to rely primarily on public financial reports conforming to GAAP. They must therefore extract as much apparent significance as they can from that information to tout their expertise and services. This excuse, while certainly valid, is not entirely satisfactory, however. Too often, when analysts have access to top corporate executives, they focus on the same outmoded performance indicators. Notice all the attention they give to earnings projections for the next few quarters. Correspondingly, notice how little attention corporate direction and long-term strategies receive. In other words, they too often seem not to probe as deeply as they might into fundamental value issues, which would require imagination, creativity, and effort.

Fundamentally, much of Wall Street peers through the back end of a telescope. Above all, it tends to be as much a captive as a perpetuator of in-the-box thinking. The safe course is not to stray too far from the herd. How can one be faulted for a wrong call when most of one's peers did likewise? Actually, staying with the herd results more often than not in riding with the market. In other words, the market itself tends to move with the herd.

Most analysts accordingly focus mostly on the past and the present, with only a very myopic view of the future. However unconsciously, they sell illusions of information and analysis with little actual relevance to enterprise values. After all, generating a trade, or doing a deal, today seems worth a lot more than the same tomorrow. Trying to look well into the future is much riskier, as the direction of the herd becomes less clear beyond the near term. An inevitable result is to impart distortions into investor and corporate decisions, thwarting achievement of shareholder value goals.

Recognizing Components of Enterprise Value

Consider again the proposition that the overriding long-term corporate objective must be to maximize its current value to its shareholders. Corporate enterprise values derive in turn from cash flows or, more pertinently, from expected cash distributions, to the shareholders. More significantly, values representing the net cash flows—cash receipts minus cash outlays—from individual investment alternatives, whether in tangible or intangible assets, represent direct value contributions to total enterprise values. Those total enterprise values therefore must represent the sums of the true (market) values of tangible and intangible assets after netting out the liabilities. Thus, they should normally be neither more nor less than the net values of their components.

One might never suspect the existence of these sorts of cash flow and value relationships from reviewing the investment literature, to say nothing of corporate financial reports. Even textbooks on finance pay little or no attention to the components of enterprise value. Indeed, in actual practice, stock analysts often pay little attention even to cash flows.

The seemingly unconventional proposition that enterprise values derive directly from their underlying components perhaps requires thorough demonstration. Similarly calling for demonstration is that cash flows and values provide the linkage between the parts and the whole. This proposition is essential to the concept of a comprehensive, integrated decision-making framework employing value criteria, yet it really relies on some very simple principles:

- The net cash flows of the enterprise are the sums of the net cash flows from its various underlying assets and liabilities.
- *Value* is simply the net present value of immediate and future net cash flows at some particular time.
- Thus, the value of an enterprise must be the sum of the values of the various underlying assets and liabilities.

Discrepancies obviously do arise among value measures, such as between an enterprise value implied by the market price of outstanding shares and the foregoing net asset value. They arise because of imperfections in how markets function, and particularly because of deficient and distorted market information. Meanwhile, achieving a comprehensive, integrated decision framework is enormously difficult, and more likely impossible, with conventional definitions and measures of enterprise goals and financial outcomes.

What Is Enterprise Value?

The most effective way to explore further the problems arising from the Wall Street mentality is first to consider how one should conceive of the value of a business enterprise. In undertaking this exercise, understand that it represents a brief primer on *values*, not *valuation.* In other words, to the extent a distinction is possible, it concerns value perspectives rather than techniques for developing value estimates.

A fundamental but often violated principle for understanding any value is to examine its value characteristics from as many different perspectives as possible. This principle applies whether the value pertains to individual assets—financial instruments, real property, furnishings and equipment, intangibles, or whatever—or to a business. Valuation theory distinguishes among three general approaches, each conceptually as well as methodologically different from the others, and each having a number of variants.

A point to keep in mind in reviewing these approaches is that stock analysts routinely follow only the largest public companies. Smaller corporations tend to attract attention only when the possibility of a bargain or business combination emerges, or perhaps when institutional investors are looking for such bargains. This fact alone acts to limit the amount of information regarding most corporations that is available to investors.

Market Values

The price at which something trades in the marketplace is a direct measure of value. Indeed, *value* means an actual or potential market price. A market price nevertheless may not be an entirely satisfactory indicator of value. Market distortions commonly arise from imperfect information and impediments to competition. Understanding the value of an asset or business thus may require specifying the relevant market context.

Valuation as a discipline usually requires estimating values when no observable price attaches directly to an asset or business. In such cases, one approach is to use a market price that prevailed at some earlier time, then adjust for any subsequent changes in circumstances. Another approach is to use current market prices of very similar, or comparable, assets, again adjusting for differences in circumstances. The choice between these approaches, and an assessment of their adequacy and relevance, depends on the quality and relevance of the available data. Examples are particularly common in real estate. In some cases appraisers adjust historical prices of property according to general trends in real estate prices; in others they rely on data on prices prevailing in recent exchanges of very similar property. They may also combine these approaches.

Thus, if the shares of a corporation are publicly traded, their price provides one measure of market value and hence of its value to its shareholders. Still, to interpret that price as indicating *the* value to shareholders requires qualification. Perhaps that price is depressed by inactive trading or concerns with where control of the company resides. Perhaps, too, that price reflects inaccurate or insufficient information. Do the directors and management truly act on behalf of the public shareholders? If not, what are the prospects for their removal? Would the shareholders realize more value through an acquisition or merger, or from paying out higher dividends? In confronting such issues, an analyst has several alternatives:

- One option is to adjust for the amount by which these factors affect share prices, perhaps by comparing acquisition terms for comparable corporations with their prior share prices.
- A more common practice is to estimate values from observable share prices of actively traded but otherwise comparable corporations.
- Another common approach is to estimate values directly from

the terms of acquisition for comparable corporations, giving no attention to the prices of their shares before acquisition.

Use of such comparables in valuing businesses usually relies on ratios of their share prices to various financial measures. Common measures for this purpose include earnings, reported book equity (net worth), and, particularly in cases of small professional businesses, annual sales. Reliance on direct adjustments for inactive trading and lack of control is most common for small, closely held businesses. Merger and acquisition analysis typically relies on terms of prior acquisitions and mergers.

Predictions of future share prices similarly rely on the comparables approach, particularly by comparing a corporation with itself at different times. For example, current market data provide ratios of share prices to earnings. Application of these ratios to projected future earnings provides projections of share prices. A result is acute interest among analysts in near-term earnings projections.

The range of possible comparables expands enormously in analyzing business components and assets. For example, market valuations of credit card portfolios are usually ratios of acquisition prices to outstanding receivables balances. Valuations of newspapers, periodicals, and broadcast audiences may rely on numbers of subscribers or listeners, or on total revenues, among other possibilities. Indeed, valuations of many types of customer lists may be simply on the basis of the number of names they contain, while numbers of clients provide a common method of valuing of stock brokerage accounts.

In virtually all of these cases, however, market valuations are likely to be as unreliable as they are common. Because comparables elude accurate identification, alternative valuation techniques tend to be necessary either in addition to, or instead of, market valuations.

Discounted Cash Flow (DCF) Values

The true economic value of an asset—something that represents a future stream of cash outlays and receipts—is the present (discounted) value of those cash flows. A market value is simply a current consensus, however well or ill informed, and however long term or transitory, as to the amount of that value. Discounted cash flow, or DCF, values are simply direct measures of those cash flows over the asset lives, discounting them back to present values by applying discount factors appropriate to their risks.

The most common DCF value concept for a corporation is the *dividend value*. As a technique of financial analysis, the usual approach is to assume the enterprise value to be the present value of the maximum amount of dividends it could pay to actual (or hypothetical) shareholders while maintaining adequate levels of equity capital. In its most conventional applications, it normally does not extend to possibilities for varying earnings retention by adding capital or, even more particularly, by reducing it by distributions to shareholders. Its most common forms rely on the following assumptions:

- The corporation is a going concern that will remain in business indefinitely, wherefore the cash flow projections reflect automatic replacement of all depreciable and amortizable assets.
- The projections extend over some finite period, perhaps 10 to 15 years. They include a hypothetical terminal value of the corporation at the end of that period—an assumed sale value at some multiple of projected terminal earnings or net worth.
- The projections are typically in terms of conventional financial statement income and expense categories. In particular, the classification of expenses is typically according to types of inputs rather than pertaining to resulting products and services.

In this form, dividend values still beg the question of what determines the capacity of a corporation to pay dividends. The approach does not probe behind conventional financial reports. It is not really the same thing as the value of an enterprise's cash flows—the cash receipts and outlays of the corporation. For example, it often simply assumes depreciation expenses to be estimates of cash outlays for asset replacement. If earnings are subject to distortion, it may misstate the amount available for dividends without causing asset impairment.

There are two rather different concepts of enterprise value that relate directly to cash flows:

- A variant of the common dividend valuation approach, expressing all income and expense on a cash basis with express recognition of investment outlays.
- Valuing only the assets and liabilities currently in place on the basis of their projected cash flows over their remaining lives, assuming no replacement.

In applying the first of these variants, analysts again typically project the cash flows over some future horizon and assign a terminal value to the end of that period. Actual asset replacement substitutes for depreciation and amortization of assets.

The second variant, which requires closer examination, represents an aggregation of the DCF values of all the individual underlying assets and liabilities. The asset values, of course, must include the intangibles to be meaningful. Thus, again, regard the market value of an asset as simply a consensus about the value of future cash flows. If so, the value of a corporate enterprise in terms of DCF values must correspond to the net market value of underlying assets and liabilities.

DCF value concepts are rare in valuing entire public corporations except occasionally in merger and acquisition analysis. Even then the analysis seldom extends to underlying assets and liabilities. As a practical matter, valuations of intangible assets nevertheless usually rely primarily on DCF methodologies. Relationship assets are no exception. One reason is that because the outlays on their development are normally internal, market transactions that might provide indicators of value are sparse. Moreover, when market transactions do occur, as in acquisitions, information on the acquisition terms is often either unreported or reported in a manner that is difficult to interpret. Even such information as is available is usually insufficient for identifying comparability among different transactions.

Replacement Costs

The common concept of replacement cost is that it normally applies to individual fixed assets such as plant and equipment and residential structures. Appraisals for property and casualty insurance, for example, are usually on the basis of the costs of replacing assets.

Costs of replacement can be ambiguous, requiring special care in detailing the assumptions underlying any estimate. For example, is a replacement cost the cost of replacing an asset with another that is *physically identical* or with one that is *functionally equivalent* even if physically quite different? How much physical wear and tear represents equivalency? Moreover, notwithstanding the costs necessary to replace an asset, it nevertheless may have little or no value. Abandoned grain elevators and feed mills, common in agricultural regions, provide examples.

Replacement costs are often difficult to identify for intangible assets. Consider, for example, attempting to value newspaper subscribers using a replacement cost approach. A daily newspaper, typically being one of no more than a few options in its territory, automatically attracts some subscribers with virtually no effort. As it seeks to expand its circulation, it must undertake more and more investment in promotion and in expanding editorial content and advertising. Is the replacement cost appropriate for valuation the cost of attracting the first few subscribers, the cost of the marginal subscribers resulting from the last few dollars of outlay on attracting subscribers, or can one consider the matter only in terms of the entire subscriber base? If those last marginal subscribers represent any positive value, a buyer of the newspaper probably would value it in terms of the entire subscriber base.

Replacement cost concepts nevertheless have been common and useful in workforce-in-place valuations—valuing the employees of an acquired business. A replacement cost estimate of value in these situations asks how much it would cost to recruit an equivalent workforce. One variant is to assume that those employees already have equivalent skills, in which case the recruiting costs might be relatively high but subsequent training costs relatively low. Another is to assume lower skill levels and to include the costs of the delay and training involved in developing the necessary skills.

Application of replacement cost concepts to entire businesses is almost unheard of, particularly in a corporate context. The main exceptions are small, closely held businesses whose assets consist mainly of real estate, machinery, and inventories; businesses of this sort often need valuation for estate tax purposes. Yet, one might view a net asset value of any business, including a large corporation, as a variant of a replacement cost value. This net asset value—the excess of the market values of its assets over the values of its liabilities, including the intangibles—essentially represents the net cost of replacing an enterprise. Moreover, an altogether consistent view of replacement cost is as the current acquisition costs of all of these assets and liabilities. Specifically, how much outlay would be necessary to acquire all those assets in their current condition, recognizing accumulated wear and tear?

Conceptually, the costs of assembling all the components necessary to create a business should approximate the value realized in selling off those components to others seeking to assemble other businesses. Those outlays, and thus the costs of replacing those components, represent a form of liquidation value—the net proceeds from the sale of the assets and retirement of the liabilities—in a competitive market.

Again, to be meaningful and relevant, this conception must include intangible as well as tangible assets and liabilities.

This net asset view of enterprise value is, to be sure, entirely hypothetical. Actual liquidation may itself be a costly process. Value impairment often occurs to the extent actual liquidations are under circumstances of distress and are perhaps in haste and disorderly. Moreover, applying this concept to industrial enterprises can be difficult. Some assets are so limited in transferability and use as to lose most of their value when removed from the context of a particular going concern. An abandoned grain elevator is an example.

Later discussion will develop the net asset concept further. For internal as well as external application, it relies on two propositions that should by now be familiar:

- The market value of a corporation—ultimately, its value to its shareholders—must be the net market values of its component assets and liabilities, including all intangibles.
- The market values of those underlying assets and liabilities are the present (discounted) values of the net cash flows that they contribute to the enterprise.

Notice how these concepts come full circle, as the sum of the underlying net cash flows is the net cash flow to the enterprise, providing its value as an aggregate.

These concepts do open up a question, however. Understanding that pursuing it is hypothetical, suppose poor management results in assets generating less cash income than they might generate elsewhere. As a consequence, suppose their market value if offered in the marketplace is higher than those actual cash flows indicate. How does one reconcile the different values? One approach to reconciliation is to assign the values obtainable in the marketplace while recognizing that, after deducting its compensation, poor management essentially is an intangible representing negative value.

An alternative approach is simply to value the actual cash flows while overlooking the management element. The resulting value will be less than the sum of the market values, as the latter is a potential value assuming superior management (as a buyer might provide). This actual value is therefore an enterprise value impaired by poor management. From this point, one might then adjust that value to reflect the effects of injecting more effective management, whether by management replacement or by corporate acquisition.

Reconciling Different Value Concepts

The different concepts of enterprise value still might seem as if they should yield different measures of value. Nevertheless, abstracting from market imperfections, a corporate enterprise surely cannot have a variety of different values. Different value concepts and valuation methods mostly represent different ways of addressing market imperfections and information deficiencies. Upon removing those problems, the various concepts merge, whereupon the different measures of value should converge.

Perhaps particularly important to decision making in a relationship context is understanding how a net asset value of a business—the net market value of its underlying assets and liabilities—converges with its overall DCF value as a going concern. The difference is in conventional assumptions about asset replacement. Net asset values represent only those assets and liabilities in place as of some valuation date. No consideration is given to their possible replacement. Conventional DCF enterprise valuations, on the other hand, assume going concerns with automatic replacement of wasting assets. In their purest form, DCF valuations consider only actual cash outlays on acquiring assets, ignoring depreciation expenses.

To illustrate, assume a mature business that replaces assets as they wear out. For simplicity, suppose the assets of this enterprise consist solely of 5 machines, with one requiring replacement at the end of each year. Also assume that each machine generates a net cash flow (after taxes) of $1,000 per year, received at year-end. Finally, suppose the cost of capital—the (annual) discount factor to apply to value the cash flows—is 20 percent. The net present value (NPV) of each machine should approximate the cost of its replacement (assuming no inflation): the present value of $1,000 received at the end of each year over 5 years, discounted at 20 percent, which amounts to $2,991. Valued as a going concern, cash inflows in the amount of $5 \times \$1,000 = \$5,000$ are received at the end of each year. Of that amount, $2,991 must be an immediate outflow in order to replace the worn-out machine. Valued over an infinite future period (an approximation for indefinite enterprise life that DCF valuations sometimes assume), the present value amounts to ($\$5,000 - \$2,991 = \$2,009$) ÷ .20 = $10,045.

In the case of a net asset valuation with no replacement, on the other hand, the cash flows at the end of each year would simply be $1,000 for each remaining machine:

Year	Cash Flow
1	$5,000
2	4,000
3	3,000
4	2,000
5	1,000

The last of the initial set of five machines thus wears out at the end of the fifth year. The present value of those cash flows at 20 percent is $10,045—exactly the same as obtained with the DCF going-concern valuation.

Because new investment and retirements match (which would normally be coincidental), this example happens also to be one in which an earnings-multiple approach based on earnings might work well. The retirement rate for these machines—one machine, or 20 percent each year—provides a reasonable basis for annual depreciation expenses in calculating earnings. In that case the depreciation rate would actually match the replacement outlays and earnings therefore would match the net cash flows. Calculating the earnings multiple as the inverse of the applicable discount factor or cost of capital (here, $1 \div .2 = 5$ for a multiple of 5 times earnings), the value estimate is $5 \times \$2,009 = \$10,045$.

Precisely the same principles apply if the assets happen to be intangibles, such as market relationships, that actually erode in terms of numbers of relationships (through attrition) as well as losing value with age. By understanding the differences among the various approaches to enterprise valuation, use of each in conjunction with the others enhances the effectiveness and validity of each, capturing its own unique element of information. In combination, they act as checks on one another. As a practical matter, however, consistency among them means only that there should be identifiable reasons for any differences.

Earnings and Value Myopia

Market valuation in the form of ratios of market prices to earnings is much the most popular method of corporate valuation. It both results from and causes widespread misperceptions that earnings actually are the primary determinants of equity values. Indeed, it encourages focusing on recent and near-term earnings as indicators of changes in equity values.

Market valuation of earnings is deceptively simple and convenient, relying primarily on observable, and often seemingly unambiguous, information. It uses current, or at least recent, prices and earnings whether they pertain to a corporation itself, to comparable corporations, or to comparable acquisitions. Projections typically are little more than extrapolations of recent trends, perhaps with adjustment for recent or foreseeable events. Stock analysts, in particular, rely heavily on the near-term forecasts provided by corporate executives, even if they do not entirely accept them. Indeed, for fear of otherwise misleading the public, corporate managers normally provide only very near-term earnings projections.

One need not assume earnings to be altogether accurate measures of financial performance. Instead, they conceivably could correspond closely enough to true financial performance for market price ratios to be tolerably accurate value indicators. Price-earnings ratio analysis therefore could be acceptable in cases of high correlation between earnings and underlying financial performance. Were that so, changes in earnings would indicate corresponding changes in corporate financial performance—their contribution to shareholder values. The required correlation of earnings to shareholder value contributions is only an assumption, however. It generally does not exist in a relationship environment, particularly within the very short time horizons that are the focus of most stock analysts and investment bankers.

Some observers argue that a myopic focus in financial analysis is actually appropriate. As the long term is too uncertain and speculative, near-term prospects are the predominant determinants of equity values. Such reasoning is circular, as it forces financial markets to emphasize the short term. Otherwise, it is inadequate and misleading. Internal corporate decision making is unavoidably long term. The consequences of many decisions extend well beyond the short horizons of most earnings forecasts. In many instances, those consequences may not even begin to become evident in those short periods.

Corporate directors and managers must in any event look beyond the sell-side analysts—those seeking to generate transactions. If the stock of an enterprise is not widely held and actively traded, liquidity considerations suggest long-term shareholder investment horizons. Too rapid accumulation or disposition of stock positions may disrupt equity markets and distort share prices. Even among actively traded shares, holdings of individual stocks by institutional investors are often so large that to avoid market disruption, it requires months to accumulate or dispose of stock positions. In other words, an important and growing segment of the investment community has to look to the longer term in its investment decisions.

Earnings Growth and Enterprise Value

Common supposition is that whatever else earnings might or might not represent, earnings growth must indicate more shareholder value. Yet, earnings trends may be false indicators of value trends. One reason is that the growth in earnings may simply reflect excessive retention of earnings—reinvestment of earnings at rates of return below a corporation's cost of capital. What essentially happens is that those additional earnings have less value than if the outlays to obtain them had been distributed as dividends. If shareholders perceive the excessive retention as only temporary, perhaps the only effect will be to reduce the growth in share prices. If they regard it as a continuing process, share prices must eventually decline. Absent corrective action by shareholders and directors, a corporation can remain in business well into the future even under these latter circumstances, providing a nice sinecure for its senior management. Its ability to obtain additional capital nevertheless would progressively deteriorate.

Because earnings retention is so pervasive, including among corporations with weak financial performance, this potential for value to decline with growing earnings requires demonstration. A relatively simple dividend valuation model for a corporation serves this purpose. First, suppose its shareholders expect it to pay out an annual dividend of $15 million per year indefinitely, while retaining no earnings. They therefore do not expect the enterprise to grow or to shrink. Assume, too, that the annual rate of return on their investment those shareholders require—the corporation's cost of equity capital—is 15 percent. Its value to the shareholders would then be the present value of an infinite series of $15 million per year discounted at 15 percent. That value (in millions) beginning with the $15 million dividend a year hence is:

$$V = \frac{D}{r} = \frac{\$15}{.15} = \$100,$$

where V is the present value, D is the annual dividend, and r is the cost of equity capital. The value at the beginning of any future year also will be $100 in this no-growth scenario. Thus, one can express the value today as the sum of the present value of next year's dividend plus the present value of all future dividends after payment of that dividend:

$$V = \frac{\$15 + \dfrac{\$15}{.15}}{1.15} = \frac{\$15 + \$100}{1.15} = \frac{115}{1.15} = \$100$$

Now, suppose that instead of paying out the first dividend, the corporation retains and reinvests it at a rate of return of 10 percent—a return lower than its cost of equity capital. Suppose, too, that investors will expect this additional return to continue indefinitely and that the corporation will subsequently revert to paying out all its earnings as dividends. The subsequent annual dividends would then be:

$$D = \$15 + (.10)(\$10) = \$16.$$

The current value of the corporation thus becomes:

$$V = \frac{\$0 + \dfrac{\$16}{.15}}{1.15} = \frac{\$106.67}{1.15} = \$92.76.$$

Thus, earnings grow from $15 million to $16 million while the value of the corporation to its shareholders drops from $100 million to less than $93 million. Obviously, a continuing pattern of reinvesting at returns below costs of capital implies declining values and share prices.

A rather different possibility for earnings growth to be misleading arises from a life-cycle model of a business. The general idea is that businesses develop as a result of entrepreneurship, then grow as they gradually come under the control of professional managers who improve operating efficiency and expand markets. In time, however, they become more bureaucratic and stagnate as managers seek to preserve rather than to innovate. Finally, stagnation leads to decline as they lose their competitive edge and other entrepreneurs stake out new market claims.

If a business follows this life-cycle pattern, even approximately, the consequences become evident in its value attributes before they appear in earnings or profit. The following illustration assumes that the earnings in each period are true earnings, reflecting investment recovery and returns on capital with no accounting distortions. The required annual rate of return—the discount factor, or cost of capital—is 20 percent.

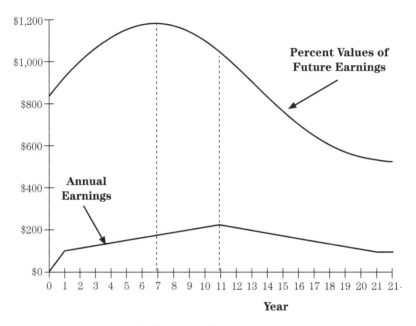

Values of Earnings.

Notice that the earnings reach their peak in Year 11, four years after the peak in value (Year 7). The earnings thus continue to grow for quite some while after their value begins to erode.

This pattern is perhaps more extreme in a life-cycle context, but it can also occur if earnings are merely fluctuating in cyclically. Thus, only if earnings follow a constant trend can they be adequate indicators of value trends. One can only speculate on how many securities analysts, as well as corporate chief executives and directors, have overrated management performance by attaching too much significance to earnings growth. Some investors may sense longer-term value significance in reduced rates of earnings growth, although the decline in value occurs only later.

To conclude these observations on the significance, or otherwise, of earnings growth, notice that the two foregoing possibilities may well reinforce one another. Suppose that a corporation is stagnating. Its earnings are approaching the peak in the above diagram. Its management might decide to boost its earnings growth by reducing dividends, even as its opportunities for value-building investment deteriorate. The result may be a transitory boost to stock prices, but accelerated deterioration is soon to follow.

Corporate Preoccupation with Earnings

Even when the tactic is contrary to their own better judgment, corporate directors and chief executives are often under pressure from the financial community to adhere to short-run, promotive tactics. If investors believe that higher reported earnings mean higher share prices, the short-run result of higher earnings normally will be higher share prices. Expectations of higher earnings generate stock trades and broker commissions, and they support stock underwritings. Sell-side stock analysts work overtime at promoting the significance of corporate earnings. In some cases the pressures on corporate manager to increase reported earnings cause them to cut back on relationship investment, creating an illusion of reduced expenses. In the long run, of course, such tactics may carry a corporation over the threshold of irreversible decline.

The widespread emphasis on earnings measures of corporate financial performance has a circular quality. To the extent that better measures are not readily available, earnings measures are by default the primary determinants of equity market values and share prices. Thus, however misleading and distorted they may be as performance measures, earnings remain important factors in management decisions. A too common result is to seduce corporate directors and managers into attempting to boost prices by improving reported earnings, even to the longer-term detriment of equity values. Similarly, corporate directors are sometimes lured into giving senior corporate executives compensation packages based on earnings.

The potential for misdirection is most severe in a relationship marketplace, where the worst distortions in earnings measures tend to occur. The consequences can be particularly perverse when earnings decline, escalating pressures to boost earnings. In severe cases, a further deterrent to relationship investment may be loss of taxable income from which to deduct those investment outlays. The resulting incentives to cut back or eliminate relationship investment may extend to failure to replace normal attrition in existing relationships.

With the perceived significance of earnings (profits) so thoroughly embedded in the financial marketplace, the onus of demonstration must be that breaking this circle can ultimately do a better job of promoting shareholder value objectives. Investment criteria in a relationship economy require value measures other than those normally encountered, requiring demonstration that those alternative measures actually do both reflect and determine market responses.

Developing an understanding of relationship investment and values among corporate directors and executives is alone insufficient. Avoiding pressures to pander to a misinformed financial community also requires educating the investing public on the true nature of their enterprise values.

A Random Walk in the Dark

A significant body of financial theory maintains the impossibility of consistently selecting corporate stocks that outperform the market. The theory rests on the proposition that when relevant information becomes known, it is available to the entire investment community. Information that indicates an increase in a share value must therefore be unexpected. The consequence is that at any particular time share prices incorporate all available market information, and subsequent changes must be random in the sense of being entirely unpredictable. Any such conclusion raises questions about what one should expect of stock analysts. A manifestation of this random-walk view of stock selection is the growing popularity of stock index mutual funds. In just a few years, Vanguard's Index Trust 500 Portfolio has become one of the world's largest and fastest growing stock funds.

The perfect information flows assumed by random-walk theories clearly are at odds with the real world. Ample opportunities do exist for out-of-the-box thinkers with imagination and creativity to ferret out information that others have tended to overlook or that they fail to understand. They exist if for no other reason than that the information on which most analysts and investors conventionally rely is faulty and incomplete. These imperfections also provide opportunities for corporate enterprises to break loose from their hostage relationships with Wall Street.

CHAPTER 7

Disorientation in the Absence of Business Theory

AN AGE OF ANXIETY

Corporate misdirection generates executive anxiety. In response, executive behavior may demonstrate a sense of disorientation and entrapment. Why else is management consulting among the fastest-growing business pursuits?[1] Most management consultants are of the buttoned-down pinstripe variety. Many are from the more prominent consultancies and faculties of the leading business schools. In demeanor, most fit in well with the corporate establishment. Some may prescribe radical organizational changes, but not of a sort that will discomfit the executive suites.

Many executives nevertheless seek something more. No business conference seems complete without featuring an inspirational speaker or visionary on the program. Senior managers enroll in droves in programs offering everything from oriental and Greek philosophy to contrived dangers in the wilderness. They listen attentively as management gurus exhort them to act a little crazily or listen to their

---

[1]For additional detail on this and other topics in this chapter, see John Mickelthwait and Adrian Wooldridge, *The Witch Doctors: Making Sense of the Management Gurus* (New York: Times Business, 1996).

inner selves. Some seminar and conference programs exist primarily to reinforce the self-esteem of senior executives. Many, apparently, are not nearly as self-assured as they would have others believe.

What is happening here? Are some executives becoming unhinged? Are these symptoms of managerial disorientation? Captains of industry of a few generations ago would be aghast at some of these goings-on. Perhaps they contain some element of entertainment, but much of the trend may represent genuine attempts to break out of the box. Are these attempts effective? Can they be effective? An immediate question is how one defines *the box*. Does the operative definition reflect the true problem? If the personality traits that give rise to imagination and creativity are already in place, maybe such programs can unlock some of the inhibitions that restrain them. Yet, how many top executives rise through the ranks by being imaginative and creative? As an alternative, perhaps these programs can create more receptivity to others' creative ideas.

Business Principles in Theory and Practice

Corporate leadership requires strategic vision, but not necessarily extending to high levels of imagination. One role of a leader is to make best use of others' talents, often giving particular attention to contributions from those whose talents differ. Lee Iacocca did not singlehandedly conceive of the Mustang while at Ford nor of the minivan after moving to Chrysler. Rather, he recognized their potential and brought them to fruition.

The fourth side of the box is not constraints on imagination so much as it is shortcomings in business theory—that body of principles, whatever they may be, that guide business practices, decisions, and strategies. Business theory is perhaps somewhat more inclusive than management theory, which seems, at least in some interpretations, to pertain mainly to organization structures and internal relationships. A viable business theory should encompass all the business disciplines—economics, finance, accounting, marketing, and management. Managing a business without an underlying theoretical foundation is rather like flying in a fog without a navigation system. The likely result is to become disoriented.

The principal difficulty actually is a dearth of true business theories. To consider this point one must distinguish mere ideas, information, and suggestions from theory. A theory is a framework for synthesizing principles and facts. A valid theory must be predictive.

By observing certain patterns, one should be able to predict others. Consider a natural science such as chemistry. A valid descriptive, or predictive, theory—one that has survived testing—allows the chemist to predict the chemical reaction resulting from combining specified quantities of different agents in a particular way.

A corresponding business theory presumably would enable a social scientist observing the characteristics of a corporation to predict its responses to different external circumstances. Maybe a few business theorists have reached this theoretical plateau. Nevertheless, most inquiries into corporate behavior tend, at best, to be explanations after rather than before the fact. Often they extend no further than mere observation.

At a higher theoretical plateau is *normative theory*—a comprehensive set of principles guiding how one should proceed to achieve certain results. The distinction may be an artificial one, for normative principles should derive directly from valid descriptive theory. A normative business theory provides practical principles of corporate strategy and management decision making that consistently direct the enterprise toward achievement of its directive. Recall Alfred Marshall's emphasis many years ago on the proposition that a valid theory must also lead to practical applications.

Today, in contrast, one first observes confusion about corporate objectives. To the extent they are articulated at all, they are too often cluttered with earnings goals, stakeholder claims, and other meaningless and often contradictory nonsense. Decision criteria normally have no direct link to shareholder value objectives, even with recognition of the overriding legitimacy of shareholder claims. Often missing as well is an integration of corporate external perceptions, as they arise from market research and information or from visioning exercises, with concepts of management responsibility and corporate organization. Instead, the modern corporation is left to seek guidance from a potpourri of disconnected ideas and concepts.

The Academic Origin of Conceptual Disconnection

The general absence of comprehensive business theory originates in the universities, primarily in their schools of business. Put aside for the moment the faddishness with which a handful of business professors promote their careers, including as consultants. One major difficulty is that many academic curricula tend to be conglomerations of disconnected subject matter. Courses of study tend to reflect the particular professional pursuits of those who teach them. Nowhere in a typical business course of study is one likely to find a course or program that integrates the subject matter into comprehensive business principles. Business schools tend to be fountainheads of tunnel vision.

Economists therefore teach pure economics. They focus mostly on microeconomic theories of profit maximization, untainted by practicality. They then move on to business cycles and macroeconomic (monetary and fiscal) policy. Any linkage between their subject matter and accounting curricula is likely to be incidental at best; mostly, the economists and the accountants go separate ways. Finance courses usually mention shareholder value objectives, but without synthesizing this idea with the economists' idea of profit or with accounting theory and conventions. Marketing and management similarly go their own different directions.

Meanwhile, with growing frequency, business school administrators are not expected to be academic leaders. Rather, their assigned roles include budgeting, fund-raising, student recruitment, and forging ties with the business community. Universities accordingly often recruit business school deans from the business community. Also detracting from curricular cohesion is the widespread and apparently growing practice among business schools of substantial reliance on part-time faculty. Although some may argue that this practice brings practical outside perspectives to business programs, a more important reason for it in many institutions is budgetary. Adjunct professors are often much cheaper than their tenured counterparts.

A further difficulty with the typical academic environment is that scholars have a tendency to be locked in their own boxes. Economists and business professors themselves remain closed in the box of industrial-age legacies. They are mostly unaware of the significance of intangible forms of capital in determining how to set and pursue business objectives. They have been particularly oblivious to the economic characteristics and significance of relationship assets. A consequence is inability to explain the sources of enterprise value and hence to develop appropriate principles for identifying and developing that value. They, like the financial community, look at a typical corporation and see an enormous void of unexplained value.

As a consequence of these difficulties, a business degree is hardly a guarantee of real understanding of what a business enterprise is or of what it is supposed to do. MBAs tend more often to be specialists and technicians than budding business leaders. Many therefore undertake various types of consulting, investment banking, marketing, and technical pursuits. While the number of MBAs vastly exceeds the availability of corporate leadership positions, many chief executives do not have MBA degrees. Similarly, entrepreneurs—originators of creative ideas that develop into new businesses—are unlikely to be MBAs.

An intriguing hypothesis, which may not be demonstrable, is that business schools tend to be most attractive to individuals seeking the security of the establishment status quo. In other words, perhaps the typical business student mind-set is the antithesis of out-of-the-box thinking and strategic vision. If so, business schools might review their curricula with an eye not only for more comprehensive approaches but also for greater receptivity to fresh ideas. Perhaps they should seek out more unconventional candidates for admission. Maybe they should even supplement their textbooks with some good science fiction.

Consulting and the Consultants

The distinctions are often vague, but understanding the role of consultancies in the corporate community may require separating management consulting from a wide variety of other types. A substantial amount of the outside consulting to corporations, and also to government and nonprofit enterprises, involves developing and implementing new information technologies. One thus hears of multimillion-dollar contracts to develop or upgrade information and communications systems. That the area around Washington, DC, is a major center for consulting businesses is hardly accidental. Much of the information technology that consultancies bring to corporations is an outgrowth of technologies developed under government contracts.

Many nontechnology consultants also provide specialized services that have little or nothing to do with corporate direction or business principles. Among them are many small consultancies specializing in market research, public opinion, advertising, engineering, environmental issues, politics, public policies, litigation, and the like. They, too, tend to be distinguishable from management consulting.

These distinctions nevertheless do not mean that business strategies are irrelevant to consulting other than the management variety. The effectiveness of a management information system depends on how it contributes to achieving corporate objectives as well as on the technology it incorporates. Consulting on such matters as marketing, advertising, and public relations similarly cannot be fully separable from strategies. Without careful client guidance, an absence of strategic foundation can distort what consultants bring to engagements that are not primarily strategic.

Consider management consulting as primarily intended to provide some form of normative guidance to business clients—to tell clients what they should do. Specialization pervades even this group. Among those specialties are marketing strategies, visioning exercises, strategy facilitation (guiding internal strategic deliberations), corporate restructuring in its various forms, executive compensation, and mergers and acquisitions. In other words, armies of consultants offer a variety of services that, one way or another, bear directly on corporate strategies and decisions.

Merger and acquisition advisory services provide an example of consulting that is often quite different from management consulting. An acquisitions analyst conceivably might go no further than to advise on the value of a merger prospect, offering no advice on whether or not a client should pursue it. Going one step further, the analyst might advise that the prospect appears to offer an attractive opportunity on the basis of comparing its underlying values with its share price. Yet, the distinction from management consulting begins to fade if the analyst offers advice on how the prospect fits in with the client's own strategic objectives.

Are management consultants legitimate arbiters of business principles? Much of what they offer actually has far less strategic content than they often promote and than many suppose. Indeed, many corporate executives perceive a widespread absence of strategic perspective even among the management consultants. Many companies have therefore internalized their strategic planning rather than looking to outside advice.

A strategic perspective requires creativity as well as intelligence. Some editors at the *Economist* have made a specialty of following the consultancies. They observe that even as their fee revenues are growing by leaps and bounds, at least some of the majors have lost whatever creative edge they may once have possessed.[2] Thus, they cite Andersen Consulting's "Andersen androids" and suggest that "[p]ooling [McKinsey's] collective wisdom seems to produce bland and homogeneous results."[3] Perhaps simply recruiting the seemingly best and brightest business school graduates is insufficient.

Many consultancies, moreover, tend to focus more on developing

---

[2]"A Survey of Management Consultancy," *The Economist* (March 22–28, 1997) 1, 20.
[3]"A Survey," 20.

gimmicks that differentiate them from rivals than on providing substantive solutions to client problems. How else can one explain the restructurings that require subsequent repair? Yet, the resulting dearth of strategic perspective among consultants is becoming evident just as their clients, confronting economic revolution, are beginning to appreciate the need for more strategic guidance.

Process reengineering, which emerged as the ne plus ultra of management consulting during the first half of the 1990s, is a case in point. With the 1993 publication of the best-seller *Reengineering the Corporation: A Manifesto for Business Revolution,* by Michael Hammer and James Champy, every major consultancy had to get onto the reengineering bandwagon.[4] Corporation after corporation, and even government departments and agencies, just *had* to reengineer their processes. For many consultants, reengineering has been a gold mine. It requires substantial resources to undertake detailed redesign of corporate organizations. It involves much more than simply instilling new concepts or senses of redirection.

Is process reengineering truly strategic? A close look suggests that its originators avoid using the term, yet when they speak of corporations reinventing themselves to confront "a new world for business," they certainly seem to imply as much. The underlying idea, widely familiar by now, is that the traditional corporation emerged from an assembly-line model of production dating back at least to Adam Smith. In *The Wealth of Nations,* Smith exults over the enormous increases in productivity that accrue when each worker specializes in a single repetitive task.

Specialization in production processes requires managers to supervise them. As businesses evolved into modern corporations and grew, they became more complex and supervision required more and more layers of management to control them. Eventually, even simple tasks such as processing customer orders and subsequent billing required piles of paperwork passing from one administrative specialist to another. Process reengineering can often eliminate much of the paperwork and some of the layers of responsibility by substituting electronic information and communications systems. Indeed, some reengineering programs apparently have been highly successful in reducing expenses by improving the efficiency of corporate communications.

Process reengineering nevertheless mostly concerns the *how* ques-

---

[4]Michael Hammer and James Champy, *Reengineering the Corporation: A Manifesto for Business Revolution* (New York: Harper Business, 1993).

tion of corporate strategy. Proponents have suggested that it can facilitate communication with customers by centralizing points of customer contact and perhaps by freeing managers from routine administrative tasks. Still, these consequences, however desirable, are normally insufficient to elevate reengineering to strategy. In particular, such benefits may vanish to the extent that reengineering is a form of downsizing.

Notwithstanding its success stories, *Reengineering the Corporation* admits to some failures as well. Part of its "reinvention" concept is that, to succeed, reengineering requires a quantum leap from the old organizational format to a new, totally reengineered configuration. It correspondingly blames failures on excessive tentativeness and insufficient commitment among corporate managers. The real problem, though, is that it is fundamentally incomplete and nonstrategic, giving too little attention to the *what* and *for whom* of business direction. Indeed, several years after publication of *Reengineering the Corporation,* Hammer admitted that that the original concept was seriously flawed by being too mechanical:

> The real point . . . is longer-term growth on the revenue side. It's not so much getting rid of people. It's getting more out of people. . . . I wasn't smart enough about that . . . I was reflecting my engineering background and was insufficiently appreciative of the human dimension. I've learned that's critical.[5]

Should those corporate managers who paid $2,200 each to hear this admission believe that reengineering has now suddenly become strategic? Still missing are the *what* and *for whom* dimensions. Furthermore, what is implied about the previous admonition that reengineering will only work as a complete, radical organizational overhaul?

Other forms of corporate restructuring, to the extent they are distinguishable, similarly may lack strategic content. Simple downsizing and other cost reduction programs may give little or no thought to the *what* and *for whom* dimensions. They often seem not even be viable resolutions of the *how* of strategic concerns, as they often unwittingly discard value embedded in middle management and corporate culture.

Focusing on core competencies may appear to be more strategic,

---

[5]Quoted in the *Wall Street Journal,* November 26, 1996, A1. The *Journal* article refers to a $4.7 billion "re-engineering industry."

and it is often touted as such. It, too, is often insufficiently strategic. In particular, it often appears more likely to be a reflexive reaction to market pressures arising from unsatisfactory corporate performance. The core competency approach is internally and not externally directed. In the case of an otherwise healthy enterprise, it may result in overlooking opportunities for diversifying or expanding into new markets. More frequently, though, an announcement that an enterprise is returning to its core competency suggests that it is in trouble.

Total quality management, or TQM, perhaps has more strategic content. In part, it concerns the cost aspects of *how* to produce. The basic concept is that reducing product defects during production is often less costly than subsequent repair or replacement of defective output. TQM nevertheless also has customer implications that capture elements of *what* and *for whom*. Satisfied customers are likely to be repeat customers and to refer others. A reputation for quality in one product line or market may help open up new opportunities. These benefits do not mean that TQM itself is fully strategic, however, which may explain some of the failures that reportedly have accompanied its successes. Before adopting TQM, corporate managers should weigh the costs of defects against the costs of preventing them. TQM may not be the surest or most cost-effective approach to quality control.

Whatever the nature or apparent pedigree of corporate overhaul, failure to achieve desired objectives often occurs simply due to haste. Wall Street often pressures corporations into seeking quick fixes to boost share prices (and generate trades). Chief executives seek and often expect quicker results, legitimate or otherwise, than truly strategic programs can deliver. Consultants as well as Wall Street often encourage unrealistic expectations with premature proclamations of success.

Corporate executives contemplating bringing in management consultants to address their problems might consider AT&T's experience. To be sure, AT&T faced the necessity of redefining itself following its court-ordered divestiture of its regional telephone companies. By turning to consultancies for guidance and ideas:

America's largest telephone company, AT&T, used to be a management consultant's dream. Since the start of this decade it has spent more than a billion dollars on consulting. At one time, more than 1,000 firms—ranging from respectable outfits such as Mc-Kinsey to way-out purveyors of psycho-babble—were crawling all over it. This army of hired thinkers encouraged AT&T to make a series of disastrous decisions. . . . It also talked the company into adopting some of the silliest management fads around.[6]

Perhaps this episode is extraordinary only in terms of its scale. What did AT&T gain from it? The party at AT&T ended in November 1996 with the appointment of a new CEO and wholesale dismissal of consultants. Perhaps AT&T's primary gain from its billion-plus dollars of consultant outlays was a new skepticism about consultants.

Clients themselves are often causes of disappointment with consultants' advice. That they typically expect too much from consultants is only one of the reasons. Instances also arise when clients believe they know what they need, and insist on it, even when it is nonsense. Sometimes it is outright nonsense; on other occasions they pick up an idea that may have made sense in some other situation but becomes nonsensical in their own.

A quite recent trend among corporations and their consultants is to pay more attention to revenue growth and less to restructuring. Observing that many of today's most successful companies have simply grown without restructuring might suggest that restructuring is not a particularly good idea. Can one conclude that those who eschewed restructuring were that much smarter? Alternatively, might it just be that they were lucky enough not to have problems requiring drastic solutions? Restructuring, albeit undertaken with more planning and care, is likely sooner or later to be necessary for competitive survival even for healthiest, best-managed corporations.

Whither Shareholder Value Objectives?

To the extent consultants do recognize the legitimacy, and perhaps even the significance, of shareholder value objectives, most simply adopt the conventional assumption that pursuing earnings goals will meet those objectives. A few consultancies nevertheless do purport to focus directly on shareholder values. While they perhaps represent a step forward in strategic perspectives, significant shortcomings apparently remain:

- Direct linkages between decision criteria and enterprise (shareholder) values still tend to be missing.

---

[6]"A Survey," 20.

- Generally absent is an adequate comprehension of the under-lying sources of enterprise values, particularly the intangible components.

At least two rather different approaches seem currently to be in vogue. One is to use multivariate statistical regression (least squares) analysis to identify statistical relationships between shareholder values as represented by share prices and sundry other variables. Reported earnings are usually but one of a number of variables.

As a purely hypothetical example, one might posit that the stock prices for some particular industry group depend on earnings and earnings growth, dividend yield, book value (net worth), ratios of operating expenses to revenues, and revenue growth. A consultant might first identify statistically the effect of each of these variables on share prices. Using that information, the consultant can advise an individual client on how to change those variables within its own organization in ways that will increase its share price. Some potential problems with this approach include:

- It still relies on surrogates for value determinants rather than probing into basic sources of value. In particular, this analysis mainly relies on external, public information. Yet, a consultant working with a client should be able to develop data that pertain much more directly to enterprise value.
- The more variables the analysis employs, the larger the number of observations—different comparable corporations (banks, for example)—necessary to identify the statistical relationships. This requirement limits the approach to clients in industries with numerous reasonably comparable enterprises.
- The predictive power of this analysis deteriorates rapidly outside the observed ranges of the variables. It therefore encourages behavior conforming to industry patterns, thus promoting reactive decision making rather than innovative, out-of-the-box strategies.

As one simple example of the third point, suppose one observes a negative relationship between share prices and the ratio of employee expenses to revenues. In the extreme, the implication seems to be that cutting employee compensation expenses raises share prices right to the point at which employees vanish—a nonsensical prescription. Actually, one need not go so far. The American Management Association reports that fewer than half of all firms that have downsized since 1990 actually achieved increases in operating profits.[7]

Consider, too, the consequences of employing this statistical approach to advise two or more competing firms on competitive variables such as pricing and marketing. It suggests that each client should adopt much the same strategies. How, then, could one obtain competitive advantage over any other? Ultimately, this approach is likely to promote conformity, deterring innovation. It might be consistent with maintaining a normal return to investors—the minimum they require on their investment—but no more.

Notice that this same general type of approach might be a relatively scientific method of analyzing mergers and acquisitions and corporate stocks. One might thus incorporate a variety of different variables into a single predictor of a stock price. Indeed, if a stock were rarely traded, frequency of trades could be included among the variables. This concept perhaps belonged in Chapter 6, except that it is rarely adopted. It is, of course, subject to the same limitations as its use as a planning device.

A quite different approach is economic value added, or EVA, with its cousin, market value added, or MVA.[8] EVA essentially recognizes that the return on investment that investors require is the cost of capital. For a real capital outlay to be acceptable, its expected return must be above that cost. By expressing EVA in terms of present values, it simply becomes a form of discounted cash flow (DCF) analysis. By applying it *prospectively* in its DCF form to internal decision making, it could become traditional capital budgeting analysis, which a later chapter examines in detail.

Common use of EVA is as a means of *retrospective* assessment of overall enterprise performance, either as an internal management tool or as a method of external financial analysis. First, measure the "normal" capital base as book equity plus debt, to which one adds back such items as deferred taxes, extraordinary losses, minority interests, and amortized goodwill from prior acquisitions to obtain an estimate of capital outlays. "Normal" returns on that capital base are estimated as operating profit plus interest expense minus extraordinary losses and, more significantly, minus the cost of equity and debt determined from the weighted-average cost of capital (discussed in Chapters 9

---

[7]"Downsizing in America: The Revolving Door," *The Economist* (October 26, 1996) 80.
[8]Both *EVA* and *MVA* are terms apparently originated by a management consutancy, Stern, Stewart and Company.

and 12). If the net result is positive, EVA analysis concludes that the enterprise has made a positive contribution to shareholder value—the enterprise has provided a surplus return on capital over the cost of the capital.

If the measured results reflected underlying realities, they would indeed indicate whether shareholder value has been enhanced. To that extent, this analysis represents a significant step forward in recognizing that the returns investors require on capital represent a cost, which conventional earnings analysis simply fails to acknowledge. In its common form, however, this analysis does not indicate whether the enterprise has developed shareholder value to its full potential—it may indicate mere value "satisficing" rather than achievement of maximum shareholder values. Fully achieving shareholder value goals requires disaggregating the analysis to individual management decisions and recasting it prospectively. In other words, it requires adopting traditional capital budgeting analysis for virtually all decision making.

A yet more severe, and often fatal, weakness of EVA is its reliance on conventional accounting data, which, among other problems, means ignoring most relationship capital. No wonder, then, that EVA analysis is generally unreliable, and is virtually useless in the context of service enterprises. Any concept that appears reasonable only in selective applications is likely to be fundamentally flawed.

MVA looks instead at whether the market value of corporate equity exceeds invested capital. Exactly how one is to measure that invested capital seems unclear. In one form it simply compares market values with book values, which is virtually meaningless in a relationship environment. Indeed, both EVA and MVA appear to have evolved mainly from industrial rather than relationship contexts. Like EVA, MVA seems not to recognize the capital nature of intangibles. If MVA measures invested capital as an outlay, it, too, seems to be nothing other than traditional capital budgeting. For both EVA and MVA, perhaps only the terminology is really new.[9]

Another concept warranting mention in this context, although not

[9]Tom Copeland, Tim Koller, and Jack Murrin, *Valuation: Measuring and Managing the Value of Companies*, 2d ed. (New York: John Wiley & Sons, 1996). This book, whose authors were or are partners at McKinsey & Company, Inc., discusses and seemingly adopts EVA and MVA. Its analysis nevertheless is readily recognizable as based on traditional capital budgeting. Probably the most widely used guide to capital budgeting over the years has been Harold Bierman, Jr., and Seymour Schmidt, *The Capital Budgeting Decision: Economic Analysis and Financing of Investment Decisions* (New York: Macmillan, 1960).

focused directly on value in any way, is customer retention analysis.[10] The basic idea, which pertains more to marketing than strategic planning, is that a corporation might improve its earnings by expending more resources on retaining current customers. Moreover, it might find simultaneously reducing outlays for attracting new customers to be advantageous. Indeed, many cases do arise when the costs (or outlays) necessary to retain customers—presumably customers with whom relationships already exist—are significantly less than the outlays that replacing them would require.

Retention analysis touches on, but fails to develop, a fundamental principle. The value of a customer relationship tends to be higher the longer it remains in place. Outlays on extending the lives of existing relationships may therefore contribute more enterprise value than investing in new relationship development. The sorts of options that confront a relationship business is a topic for later, more detailed discussion. The shortcoming of retention analysis as its proponents promote it is its lack of value content.

Conflicting Perspectives of Management Theory

The primary reason for widespread discordance in approaches to business principles is the lack of a common foundation. If a comprehensive business theory ever did exist, it is no longer workable. A strategic void thus arises from a theoretical void, opening the door to management fads. Everyone seeks *the* key to achieving corporate objectives, and all sorts of consultants purport to offer it. Actually, the existence of any single key is highly unlikely.

The search for a magic key to corporate prosperity brings to mind when Peter Snell won gold medals in both the 800- and 1,500-meter runs in the 1964 Olympics. Upon learning that Snell trained by running some 100 miles per week, thousands of aspiring Olympians around the world adopted a similar regimen. Instead of finding the key to success, many achieved little more than exhaustion. Then, in 1980, 1,500-meter gold medalist Sebastian Coe revealed that his training secret was intensive running with low mileage. Again, thousands of aspirants adopted his regimen, with similarly mixed results. The difference was that Snell, much the larger man, was able to endure

---

[10]This idea attracted widespread attention with the publication of Frederick F. Reichheld and W. Earl Sasser, Jr., "Zero Defections: Quality Comes to Services," *Harvard Business Review* (September–October 1990) 301.

high mileage, whereas Coe could not. No one training regimen could be universally appropriate. Among business enterprises as well, no one management approach can be suitable for all. Indeed, the idea of developing a break-out strategy—separating oneself from the competition—suggests otherwise.

Consider a clash among theories of human resources management. The more traditional, industrial-age view of employees is as representing costs of production. Quantitative theories for organizing production focused on how to minimize those costs, drawing on engineering concepts and time and motion studies. They regarded laborers as fundamentally homogeneous cogs in the great wheel of assembly-line production. An inherent problem with this old-fashioned quantitative view is that it encourages reducing inputs without adequate attention to outputs. Treating workers as wheel cogs encourages them to behave accordingly. TQM at least demonstrated the potential pitfalls.

TQM and process reengineering represent more modern empowerment management concepts. Instead of treating production workers as if they are effectively automatons, they become decision makers. The need for middle management supposedly diminishes as it relinquishes more responsibility for decisions. At some extreme, at least conceptually, is the emergence of the horizontal corporation, with a few senior executives responsible for strategic direction while everyone else is some sort of partner or team member. The result is something radically different from the familiar hierarchical organization model.

One difficulty with empowerment is that individual responsibilities may remain ambiguous. If so, partners and team members will trip over one another. A further difficulty is likely to be that many employees do not want the requisite decision-making responsibility. Exercising that responsibility means that somehow, sometime, rewards and penalties result from good and bad decisions. Some workers may welcome that risk with a potential for more reward, while others might prefer a safer, if possibly less remunerative, course.

Maybe a solution to this sort of impasse is for an organization to adopt one model or the other. If it adopts the empowerment model, it should exercise care that its employees are in step with that model. A rather different approach might be a hybrid of the two models, with different employees assuming different levels of responsibility. Decision-making production workers would nevertheless not supervise those who eschew decision responsibility. Otherwise, this model is likely to collapse back to the hierarchical one. This second approach might be a bit like market segmentation, with customization of organizational management according to different employee proclivities. Simply mentioning this possibility here is not to imply any opinion about its workability, however.

The Japanese management model is yet rather different, involving management by consensus. It implies a team approach to decision making, perhaps at multiple levels of management. While perhaps drawing on a broader base of information and judgment as well as promoting internal harmony within an organization, it tends to slow down the decision-making process. The resulting delays in reaching decisions may become more costly as economic change accelerates and response lags increase.

As enterprise decision making tends to be hierarchical according to the significance and scope of decisions, the pyramidal form of corporate organization will surely survive, albeit perhaps in modified forms. The logic that will preserve it does not mean that it is without pitfalls. It first implies severe constraints on abilities to import different experiences, perspectives, and creative ideas. This limitation alone can lead to internal rigidity, effectively locking an organization in the box. It further implies a constant exodus of employees who can only advance their careers elsewhere. Poor management of that process may result in exporting an organization's most creative elements. Indeed, it may do so if only because those elements are often the most critical of maintaining an ineffective but, for many, comfortable status quo.

A question nevertheless arises with this organizational form, which has no ready answer. How much decision-making authority should a corporation centralize in one individual? In particular, should the same individual serve as chairman of the board of directors, president, and (thus virtually by definition) chief executive officer? Is this centralization the most effective, if not the only, means by which to expedite essential decisions in a fast-paced business environment? Alternatively, is it a form of hubris that results in decision-making overload, detracting from management effectiveness?

The limitations of the pyramidal organization model are also pertinent in the present context because many consultancies themselves tend toward that form. A common modus operandi is to recruit hordes of top business school graduates who must then face a progressive weeding out process. Without progressive thinning of the ranks, too many senior consultants spend too much time on relatively menial tasks. In the same manner as for any business organization, a likely result is homogenization and eventual internal ossification.

Fad Culture in Corporate Society

In part because of expectations or desires for quick results, conflicting management ideas induce many corporate executives to bounce peripatetically from fad to fad. In many cases they adopt a number of fads simultaneously. Consultants encourage this behavior by claiming success on the basis of near-term results, never minding that longer-term outcomes tend to be quite different. At least some corporate restructuring programs have been doomed to this pattern from the outset. Success appears as higher reported earnings when it reflects an erosion of capital.

Even situations giving rise to legitimate cost reduction opportunities can easily go awry. Downsizing requires decisions on who stays and who goes. One common tendency is again to focus on the near term. Thus, more senior managers (other than occupants of the executive suites) are more likely to be expendable because they represent higher compensation costs. Another tendency is to retain managers and employees who seem to fit best in the organization. Gone, then, are likely to be the gadflies, creative thinkers, and innovators. What is likely to remain is a reduced but reinforced status quo.

How, indeed, can one avoid some degree of conflict between, say, emphasizing core competencies and process reengineering? The former seems to imply taking advantage of management experience and expertise that has developed over a considerable period of time. The latter implies removal of much of that management. Similarly, how credible is employee empowerment amid widespread layoffs?

Corporate Dependence on Consultants

Why is it that for all its conflicting ideas and deficiencies, management consulting continues to expand its influence? What drives what often seems to be a peripatetic corporate reliance on outside consultants? To what extent do these tendencies reflect greed, fear, desperation, or ignorance? Among the possibilities, consider that:

- A sense of runaway economic transformation accentuates legitimate incentives to draw on outside knowledge, experience, and perceptions. One constructive role of consultants is to accumulate and provide industry or market information that is otherwise not accessible by individual clients.

- Many corporate executives persist in expecting more advice from consultants than the consultants have the expertise and experience to deliver.

- One function of outside management consultants may be to validate management decisions and overall corporate direction. Thus, a chief executive can tell directors that "Our consultants advised us. . . ." Consultants may thus serve as a prop for losses of managerial confidence.

- At least some corporate executives rise through the ranks due to qualities other than their true leadership, vision, or decisiveness. Consultants may act as surrogate management, perhaps while many managers themselves, not really knowing how to lead, immerse themselves in administrative chores, endless meetings, and other forms of avoidance.

- Senior executives, in particular, may tend to isolate themselves within their own organizations. Consultants provide them with opportunities for peer networking, and may also serve as an information conduit within an organization.

The final point regarding executive isolation has yet a further dimension. Some critics of today's corporate culture argue that much of what senior executives call upon consultants to provide actually is available at much less expense, and with more relevance, from their own employees. Is it ignorance, arrogance, or defensiveness that deters them from looking to these sources?

Consultants seem in any event to be as much captives of in-the-box thinking and as afflicted with tunnel vision as many of their clients. As products of the business schools, they typically lack sufficient foundation in business theory. How, then, can they apply fundamental, workable business principles in meeting client needs? Their own primary incentive is to sell their own particular specialties, which may not be what clients need. The inability of many clients to understand, and even less to articulate, their needs is an invitation to a certain degree of charlatanism.

Resurrecting Strategic Thinking

As suggested earlier, a business cannot avoid having some sort of strategy, even if is nothing more than avoiding making decisions.

Moreover, visioning is no substitute for strategic thinking. While it may be a useful exercise in preparing managers for possible but unforeseeable future events, developing an effective strategy further requires a decision framework.

Visioning runs the danger of being a vehicle for avoiding strategic choices. It may, however, represent a step forward from the old-fashioned strategic planning that was popular a generation ago. That sort of exercise has fallen into disrepute, and deservedly so. Its shortcoming was not the underlying idea of strategic thinking but that there was so little of it. It, too, suffered from a dearth of underlying principles. The preparation of strategic plans was too often a mechanical process of document production by strategic planners who relied substantially on extrapolating past experience into the future and typically made little allowance for contingencies. Much more often than not, subsequent events departed from those projections. The resulting plans often were obsolete even before completion.

The business community will either commit to strategic thinking or continue to flounder. By being carefully selective, an enterprise can obtain useful ideas from outside advisors, but outsiders are hardly capable of delivering strategies. Processes of strategic thinking must be mainly internal. Strategic planning does require some type of structure, but obviously must avoid bogging down in mechanical procedures.

The foregoing review of the four sides of the box—the institutional constraints deterring effective strategies and decisions—has contained a fair amount of criticism. The corporate landscape is cluttered with insubstantial, misguided ideas. By way of summary, then, instead consider briefly that this clutter also contains many nuggets suggestive of forward thinking. Have significant elements of the business community itself begun to perceive needs for new ways of thinking? Among the possibilities are:

- Some understanding that required returns on investment are costs rather than profits. Among other things, this principle underscores the formidable challenges confronting efforts to develop more shareholder value. It also makes clear that apparent increases in shareholder value may be merely illusory.
- Some recognition that many business decisions have long-term outcomes. As they are therefore investment decisions, they require a time dimension which in turn requires translating outcomes into present values.

- Understanding, particularly among economists, that a value is a price, or a composite of prices, that can exist only at some particular time. In other words, historical prices drawn from different times cannot represent a value.
- Accounting procedures that depart from conventional book accounting to revalue balance sheets at the market values of assets and liabilities, with inclusion of market values of intangible assets. (A later chapter considers this purchase accounting in more detail.)
- Recognition among at least some accounting professionals, even if not widely communicated outside the profession, that conventional accounting otherwise has serious, growing, and possibly insurmountable problems in achieving economic relevance.
- A slowly emerging concern, most importantly among large institutional investors, with lapses in accountability of corporate directors and chief executives to shareholders.
- Recognition among some consultants, primarily marketing specialists, of the significance of customer relationships to a business, even if this recognition does not extend to assigning values to such relationships.
- A growing understanding among some management consultants that middle managers and other employees possess experience and skills that are costly to eliminate and are not readily replaceable.

A continuing process of corporate restructuring is clearly necessary and inevitable. Financial performance and economic prosperity still require substituting machines for people. Increasingly, however, they require using both machines and people in very different and more effective ways. Whether to restructure is not even an issue, and perhaps has never been. When to restructure also is not an issue—the need to restructure is unremitting. The only legitimate issue is how to restructure. Thus, subsequent chapters consider in detail how business enterprises should proceed in developing effective strategies that are responsive to the demands of a relationship economy.

A final question before leaving this topic is whether or not a value-based decision model represents a management theory. However one might choose to regard it, it certainly is essential at least as a foundation for developing management theories.

PART 3

Breaking Out of the Box

A good name, then, or almost any kind of notoriety, may be a factor of production in the commercial sense just as much as tools, site, raw material, strength, intelligence, or conscientiousness.

Philip H. Wicksteed, *The Common Sense of Political Economy* (1910)

CHAPTER 8

Recognizing Shareholder Value Objectives

POSITIONING FOR A BREAKOUT

Part One of this book made the case that today's relationship economy is something vastly different from the industrial economy that preceded it and that shaped contemporary business thinking. It also touched on the need for developing business strategies with which to confront that newly emerged relationship environment.

The mere fact that economies are developing relationship configurations nevertheless does not mean that business communities have adapted to those circumstances. For the most part, corporate enterprises have not adopted policies and procedures for effective relationship building. Indeed, they may have developed their relationship potentials more fully in an earlier, simpler environment than is the case today. A problem seems to be with managing an overload of communication and information, often with breakdowns in common courtesy. Unreturned telephone calls, unanswered invitations, and unacknowledged correspondence are commonplace, as responses often depend on perceptions of immediate need or advantage. A consequence is reduced communication and more uncertainty.

Part Two examined the four major types of impediments to recognition of, and effective responses to, rapid economic change in a relationship environment. Retrogressive institutions, conventions, and assumptions still confine business principles and practices to the box. Each side of the box of institutionalized convention acts as such because it is itself trapped in the box. Each side, moreover, reinforces the others. Moving ahead means breaking out of that essentially inward-looking, defensive, and ultimately self-destructive status quo.

Much of today's corporate society faces gradual loss of control over its destiny. The widespread absence of viable business strategies guarantees as much—the purpose of a strategy is to gain that control. The four sides of the box suggest four corresponding initial steps in that direction:

1. Substitute shareholder values for profit objectives.
2. Eschew conventional accounting measures as primary decision criteria.
3. Break loose from untoward influences of the sell-side of Wall Street.
4. Develop more skepticism toward outside advisors.

Each of these steps requires better understanding of the characteristics of economic relationships and their significance as underlying value elements of corporate enterprise. With that understanding, one can then explore how those value elements relate to strategic objectives.

The Supremacy of Shareholder Values

A necessary starting point is to accept the principle that shareholder values are the supreme, uncompromisable objective of a corporation. Another is to recognize that current and expected dividend distributions are the ultimate sources of those values. With those propositions in place, the next step is to look in detail at the underlying sources of a corporation's capacity to pay dividends. Therein lie the sources of its value to shareholders.

Much of corporate society pays lip service to shareholder value principles without installing the mechanisms for directly pursuing that objective. Pursuit of other, often inconsistent objectives is commonplace. Insensitivity to shareholder interests remains too common, undoubtedly arising from a lack of a sense of urgency. Although its consequences include reduced access to capital and impaired competitiveness, these may seem too far in the future to cause concern for today's management.

In time, perhaps failures to manage on behalf of shareholders will give rise to shareholder disgruntlement. Such dissatisfaction must be taken more seriously as more corporate stock comes into the hands of institutional investors. Lapses in accountability may also lead to hostile takeover offers, although the wayward chief executive may by then be long gone with a handsome retirement package. If not, perhaps a golden parachute reduces his concerns.

Is paying the piper for neglecting shareholder interests really so remote? The problem seems not to be the basic principle of shareholder value maximization as it is the myopia prevalent throughout much of corporate society and the investment community. As a simple hypothetical illustration, imagine a corporation that historically has emphasized shareholder objectives. The CEO then retires. His successor, recruited from outside with a handsome compensation package tied to earnings performance, undertakes a different course. A somnolent board of directors takes little notice. What might happen?

1. Perhaps no adverse consequences initially become apparent. Suppose, for example, that to increase reported earnings the new CEO slashes marketing expenses. Wall Street cheers the higher earnings, institutional shareholders initially nod approval, and the share price rises. Nevertheless, if the previous marketing program had been generating net value to the enterprise, its underlying value is already compromised.

2. The initial ploys to boost reported earnings were essentially a form of borrowing from the future. Thus, following the initial cosmetic improvement in financial performance, earnings begin to falter and share prices weaken. Perhaps corporate insiders have already sold some of their shares.

3. Weakened share prices mean higher costs of equity capital. The company therefore cannot raise outside equity on as favorable terms as before. Viewing this development, the credit markets will be less willing to provide debt financing, and costs of new debt also will rise.

4. The CEO recognizes that the company cannot allow its real capital, including that embedded in customers and employees, to continue to erode, yet still remain competitive. The company therefore must at least fund investment in replacing that capital or gradually wither away.

5. With impaired access to external equity and higher costs of debt, the CEO decides to rely more heavily on internal funding for investment, including for replacement. Notwithstanding accounting intricacies, more internal funding of investment means lower dividends.

6. Nevertheless, projects that had prospective returns above the company's cost of capital now encounter a higher cost of capital. The company either must invest less than if it had been more attentive to shareholders, or it must invest on terms that further erode shareholder value.

7. The CEO might decide to proceed with suboptimal projects anyway rather than paying earnings out as dividends, which would imply corporate shrinkage. As Chapter 6 discussed, the consequence is further weakening of returns on their equity, with further weakening of share prices.

8. The CEO might instead decide to issue more long-term debt to fund new investment, even at the higher costs of borrowing. Doing so increases the risks on both the company's debt and its equity, further raising its costs of capital with consequent weakening of share prices.

9. As the downward spiral accelerates, the CEO may bring in consultants who will suggest downsizing, perhaps to focus more on its core competencies. Wall Street might again cheer, if only because the move implies less investment with prospective returns below the cost of capital.

10. Before actually moving very far on a restructuring track, a hostile takeover may materialize, or the CEO, sensing that the situation has deteriorated to the point of being irreversible, will begin to seek an acquirer. He therefore engages investment bankers to explore the company's strategic options.

If this scenario seems far-fetched, perhaps it is mainly in assuming that the predecessor CEO was uniformly committed to serving the shareholders. Observe that actual deterioration in both value and competitive resources sets in immediately, even if it becomes apparent only gradually. A consequence of this lag is a discrepancy between the true underlying value of the enterprise and its value as reflected in share prices—a discrepancy that should itself gradually disappear.

Indeed, ploys for boosting earnings cannot go unnoticed indefinitely. Here, a shrinking customer base would begin to raise questions about competitiveness. Observe, too, that shareholder disgruntlement would emerge as deteriorating share prices well before it is likely to break into the open at annual shareholders' meetings. Hostile takeovers are usually slower to develop. Information suggestive of opportunities is slow to emerge, and mounting a hostile takeover is usually costly. Thus, except for weakening share prices, the penalties for inattentiveness to shareholders usually take shape internally well before breaking to the surface. The main point is that when capital markets are competitive, an enterprise must behave accordingly. Being competitive in attracting capital is an essential predicate to competing as a business.

More on Stakeholders

The idea that corporations have stakeholders in addition to shareholders, while by no means absent in the United States, is far more prevalent in many foreign countries. Indeed, a recent book, *Valuation: Measuring and Managing the Value of Companies* indicates that many corporate managers in countries such as Germany and Japan believe they cannot and should not seek to maximize shareholder values.[1] Rather, they must be substantially attentive to other claims, and particularly those of labor. The book goes about analyzing that view in a rather intriguing way—by comparing the differences in changes in market value added (MVA) in the United States, Germany, and Japan. Thus:

1. It defines MVA as the difference between the total market capitalization (the value of all outstanding shares) of a corporation and its book value, or net worth.[2]
2. It then measures the *changes* in MVA for large corporations in each of the three countries over the period 1983 to 1991.
3. It concludes that larger increases in MVA occur in the context of higher levels of national gross domestic product

[1]Tom Copeland, Tim Keller, and Jack Murrin, *Valuation: Measuring and Managing the Value of Companies,* 2d ed. (New York: John Wiley & Sons, 1996), p. 4.
[2]Chapter 1 of *Valuation* develops this analysis. For the purpose of measurement, it measured MVA as the total market value of corporate debt plus equity minus the book value of invested capital, as financed by debt as well as equity. The debt portion thus cancels out in measuring changes in MVA.

(GDP) per capita, higher industry productivity, and higher employment growth.

Exactly what is cause and what is effect is unclear. Also, the analysis suffers from a difficulty that perhaps is now familiar, which is how to measure MVA for services. Actually, the same problem presumably arises to a lesser degree, although for many of the same reasons, among other sectors. In any event, the analysis concludes with:

> The link between productivity and shareholder value maximization is too strong to ignore. If more output is produced with fewer inputs, the shareholder's value is greater. But in the long run, all claims, including the employment of labor, benefit when a company is a winner in its industry.[3]

This conclusion ties back into the earlier issue of competitiveness. Indeed, "companies that do not perform will find that capital flows toward their competitors."[4]

Just what foreign managers and various management theorists believe to be legitimate labor stakeholder claims beyond competitive wages is also unclear. Perhaps part of the problem in comprehending this concept is that it emerges from countries where markets for labor and capital are fundamentally uncompetitive. Capital markets abroad are only gradually breaking loose from their traditional intertwinings of management and sources of capital, particularly banks. Similarly evaporating only very gradually are the politically powerful labor organizations in Europe and the lifetime guarantee of employment system in Japan.

The idea of stakeholders other than shareholders suggests that they somehow receive compensation for their services lower than their economic contribution. If markets are truly competitive, competitors willing to offer more should be ready to bid away any employee who is thus undercompensated. Suppose, for example, that an employee contributes $20 per hour to output but receives only $15. Contributing that amount means that if the employee were to depart, and nothing else changes, the employer would have a net loss of $5 per hour. A competing employer might see an opportunity to expand output by hiring that employee at some higher amount, say $18 per

---

[3] *Valuation,* p. 28.
[4] *Valuation,* p. 22.

hour. The process would continue until the employee's compensation converges on $20 per hour.

The argument may seem to become more complicated in a relationship value context, but it is essentially the same. The value of an employee to an employer should tend to converge with its value to the employee. Thus, apart from direct compensation, an employer will invest in employee training to the extent that doing so produces a positive marginal net present value to the employer. Here, though, one might ask what happens to the surplus net value prior to reaching that point. As this type of question may underlie a variety of stakeholder misconceptions, consider the employer's situation in the following diagram:

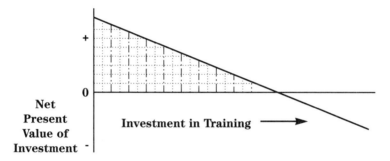

Net Present Value Contributions of Training Investment.

The shaded triangle in the diagram represents net value accruing to the employer—the employer is getting back more than it is investing. Does the worker undergoing training have a claim on some portion of this net value? Again assuming a competitive marketplace, one or both of two things could happen:

- A competitor to this employer sees opportunity to obtain similar value by offering employees similar training.
- The employee takes the value of the training to a competing employer.

In either event, it is the same old story—competition quickly comes into play that eliminates the surplus, reduces the net present value to zero, and provides the investing employer with recovery of the investment at a normal return on the outlay. Correspondingly, an employer undertakes this type of investment to the extent and in such manner as it expects its recovery with a return equal to its cost of capital.

More complicated perhaps are circumstances arising from the development over time of a corporate culture—a common sense of direction and how to do things that is specific to a particular company. It cannot exist as something separable from the employees who share it. Does that mean that the employees somehow have a stake in it? Because it has no value outside the context of that one enterprise, the employer would seem to have the primary incentive to invest in its development. Perhaps employees would also participate, but only to the extent they expect something in return, knowing it not to be transportable. Meanwhile, competing companies presumably have similar incentives to develop their own internal cultures, again with the result that surplus values evaporate with competition.

Competition, of course, does not always work the way theory suggests. Markets for employment are by no means perfect, as information about opportunities and prospects is quite imperfect. That problem, however, is in large part a social one, at least partly beyond the scope of individual employers. To the extent it is in part internal as well, it is because many employers have yet to break loose from the concept of employees as representing costs rather than investment opportunities.

A rather different concept of stakeholders does have some legitimacy. A corporation's creditors are stakeholders in essentially the same way as shareholders to the extent that they share in the risks. An extreme example is junk bonds, which many financial professionals regard as closer to equity investment than to debt. Indeed, the main difference seems sometimes to be that distributions to the holders of these instruments, unlike true dividends, are deductible for tax purposes from corporate income. Normally, however, whatever equity risk creditors assume is substantially smaller than that borne by shareholders, and their stakeholder claims are much less to that same extent.

Dividends as Determinants of Corporate Values

Maximizing the shareholder value of a corporation means maximizing its capacity to pay dividends. Specifically, it means maximizing the present value today of all expected dividend payout to shareholders over the entire future life of the enterprise. Dividends thus include whatever cash proceeds shareholders realize from sale or liquidation of the corporation, which in turn includes whatever dividends they receive from any successor corporation. The latter situation arises in an exchange of stock whereby the shareholders receive shares of some other, acquiring corporation.

Keep in mind that the only means by which a shareholder can realize any value from the shares is either directly from dividends or from selling those shares. Consider an investor who buys shares today. Suppose the issuing corporation has been paying dividends per share of $12 per year, the next payment to be a year hence (which arrangement the investor expects it to maintain indefinitely), and that all investors require an annual return on investment of 15 percent. Initially assume, too, that the investor plans to hold the shares virtually forever, passing them on to later generations. Then, as in the Chapter 6 example except on a per share basis, the value of a share to this investor is:

$$\frac{\$12}{.15} = \$80.$$

Next, suppose instead that the investor firmly intends to sell the shares one year from now and expects the sale price at that time to be equal to his own valuation of the dividends. He expects the corporation still will be paying the same dividends and that the return on investment that other investors will require will still be 15 percent. The value of each share, and thus its price at that time, will still be $80. What happens is that the dividends paid in the previous year ($12) exactly equal the addition to the present value as a consequence of all future dividends moving one year closer in time. The value today of a share now becomes:

$$\frac{\$12 + \$80}{1.15} = \$80.$$

To be sure, this investor's expectations and required rate of return may differ from the market consensus. If the price is below his own value assessment, he should buy the stock. If the price subsequently rises above it, he should consider selling it. His own assessment undoubtedly will change with subsequent events, as will also the market consensus. The stock price therefore will surely fluctuate.

A possible objection to this sort of analysis is that investors simply do not think this way. They normally base investment decisions on current financial performance and how they think stock prices will behave, usually over no more than the next few years. To leave the matter there, however, is to have the grin without the cat. Somehow values must, and do, adopt some direction of central tendency, even if they never quite reach it. Share prices and values therefore always gravitate toward the dividend values.

The significance of dividends to share values and prices assumes special importance with corporate decisions either to buy back shares or to reinvest net cash flows rather than to pay them out as dividends. The emphasis here on cash flows arises because earnings are net of depreciation. Whether or not to replace capital that is eroding or wearing out is no less an investment decision than whether to invest in some altogether new venture. Even if a corporation distributes all reported earnings as dividends, it would normally engage in some reinvestment. Investors often assume that reinvestment at least equivalent to depreciation is reasonable and prudent. Chapter 6 suggested that reinvestment of all earnings may actually be possible only with some returns below the corporation's cost of capital. That situation seems especially likely in cases of poorly managed enterprises. Unfortunately, the income tax system, which taxes both corporate earnings and dividend income, encourages reinvestment that otherwise wastes capital.

Corporate repurchase of shares is a potential substitute for paying dividends that has become fairly common in recent years. Many stock buybacks are illusory, at least in part, as the repurchases are merely offsets to employee stock options. When repurchases actually do reduce the numbers of outstanding shares, they increase future dividend flows per share and thus increase share prices. They, too, are a way of deferring income taxes on dividend income. Typically, however, share repurchases tend to occur among relatively healthy enterprises that have accumulated excess cash and believe their share prices are undervalued. They are not common among poorly managed corporations that actually should be shrinking and distributing their capital for lack of opportunities.

The main reason for emphasizing the significance of dividends to shareholder value is to come back to the fundamental proposition that value derives solely from cash flows—how much and when:

- Net cash flows from different asset components determine their individual values.
- Those same net cash flows determine the net cash flows of the

total enterprise upon deducting outlays for servicing debt (to the extent debt service is not allocated among individual assets).

- The net cash flows of the total enterprise (net of debt service and income taxes) are what it has available to pay dividends to shareholders.

Were it not for income taxes, the *only* justifiable reason for not distributing all net cash flows as dividends is if opportunities exist for investing them at returns above the appropriate costs of capital, implying enhancement of future dividend capacity, and thus additional value. This proposition remains intact if modified to recognize the tax distortions that reduce the effective returns on capital from reinvestment. Adding depreciation and amortization back to earnings sometimes provides a very rough approximation of corporate cash flows, at least in a nonrelationship environment.

Convergence of Value Concepts

Business executives, financial analysts, and academicians alike tend to have blind spots when considering enterprise values. Whatever methods they use to identify those values, they typically focus on some of the components while overlooking others entirely. Previous chapters have indicated that the components they are prone to overlook—typically relationship assets and other intangibles—are often at least as important as those capturing their attention. Indeed, the intangible components have become so important that economic and business principles become sterile by ignoring them.

Appearances perhaps to the contrary, the sum of the components must always converge with any valid measure of total enterprise value. Correspondingly, the total market value of an enterprise must always tend toward the sum of its underlying value sources. Recognition of this convergence means that corporate management is in large part a process of managing, or engineering, the value contributions of the different current and potential components. Recognition of the intangibles is often the key to closing the loop between a building-block view and other indicators of enterprise value.

A building-block or net asset enterprise value is similar to a hypothetical liquidation or break-up value. It nevertheless excludes both costs of liquidating and any adverse effects on asset prices that an actual liquidation might cause. Financial analysts normally do not think of corporate enterprise values in these terms. This approach is not without precedent, however. For example, some years ago mortgage bonds were a common method of corporate long-term debt financing. A mortgage bond is secured by a lien on specified corporate assets such as railway equipment or even sections of track. Mortgage bonds eventually grew less common as it became evident that the liens often provided little protection to creditors. A section of track might be a good bargaining chip in bankruptcy proceedings but of little use otherwise if detached from a going concern.

Another, much more recent, view of the convergence of market capitalization—total market values of corporate equity—with underlying real asset values is the Q Ratio. Its origin goes back at least to 1960, with graduate students querying James Tobin, later a Nobel laureate in economics, about the economic significance of the stock market. Many economists tended at that time to dismiss the stock market as mostly a sideshow. Professor Tobin, however, suggested regarding stock prices that substantially exceed the replacement costs of real assets as a signal for more real investment. The discrepancy means that the costs of equity capital are lower than the returns on real capital. Stated another way, higher stock prices enable buying more real capital.

Conceptually, the Q Ratio itself is the ratio of corporate market capitalization to net asset values. A variant is the ratio of market capitalization plus debt to assets. Either way, as a practical matter, its calculation is usually with reference to book net worth as shown on corporate balance sheets. Because the denominator is substantially understated, particularly because it omits most intangible assets, calculated values of the Q Ratio are usually rather meaningless and nearly always well in excess of one (1.0). A corporation might nevertheless obtain guidance on its real investment by undertaking an internal estimate of its Q Ratio, including intangible as well as tangible assets and capital.

Value Building Blocks

Many business decisions can incorporate value concepts without requiring valuations of assets and capital already in place. After all, past investments are essentially irreversible. Capital budgeting decisions therefore normally compare present values of current and future cash outlays with inflows associated with new investment. They presumably reflect market phenomena, and thus market values, at the time of making those decisions.

Yet, assessments of values of assets already in place can be important for any of a number of reasons:

- Corporate directors and managers who fail to understand fully the value attributes of their businesses—where those values come from and what they represent—cannot fully understand those businesses. They are inevitably prone to uninformed, haphazard decision making.
- A test of that understanding is the ability to conceptualize and measure enterprise values in terms of their underlying sources—their component assets. In particular, net asset valuation of an enterprise should focus more attention on essential intangibles, including relationship assets.
- Understanding the future prospects of investment alternatives usually develops from past experience. Existing components of enterprise value thus provide an invaluable base of information for future strategies and decisions.
- Investment opportunities may include acquisitions or divestitures. In those cases, decisions require valuing the existing assets representing those opportunities.
- Many cases of developing additional value take on the characteristics of acquisitions. Thus, considering investment in entering a new market requires analyzing the value characteristics of the prospective customer relationships.
- The ability of a corporation to attract and retain capital depends in part on how effectively it communicates its value story to the investing public. Many executives fail to recognize the importance of conveying this sort of information.

Actually, continuous internal monitoring of corporate value characteristics seems to be uncommon, despite its potential importance. From the standpoint of corporate management and direction, periodic internal value audits should certainly be as important as more conventional forms of internal and external auditing. Improper recording of transactions—the focus of conventional audits—is hardly the only way corporate ineptitude and misdirection can fritter away shareholder values.

Thus, before focusing more directly on value principles of decision making, consider further how to identify the value of an enterprise. Obviously, conventional accounting measures fall well short of providing value information on which corporate managements and investors can rely for decisions. A relationship economy requires decision criteria representing very different measures of financial condition and performance.

A discounted cash flow, or DCF, basis for business decisions implies market value criteria. Ultimately, market values represent consensus estimates of DCF values. Correspondingly, DCF values are simply estimates of market values, more specifically of potential additions to the market value of the corporate enterprise. The significance of market values to decision making suggests measuring corporate financial condition and performance in terms of these values, at least for purposes of management information and decision making if not for public financial reporting. Indeed, this sort of market value accounting is precisely what yields estimates of net asset values.

For certain selected types of businesses, and specifically for financial services, including banking, accounting standards have been moving slowly toward market value principles. In part, this trend reflects recognition of the enormous discrepancies between the values of financial enterprises as shown on their balance sheets and their true values. Financial institutions periodically revalue their balance sheets using the market values of their financial assets (which are tangible) to the extent they are determinable. Banks, moreover, currently have the express option of disclosing values of customer intangibles in the footnotes to their financial statements. Perhaps more portentously, the Financial Accounting Standards Board (FASB) commenced a project during Summer 1997 to determine the feasibility of *requiring* that those intangibles be reported in bank financial statements.[5]

Present accounting standards also provide for market value accounting for many types of business combinations and acquisitions. Specifically, purchase accounting for such transactions requires recording all the various acquired assets and liabilities at their market values as of the transaction date. If a purchase involves only a single asset, such as a manufacturing facility, the value for accounting purposes would normally be its purchase price.

Many purchase transactions, however, involve more than one asset, and often entire corporations. The accounting rules then require allocating the total purchase price among all the different types of assets. For example, if the purchase of a manufacturing facility includes the

---

[5]Market value principles for decision making and financial reporting in banking are discussed at length in Bruce Morgan, *Foundations of Relationship Banking: Structuring Decisions to Build Shareholder Value* (Dublin, Ireland: Lafferty Publications Limited, 1994).

machinery as well as the building, appraisals are necessary to allocate the purchase price between the two types of assets. This purchase price allocation does not affect the total amount of assets or net worth initially appearing on a buyer's financial statements; the purchase is normally an outlay of cash or cash substitutes (marketable securities) equal to the purchase price, with the acquired assets also valued at that amount. Net worth remains unchanged. Nevertheless, the depreciation of each type of asset for subsequent financial reports would differ according to its particular wasting characteristics. The result is that the allocation of the purchase price may very well affect the total amounts of assets and net worth in future financial reports.

The same purchase accounting rules apply to intangible assets. Simply recording a premium over the values of the tangible assets as goodwill is supposed to be unacceptable although, as a practical matter, enforcement of this rule is sometimes rather lax. The rules further require amortizing—writing off—the value of each acquired, identifiable intangible according to its own particular wasting characteristics.

Purchase accounting is of particular interest here because conceptually, at least, it is effectively an exercise in market value accounting. Assuming appropriate allocation of the purchase prices, the values upon purchase receive the endorsement of arm's-length transactions. If so, they provide a new cost basis for historical-cost accounting for each asset. The accounting treatment thus should meet verifiability as well as value objectives for financial reporting. The intended end result is initially stating assets and liabilities exactly as would be necessary for a net asset value financial statement.

Does purchase accounting suggest that market value accounting thus offers sufficient reliability and verifiability attributes to be a potential substitute for historical-cost accounting? The primary control over purchase accounting is that at least in the first instance, the addition to assets from a purchase can be neither less nor more than the total purchase price. A more generalized market value accounting model, removed from this purchase context, would lack this control.

A Market Value Balance Sheet

As an illustration of market value accounting, consider what the balance sheet of a hypothetical bank might look like both with conventional historical-cost accounting and after conversion to a market value basis. In general, the most common types of purchase accounting adjustments are for the effects of interest rate changes on financial instruments, differences between current prices of fixed assets and their depreciated book values, and recognition of intangible assets. Banking provides a useful illustration of all three of these types of mark-to-market adjustments. Because of the large number of bank acquisitions during the 1980s, a good deal of information is available about bank intangibles. Also, their primary source of intangible value—their depositor relationships—tends to have similar value characteristics among different banks. This intangible typically represents a substantial portion (roughly half) of bank net asset values (true net worth). True net worth in banking, in other words, tends to be about twice the reported net worth. Suppose that:

- Interest rates have been rising, causing the market values of the bank's loans and securities to drop below their book values.
- Inflation has caused the market values of the bank's main office and branch facilities to rise above their (depreciated) book values.
- As is typical in banking, this bank has developed extensive market relationships with deposit customers.
- The bank's liabilities, predominantly deposits, are too short term to require price adjustment for interest rates.

The value adjustment for loans and securities obviously would be positive instead of negative if interest rates had been rising. Inflation, indeed, typically results in positive adjustments for facilities and often for equipment. The assumption that the liabilities need no adjustment is not totally realistic but is sufficiently close to be a reasonable simplification. Finally, to anticipate some possible questions, most types of bank loans have little or no customer relationship value; their role is mainly to attract and service depositors. Important exceptions are credit card loans and, more recently, home equity lines of credit. Because their significance varies widely among banks, simply ignore them for this illustration.

XYZ BANK
STATEMENT OF CONDITION
[Acquisition Date]
(millions of dollars)

Assets	Book Value	Adjustment	Market Value
Cash	$ 200	$ 0	$ 200
Loans and Securities	2,000	(100)	1,900
Facilities, etc.	30	20	50
Depositor Relationships	0	125	125
Liabilities			
Deposits, etc.	$2,100	0	$2,100
Capital (Net Worth)	$130	$45	$175

The depositor relationships represent about six percent of the deposit balances, which is rather typical. So, too, is the ratio of book net worth to deposits (at a bit above six percent). Thus, were it not for the market adjustments for the financial instruments (loans and securities) and facilities, this marking to market would result in nearly doubling the net worth.

Shifting from book to market values obviously can convey very different impressions of the financial condition of a corporation. To a more limited extent, of course, this point has long been familiar to industrial enterprises, for which depreciated book values may depart substantially from market values. Situations involving relationship assets tend to be even more extreme, as those assets normally remain entirely invisible absent an acquisition by purchase.

In the event of an acquisition, the above purchase accounting adjustments would actually be correct only if the acquirer paid a price equal to the market value of the capital, or $175 million. In that case, different but equivalent ways to look at the purchase price are:

- Book capital of $130 million plus a book premium of $45 million.
- True tangible capital or net worth of $50 million—book capital ($90 million) minus the write-down in loans and securities ($100 million) and plus the write-up in fixed assets ($20 million)—plus a true premium of $125 million representing intangible assets.

- True capital or net worth of $175 million, with no premium.

All of these different measures are in common use in describing purchase situations. Care is therefore necessary in defining terms.

Next, assume instead a purchase price of $185 million, or $10 million higher than the market value of the net worth, with no identifiable asset explaining the discrepancy. In this case the accountants would insert another asset, goodwill, as a purchase accounting adjustment to balance the balance sheet. This amount might be nothing more than a plug item, perhaps because the acquirer paid too high a price. Instead, it could represent a positive contribution such as value that customers associate with the name and reputation of the acquired institution. Which of these interpretations is correct is of little concern to the accountants.

Suppose, on the other hand, the actual price was $165 million, or $10 million below the true market value of the acquired net worth. This situation represents a bargain purchase. As accounting makes no provision for negative goodwill, conventional accounting practice is to apply a proportional reduction in the values allocated to the identified intangible assets so as to eliminate the discrepancy. The accountants would therefore assign $115 million instead of the true $125 million value to the depositor relationships (the only intangible in this illustration).

When only for accounting purposes, the allocations among different assets are often imprecise, with independent valuation studies being rare. The overriding concern of auditors, who presumably police these allocations, is to avoid overstatements of total assets. As the total purchase price in an acquisition objectively establishes any change in the assets and capital of the purchaser, auditors tend to have little concern with the allocation of that total.

Market Value Accounting and Net Asset Values

Purchase accounting is essentially market value accounting except that it applies only to one-time balance sheet adjustments. Full market value accounting measures corporate financial performance—its periodic contributions to shareholder values—as dividends plus changes in net asset values from one time point to the next. Unlike in conventional accounting, changes in those values can occur in the absence of transaction events. Unrealized capital gains and losses are common examples.

Notwithstanding occasional applications of purchase accounting, this net asset, market value concept is the least familiar of the different ways of viewing enterprise values. It treats the enterprise as a conglomeration of assets and liabilities that it hypothetically could buy or sell as separate pieces, either as if assembled into a going concern by a start-up enterprise or as if in liquidation. It represents the market value of an enterprise by focusing on the market values of the underlying components, which constitute its sources of value. Keep in mind that the ultimate determinants of market values of assets are the discounted values of the net cash flows they are expected to generate. Indeed, purchase price allocations for most intangible assets rely on DCF values. Effectively, then, market value accounting represents using DCF values of the underlying capital components to determine the DCF value of a corporation.

The significance to decision making of net asset values that they require identifying the individual value components, including otherwise oft-neglected intangibles. Viewing the value of a going concern as an assemblage of various value building blocks imparts more precision to decisions pertaining to its components. Anything less suggests inability to manage the business properly.

General adoption of market value accounting would encounter difficulties that need no further comment for present purposes. Here, market value concepts are of special interest for two rather different reasons:

- Because most relationship and other intangible assets lack any historical cost basis, market valuation is usually the only feasible means of recognizing their values, whether for external reporting or internal decision making.
- Market value principles are the only reliable basis for business investment decisions and strategies, for which their adoption need not encounter many of the impediments confronting their adoption for external financial reporting.

Market value concepts and measures provide a much more substantial foundation for corporate decision making than conventional accounting's historical-cost measures. They essentially adhere to capital budgeting principles, and they need not distinguish between tangible and intangible assets, yet recognition of the importance of market value principles could confront a catch-22 situation. Corporate chief executives may resist them absent endorsement by public financial accounting standards. Development of such standards, on the other hand, would require experience with applying those principles that that can only come from extensive experience with internal applications.

From a normative standpoint, impediments to revising public accounting standards should not impede development of superior measures for internal decision making. Furthermore, they need not deter corporations from responsible, and potentially advantageous, supplementary disclosures of value information and what it implies about enterprise value and performance. At the risk of some repetition, here are a few points to consider:

- Because conventional public financial reports give rise to serious misperceptions of corporate equity values, performance, and risks, management decisions often become hostage to misleading information and misinterpretations.
- Enterprises investing most heavily in developing market relationships are likely to be the most severely penalized by the financial markets because of accounting overstatement of their expenses and corresponding understatement of their earnings.
- Managers and directors of relationship enterprises have a fiduciary responsibility to their shareholders to promote corporate equity values by conveying their value stories to the financial community, the investing public, and public policy makers. No one else will take this initiative in investor communications on their behalf.
- Corporate communications must recognize in particular the significance of intangible as well as tangible forms of investment in explaining corporate direction and strategies to investors, many of whom are unfamiliar with these concepts.
- The value concepts underlying relationship investment and capital are unlikely to have credibility in the investment community until corporations themselves manifestly adopt them as the primary basis for decision making and planning. The causes and effects of misperceptions of value thus form a closed circle.

A focus on individual value elements and their value characteristics is essential at all levels of management to develop techniques and data for analyzing and managing their contributions to enterprise values.

CHAPTER 9

Foundations for Value-Based Strategies and Decisions

LINKING DECISIONS TO ENTERPRISE VALUES

To repeat a basic theme, a shareholder value objective requires making each decision on the basis of its contribution to that value. If the entire outcome of a decision is immediate, so, too, is its value impact. If outcomes stretch out into the future, investment criteria employing discounted cash flow (DCF) analysis are the only possible way to identify optimal decisions. Because economic relationships extend into the future virtually by definition—that is, after all, their purpose—their significance and pervasiveness require formulating most if not all management decisions as investment decisions. That means replacing mere profit criteria with value criteria. The effect is not to deny the significance of profit motives. Rather, it is to make them more robust by endowing them with an additional dimension—time.

How, then, should corporate managers apply investment criteria to decisions on such matters as pricing services and products, offering new products and services while discontinuing others, marketing strategies, personnel policies, and even government relations? In other words, what sort of decision framework is appropriate for a relationship marketplace? Earlier chapters hinted at some answers to these questions, which now require a closer look.

Application of value principles means focusing on specific sources of value, their individual contributions to total enterprise value, and how alternative decisions and strategies affect those contributions. Decisions affecting economic relationships must therefore focus on relationship values. With the development of the necessary data for identifying and allocating cash flows and for measuring and projecting relationship lives, techniques are available to value market relationships. Decision making nevertheless requires focusing on the incremental, or marginal, value contributions associated with different decisions—how much each alternative is likely to add to (or perhaps subtract from) shareholder value.

Decisions, by definition, represent choices among competing alternatives, often including the alternative of doing nothing. Thus, for each decision, which particular alternative is most likely to enhance the value of the enterprise? More specifically, does one particular alternative represent additional value relative to its next-best substitute?

Selecting among alternatives defined in terms of values and value increments is exactly what traditional capital budgeting principles are all about. Capital budgeting is a framework for making investment decisions. Indeed, it is the only appropriate framework for investment decisions. Its principles have long been familiar and in widespread use in determining outlays on plant and equipment. Relationship investment decisions mean applying exactly the same value-based decision concepts to intangible capital, such as to customer (or supplier) relationships and databases, as are applied to machinery and equipment.

Tangible and intangible forms of investment are perfectly analogous. The principles governing them are identical. Much as if the investments were in specialized machinery, relationship investment must be consistent with the overall direction and composition of the corporate enterprise. How does it fit in and contribute to the total output flow and market positioning? Similarly, economic relationships probably require some amount of regular maintenance if they are to remain productive. They may even become more productive with overhaul, upgrades, and enhancements.

As it provides much of the decision framework for a relationship environment, a brief review of capital budgeting is appropriate, and perhaps necessary. The purpose here is to convey some understanding of the topic, not to provide a textbook treatment. Even though the basic concept and the techniques may seem familiar, some of the finer points are easy to forget. They surely are not, in any event, familiar within a relationship investment context.

Basic Principles of Capital Investment

Investment principles are essentially identical whether they involve fixed assets such as plant and equipment, intangibles such as market relationships, or intangibles in the forms of intellectual property and proprietary data. To invest is to divert economic resources to future use with an expectation of receiving some form of future benefit. *Economic resources* simply means that those resources are not in unlimited supply, and thus their use entails some cost—selecting one alternative means foregoing some other desirable, if inferior, alternative. Whatever its nature, corporate investment ultimately means deferring dividend payments to shareholders. Shareholders therefore have less to spend or invest elsewhere than otherwise.

A business enterprise may commit resources to investment by means of direct cash outlays, as with expenditures on equipment. Alternatively, the investment process may be implicit rather than explicit, as with the commitment of management and employee time to marketing, planning, and training. An often-cited example of the latter is Andersen Consulting, which reportedly spends some 10 percent of its annual revenues on training. Certainly, management resources and time are significant components of investment in many types of relationships.

The benefits of business investment typically, but not always, take the form of higher future net cash flows representing additional income or reduced expenses. Among the possible exceptions are measures that reduce the risks associated with the cash flows. Promoting shareholder value goals should certainly include seizing opportunities to invest in risk reduction, as by reducing internal risks and improving investor communications. Lower risk associated with some given set of expected cash flows increases their value.

Value-based, or investment, principles of business decision making require identifying the specific revenues, or cash income flows, and the cash outlays resulting from each decision alternative. This requirement is in direct contrast to conventional accounting classifications of expenses, or costs. The conventional classifications are according to the inputs—what the enterprise buys, including labor, materials, machines, advertising, and so on—instead of according to outputs. In other words, conventional cost allocation principles are the opposite of what informed decision making requires.

Company income statements, for example, typically break out total personnel compensation expense, and perhaps differentiate wages and salaries from fringe benefits. For financial reporting purposes they need not provide any information on the personnel costs allocable to different products, services, markets, or customers. Also, some of the expenses, such as certain types of executive compensation, may represent future liabilities rather than current outlays. Here, again, accounting convention is driven by observable transactions and verifiability rather than by management decision needs.

By focusing on values of cash inflows and outlays, moreover, investment decision making need not distinguish between current expenses and capital outlays. Cash receipts and outlays occur at specific, identifiable points in time, with values at any prior point in time determined by discounting. Income and expenses as reported in company income statements are measurable only with reference to periods of time such as months, quarters, or years.

Capital budgeting involves formulating investment decisions on the basis of net present values (NPVs) of cash flows. If the expected net cash flows—inflows minus outlays—from an investment alternative are positive, the net present value is similarly positive. The investment therefore represents a net addition to enterprise value.

The mere fact that it adds enterprise value does not alone mean that a particular alternative is the most appropriate one, however. Alternatives may be inconsistent with one another or with prior investment. Selection of any one alternative typically precludes selection of many others. Among them, many may be attractive, just not as attractive, in terms of contribution to enterprise value, as the one selected. In other words, whenever acceptance of an investment alternative means rejecting others, the objective is to identify and select the best one so as to obtain the largest possible addition to enterprise value.

Capital budgeting therefore means sorting investment opportunities into separate groups so that within each group, selecting any one opportunity automatically precludes selecting any other. More specifically, it focuses on the additional (incremental or marginal) net cash flows and net value obtainable by selecting each opportunity over each competing opportunity. In each comparison the incremental NPV represented by one alternative will be positive and that represented by any other will be correspondingly negative. The objective, in other words, is to identify the alternative representing some positive additional value increment beyond that obtainable from any competing alternative.

Selecting among Alternative Investments

The discounting (DCF) process by which to calculate an NPV can employ any of several procedures. Each is simply a variant of the others, differing only in the order of the same basic calculations made using the same underlying data. In particular, the calculation can be by separately summing the present values of the different components of inflow and outlay. Instead, it can be by calculating a present value of the net cash flows—the differences between the inflows and outlays—in each future period. Whatever the order, the results of the alternative procedures should be identical.

Textbook treatments of capital budgeting typically devote considerable attention to demonstrating the superiority of applying NPV criteria using DCF analysis for evaluating and selecting among investment opportunities. Summarizing some earlier points:

- DCF analysis directly recognizes the time value of money, unlike simple profit comparisons.
- DCF analysis adjusts for the risks associated with the cash flows, which is also beyond the capability of simple profit comparisons.
- Unlike all alternative methods of analysis, NPV comparisons capture the value effects both of investing different amounts and of investing for different periods of time.

The most common substitute for present value analysis is internal rate of return (IRR) analysis, which is superficially similar to the long-run profits of economics. Indeed, although it is inferior, IRR may be in more widespread use than NPV analysis. One reason for its popularity is that many businesses ration their available capital by assigning hurdle rates to their different business units. A *hurdle rate* is the minimum rate of return obtainable from a proposed investment project that management considers acceptable. Evaluating an investment project thus involves determining whether the IRR is above or below some hurdle rate.

An investment IRR is that discount factor at which the NPV—the present value of future net cash flows (inflows minus outflows)—is zero. If an IRR is above some required rate of return (a cost of capital or hurdle rate), that investment is deemed acceptable. The excess return necessarily indicates a positive NPV, even if not calculated directly, indicating in turn some net contribution to enterprise value.

Moreover, when comparing different investments with identical outlays and investment horizons, the alternative with the highest IRR
would provide the largest value contribution.

IRR analysis is mainly useful for deciding whether to select or reject
a stand-alone investment opportunity. It is common in acquisition
analysis, for example. Decisions in those situations may simply be
whether or not to proceed with a specified opportunity. Because it
does not capture the scales and time dimensions of different investments, however, IRR analysis is normally inappropriate for selecting
among competing investment alternatives. This shortcoming can be
significant in analyzing relationship investments because of their
often complex patterns of cash outlays and inflows.

To illustrate this problem, consider a simple example consisting of
three alternative investments from which an enterprise can select
only one. Each case involves an initial cash outlay at Year 0 and a cash
inflow at the end of each year.

Year	A	B	C
0	$(100)	$(200)	$(200)
1	120	240	120
2	0	0	144

The IRR in all three cases is 20 percent per year. In other words,
the NPV at Year 0 of each set of cash flows, including the initial outlays, is zero if discounted at 20 percent per year. If the required rate
of return, or cost of capital, for this enterprise were, say, 15 percent,
all three alternatives would represent a net addition to enterprise
value. This result would be the end of the matter absent having to
choose one to the exclusion of either or both of the others. Moreover,
by itself, an IRR analysis indicates that all three investment opportunities are equally acceptable.

Yet, because the IRR is identical for all three, it fails to indicate that
the amount of added enterprise value is much larger for investment B
than for A. Discounting at the cost of capital, at 15 percent, the net
value added by B is $8.70, while that added by A is only half that, at
$4.35. Viewed another way, the additional $100 investment represented by B represents an additional NPV contribution of $4.35. Put
yet another way, B is essentially twice A. IRR analysis also fails to re-
veal that option C contributes much more additional (marginal) value
than either A or B, at $13.23.

True capital budgeting analysis normally estimates net cash flows after taxes, but without deducting depreciation or amortization expenses, which do not represent cash flows. Because capital outlays are reflected in the cash flows, deduction of depreciation and amortization would be a form of double counting. Meanwhile, capital investments receive recognition only when represented as cash outlays.

In practice, the cash flows for NPV analysis commonly exclude the costs of long-term financing of investments, such as interest on long-term debt. This exclusion is because the discount factors commonly used to translate future cash flows into present values reflect those long-term (permanent) financing costs. Those discount factors, in other words, are usually weighted-average costs of capital. That means they are averages of the required returns on equity and the interest costs of long-term debt, each weighted by its relative contribution to long-term financing. On the other hand, the net cash flows are normally, after deduction of interest on short-term debt, treated as a current expense. To the extent that short-term debt maturities are somewhat less than the lives of relationship assets, that debt presumably is not normally a means of their financing.

A weighted-average cost of capital is simply a type of average of the net (after-tax) cost of long-term debt and the rate of return that shareholders currently require—the cost of equity capital. Thus, suppose:

- The current interest rate on new long-term debt financing is 9 percent before tax, but because it is tax deductible, its net cost is 6 percent.
- Shareholders, whose risks are somewhat higher than those of long-term creditors, require a return on any new equity (stock) financing of 15 percent.
- The total long-term financing of the corporation consists of one-third debt and two-thirds equity.

The weighted-average cost of capital is therefore:

$$(2/3)\ 15\% + (1/3)\ 6\% = 10\% + 2\% = 12\%.$$

This particular construction nevertheless represents common practice rather than conceptual necessity. A variant would be to deduct the costs of long-term debt for financing investment projects directly from the cash flows they generate. The appropriate discount factors for calculating present values would then be costs of equity appropriate to the investment risks. In theory, at least, the resulting NPVs from this procedure and those using weighted-average costs of capital (including long-term debt) must be identical. The idea of allocating long-term interest costs among different types of capital is, to say the least, as unfamiliar as it is awkward. The general idea is nevertheless the same as a previous one—if done properly, treating a cost of capital as a direct expense should always lead to the same conclusion as discounting to present values.

Classifying Investment Alternatives

Investment opportunities tend to fall into three different categories:

- *Independent investments.* The decision to proceed with one investment opportunity is unrelated to decisions to proceed with any others. For example, the decision to open a retail outlet in Town A may be entirely independent of whether to open one in Town B.

Of course, unless the amount of investment is very small relative to the size of the enterprise, independence is a matter of degree. Without an unlimited supply of capital, absolute independence cannot exist. Particularly in the short run, an enterprise quickly encounters a rising supply curve for capital—costs of capital increase the more rapidly it seeks to expand. Ultimately, then, any one investment can affect the cost of capital applicable to any other.

- *Substitute investments.* Acceptance of one alternative precludes acceptance of others. For example, selection of one retail site probably precludes the selection of another in the immediate vicinity.

Earlier examples demonstrating the superiority of NPV analysis concerned comparisons among substitute opportunities. Substitutes may represent different means of production or distribution, different products or services, or even different time periods. Thus, should a new service or product be introduced now, before it is fully market tested, or should its introduction be deferred? What is the effect of investing in a new product or service that effectively displaces an existing offering? In that case, part of the investment outlay is the value lost due to the displacement. Even if a loss due to displacement is insufficient to preclude an investment, it may affect its timing.

- *Complementary investments.* Investments are complementary if one somehow adds to the net cash flows that are expected to be obtained from others. For example, opening retail outlets in both Towns A and B may add more value than the sum of the two individually, perhaps because the same advertising media cover both communities.

Complementary investment decisions are common in developing marketing programs.

Comparing Alternative Investments

The first step in capital budgeting is to identify the different investment opportunities according to their projected cash flows and appropriate discount factors (costs of capital). To compare them, next organize those opportunities into groups of substitutes. There are at least two alternatives in all cases. Even for an independent investment opportunity, there is always the alternative of rejecting the opportunity altogether and doing nothing. Acquisition opportunities are common examples.

Complementary investments group themselves into competing combinations. Suppose, for example, that a restaurant chain is considering entry into a new community. It might have three alternatives. One is to open just a single full-service restaurant. A second might be to open a take-out facility on the opposite side of the community that would be in addition to the full-service restaurant. A third might be a second full-service restaurant in addition to, although perhaps smaller than, the first one instead of the take-out facility.

Notice the lack of symmetry in this example. The initial restaurant may very well be viable without either the take-out facility or the second, perhaps smaller, restaurant, but its establishment may be essential for either of the other two to be viable. Of course, the complementarities might be so important that the one restaurant is simply not viable without either a second one or the take-out facility. Apart from a possible need to achieve a minimum volume to support local advertising, perhaps some prospective diners will patronize this chain more frequently if they have access to it at more than one location. In that case, the alternatives reduce to two—two full-service restaurants, or one full-service restaurant plus a take-out facility.

Taking this example a step further, suppose that the three alternatives with which it began are independent of any others the company is considering. Suppose, too, that the investment in each case generates a constant stream of net cash flows over 25 years, at the end of which it loses all value. (Maybe the facilities will require total refurbishment or relocation by that time.) To simplify further, assume that all cash flows are either immediate or at the end of each year, and that the cost of capital is 12 percent.

Option A: A single restaurant. The initial cash outlay to obtain a site and to construct, equip, and staff it is $1 million. The projected future *net* cash inflows after all direct expenses, maintenance, overhead allocation, and taxes are $200,000 per year for each of the ensuing 25 years. At a discount factor of 12 percent, the present value of the cash inflows is $1,568,600. Because the present value exceeds the outlay—the net present value is $1,568,600–$1,000,000 = $568,600—this investment should represent a net contribution of that amount to the net asset value of the enterprise. The IRR on this investment, at $200,000 on a $1,000,000 investment, is 20 percent, or well above the 12 percent cost of capital.

Option B: A full-service restaurant plus a remote take-out facility. In addition to A, this option requires a further initial outlay of $400,000. The projected future net cash inflows are $75,000 per year, a portion of which might result from additional patronage at the main restaurant by customers seeking two points of access to this chain's offerings. At a discount factor of 12 percent, the present value of the additional cash inflows generated by the take-out facility is $588,225. This investment opportunity thus represents a net value contribution to the enterprise of $588,225–$400,000 = $188,225. The IRR in this case, at $75,000 per year on an investment of $400,000, is 18.75 percent. This alternative certainly would warrant acceptance in the absence of any more attractive competing alternative.

Option C: Two full-service restaurants. In addition to A, this alternative requires an initial outlay of $800,000 with its projected future annual cash inflows at $140,000. Some cost economies should be obtainable from operating two restaurants in the same community, and there should be the same sort of marketing and service complementarities as provided by the take-out facility. The present value of the cash inflows at 12 percent is $1,098,020, and thus this option has a net present value to contribute to the enterprise of $1,098,020–$800,000 = $298,000. Here, the IRR is $140,000 per year on an investment of $800,000, or 17.5 percent.

This alternative also is highly attractive and should be acceptable absent competition with a more attractive substitute.

The expansion program certainly should include either the take-out facility or the second restaurant, but B and C are substitutes. Both represent value contributions additional to what is obtainable from the single restaurant (A). Yet, which is the more attractive? IRR analysis favors B, the take-out facility, at 18.75 percent, instead of 17.5 percent for C, the second full-service restaurant. This selection is not the better one, however. The second full-service restaurant adds net value of $298,020, which is $109,795 more than the additional value contributed by the take-out facility. Compared to the second best alternative, it has a positive additional, or incremental, NPV contribution of another $109,795.

Only the incremental, or marginal, NPV points to the best alternative in the example. Notice how the IRRs fail to capture the effects of differences in investment scale. To illustrate, suppose that in addition to options A and B above the company can also select an alternative, option D, which involves an initial outlay of $400,000 with the expectation of generating future net cash inflows of $65,000 per year for 25 years. Should this option be selected as well? The present value of the future inflows is $509,795, indicating an NPV contribution of $109,795. The IRR is 16.25 percent, which, while not as attractive as the others, is nevertheless still well above the required rate of return represented by the discount factor. This new alternative actually represents nothing other than the incremental cash outlay and inflows represented by moving from the second (B) to the third (C) of the original options. C is simply the sum of B and D:

$$C = B + D.$$

Breaking alternatives down into these sorts of increments may extract the right answers using IRR analysis. In other words, simply array the substitute alternatives in ascending order of outlays, calculate the incremental outlays and inflows, and determine the IRR indicated for each increment. This method is more awkward than NPV analysis, however, and special care may be necessary to define each increment in terms of each alternative relative to its next best substitute.

As a practical matter, the number of substitute options that some types of decisions must consider within any set of alternatives may be virtually infinite. Discrete options, as in the above illustration, are most likely for plant and equipment outlays. Even there, however, alternatives representing small differences in investment amounts—a little bit more, or a little bit less—are likely.

Net Value Contributions and the Scale of Investment

Continua of alternatives are typical for market relationship investments. As an illustration in the context of relationship investment, imagine a magazine publisher considering a direct mail campaign by which to increase its subscriber base. It has access to a variety of mailing lists with sufficient information to enable predicting responses to this solicitation. Logically, the publisher would give top priority to mailings to those prospects most likely to respond. It would then expand its mailing list step by step to include prospective subscribers with lower expected response rates.

A diagram of this investment problem might appear as follows:

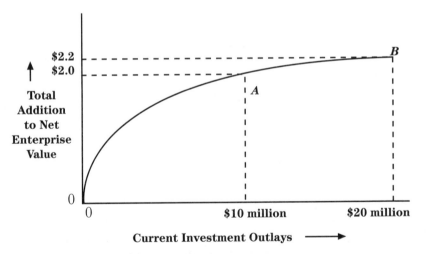

Declining Rate of New Value Contributions from Increasing Investment Outlays.

The amount of outlay on the mail campaign increases in moving from left to right in the diagram. The outlays are current, so no discounting is necessary. They are by definition present values. The net present values—the present values of future cash inflows (subscription receipts) minus the corresponding level of current investment outlay—increase in moving upward in the diagram. For example, point A on the diagram might represent a present value of future subscription revenues of $12 million obtainable by investing $10 million in current mail solicitations, for an NPV of $2 million. Similarly, point B might represent subscription revenues of $22.2 million with current solicitation outlays of $20 million, for a total net present value of $2.2 million. Up to B, each additional amount of outlay produces some additional net present value—the increases in the present values of the future cash flows (subscription revenues) exceed the additional outlays necessary to obtain them. Stated differently, but meaning exactly the same thing:

- Up to B, the incremental, or marginal, present values of the future cash flows exceed the incremental, or marginal, (present values of the) outlays.
- Up to B, the incremental, or marginal, NPVs obtainable by additional investment are positive.

The upward (positive) slope of the line in the diagram means that more investment outlay results in more NPV from new subscribers. Its curvature indicates that the additions to NPV decline with more investment. Where the curve flattens out, at B, additional outlays will result in no additional NPV. Indeed, the curve would normally turn downward somewhere beyond B, meaning that additional outlays would exceed the present values that they would generate.

- The basic rule is to extend the outlays to the point where the additional (marginal) present values of future cash inflows (receipts) exactly equal the additional (marginal) present values of the outlays.
- A restatement of the basic rule, leading to an identical result, is to extend the outlays to the point where the additional (marginal) net present value of all cash inflows and outlays declines to zero, and no further.

The most effective way to approach investment decisions involving continua of mutually exclusive alternatives, such as here, is normally in terms of net value gained from another dollar of outlay—the net present value approach suggested in Chapter 4, and used in an example in Chapter 8.

A refinement in the example is to recognize what magazine publishers understand all too well: Subscribers vary widely in the periods over which they maintain their subscriptions. The longer the life of a subscription, the greater its value. To some extent, these variations may be predictable. The projections of future subscription revenues should therefore reflect both probabilities of response and the expected lives of subscriptions. The probability of response pertains to the amount of outlay required to obtain a new subscription, while the life of the subscription determines its value after it is obtained. The marginal NPV schedule would decline more rapidly as there would now be two sources of diminishing returns from additional outlays.

The net present value principle makes matters easier in considering more complicated but also more realistic relationship investment alternatives, which typically have two characteristics:

- Cash outlays to develop market relationships often are not limited to the inception of those relationships; rather, they continue well into the lives of those relationships.
- Some of the future investment in maintaining and enriching customer relationships takes the form of lower revenues, or cash inflows, rather than cash outlays.

The first situation occurs when an initial outlay will require yet further outlays, even if only to recover the initial outlay with a return on investment. A common example is when a customer or client base must attain a critical mass to be sustainable, as for retail establishments. The second situation can arise in a number of ways. A common example is promotional pricing, such as initial discounts offered by long-distance telephone services. Another common example is the effect on revenues of the high rates of credit losses common among new credit card accounts. Yet another type of situation is when developing a customer base provides cost efficiencies as well as more revenue.

Again, the most reliable way to analyze these situations is to array the alternatives in diminishing order of additional (marginal) NPVs according to the commitments of capital they represent, taking care to include:

- The present values of future as well as the current cash outlays that the investment will require to be complete.
- The present value of the sacrifices in future cash inflows necessary for the investment to be complete.

Constraints on Total Investment Opportunities

As a practical matter, an enterprise simply may not have the capital resources to invest in all of the opportunities that it sees as attractive from their capital budgeting implications. How, then, should it ration what capital as it can obtain in a way that achieves the most enterprise value? The question itself assumes that choices are necessary among various competing alternatives. The above basic rule remains intact: Each increment of investment should yield the highest additional (marginal) NPV.

The following diagrammatic illustration best conveys the basic idea. To simplify it, suppose that the total available investment funding is some fixed amount. Again, the diagram is in terms of marginal net present values as they result from various levels of capital commitment expressed as present values. Each increment in outlay results in a corresponding net value contribution (extending from positive to negative) to the enterprise. As before, the normal rule is to increase investment outlays as long as the marginal NPVs are positive. The problem posed here arises from assuming the amount of available funding to be insufficient to pursue all investment opportunities all the way to the zero net present value point.

The illustration assumes two alternative programs (perhaps entry into two different new markets), A and B, each of which represents a continuum of investment alternatives. In the diagram, if the total amount of investment resources available is no more than the amount shown as point a, all investment should be in alternative A. Further investment beyond point a should be in both A and B, with more in A than in B up to point b, and more in B than in A up to point c, which is approached simultaneously. Investment in A should cease at c. Even with unlimited capital, no additional investment whatever should occur beyond d. Over the range between points a and c, the optimal investment allocation rule is that the marginal NPVs of the two programs A and B should always be equal. Otherwise, more NPV is obtainable by allocating some capital from that with the lower marginal NPV to the other alternative. To complete the example, the diagram shows the optimal allocation of investment between A and B when the total available investment resources amount to $m + n$.

A variant of this approach is to combine the schedules for the two alternatives into a single, composite schedule. In that case, keeping track of how to allocate each increment of investment between the two alternatives is both necessary and more difficult.

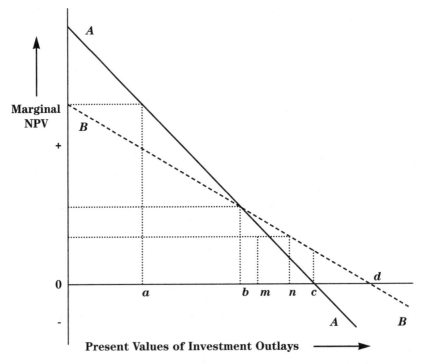

**Schedules of Marginal Net Present Value Contributions
from Alternative Investments.**

One common method of rationing capital internally is to allocate the available capital among different divisions and activities. Another is to assign hurdle rates to those different business units. Both methods can give rise to problems. Internal capital allocations may not be entirely consistent with opportunities, while hurdle rates may be inconsistent with the relative risks. Indeed, companies often seem to set hurdle rates artificially high, perhaps to offset excess optimism or empire building among lower level managers. Whatever the approach, careful monitoring is required to assure its current relevance.

Perhaps it goes without saying that when capital funding is limited in amount, intangible forms of investment are likely to compete with investment in producer goods. An enterprise might, for example, need to choose between more research and development investment, more investment in equipment, or investment in developing more customer relationships.

Information Requirements for Relationship Investment

Traditional capital budgeting analysis assumes that engineering analysis, marketing studies, and so on have already identified the expected cash flows and risks associated with each investment alternative. A relationship environment similarly requires compiling a substantial amount of information, hence the marriage of relationship investment and management with modern information technologies. The design and structure of management's decision framework determine the necessary information inputs.

The information that is actually obtainable may be too uncertain to warrant such precise techniques of analysis as comparisons of present values. If the information is imperfect, perhaps to the point of being speculative, why not just use much cruder and simpler techniques? Indeed, why use any type of formal analysis rather than rely on management judgment? Perhaps this sort of informed judgment is one of the important functions of management, implying that experienced executives may be substitutes for good analysis.

No matter how crude the information or how experienced the management, better analytical techniques tend to provide better answers. First, they provide a guide to more meaningful information. Moreover, it is easy to demonstrate that cruder analytical techniques often provide incorrect answers even with the best possible information, and susceptibility to analytical error presumably escalates as the quality of information deteriorates.

The Short Run and the Long Run

Forms of response to an emerging opportunity follow a pattern reminiscent of the economists' distinction between a short run and a long run. Some types of responses lend themselves to immediate implementation; others require extensive planning and preparation. Short-term responses usually are not stand-alone alternatives, however. The initial response to an emerging opportunity may affect both what responses are available for the longer term and their outcomes. For example, offering a new service may require future expansion into related service lines if it is to be viable. Investment alternatives therefore often consist of sequences of responses stretching out over future time.

Does maximizing shareholder value require focusing on short-run results, as Peter Drucker has suggested?[1] Drucker goes on to argue that "[l]ong-term results cannot be gained by piling short-term results on short-term results." The problem with this view is failure to recognize that shareholder values necessarily derive from expected long-term results, however much the stock markets may gyrate in the short run. To be sure, some corporate chief executives seem to behave as if only the near term matters, but the cost of doing so is to subvert shareholder values. Perhaps Drucker is correct in a sense he apparently did not intend. Because piling short term on short term does not make for a viable long term, focusing only on short-term results cannot promote shareholder values. Recall the earlier definition of the long run pertinent to management strategies and decisions. It is the future period that captures the consequences of all present decisions.

Future Dimensions among Alternatives

Distinguishing between short- and long-run responses to opportunities raises another issue. As already observed, investing in a program today may be but a first step in a sequence of investments over future time. The simplest case is when it is clear that once commenced, the process must follow a fixed sequence, with B occurring at some time later than A, and C sometime after B:

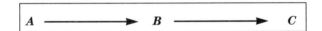

Time Sequence of Investment Outlays.

This situation simply requires keeping track of the timing of the cash flows.

Almost as simple is when either B *or* C would follow A, knowing in advance the cash flows associated with each. This case merely requires selecting which of two options, $A+B$ or $A+C$ has the higher net present value.

Matters become more complex when the cash flows associated with B and C will not be known until some later date. Suppose, for exam-

[1]Peter Drucker, *Post-Capitalist Society* (New York: HarperBusiness, 1993), p. 73, as cited by John Micklethwait and Adrian Wooldridge in *The Witch Doctors: Making Sense of the Management Gurus* (New York: Times Business, 1996), p. 181.

ple, that option B is to do nothing more following A, while C is to undertake further investment at a later date. A might be to open the full-service restaurant in the previous example, deferring any decision on whether to open a take-out facility as well to later, when information on the actual results of A begin to emerge. Observe that:

- The risk associated with A is less if it does not automatically entail a commitment to B.
- The risk associated with A also may be less with the possibility of later enhancement by B.

The second possibility arises if, for example, it becomes evident that the patronage of the full-service restaurant would be higher than otherwise because of the additional visibility and reputation of the chain resulting from B. This situation is often important in establishing banking facilities, for which convenience is an important factor in drawing customers. The evaluation of this opportunity can focus simply on A, but by discounting the cash flows at a lower rate commensurate with any reduction in risk resulting from having B as a future option. To evaluate it as if the option were $A+B$ would overstate the risks.

Matters would be a bit different if B is an option that might be imposed externally at a later date. Perhaps the restaurant chain recognizes that the amount of parking envisioned in A may prove to be insufficient, so A includes an option to purchase additional land to expand the parking facilities. The problem here is that the chain, in deciding whether or not to proceed with this opportunity, cannot be sure whether it is committing to A alone or to $A+B$ with B representing the exercise of the option and the necessary improvements. As an irrevocable decision on A is necessary today, one way to approach it is in terms of probabilities. To do this, first estimate the NPVs of the two options, NPV_A and NPV_{A+B}, with the latter being lower because it represents additional outlay. The NPV for the investment opportunity is then a weighted-average of these two NPVs, the weights being the respective probabilities of their being the appropriate options. Suppose the chain assesses the probability of the additional parking being necessary at 30 percent, immediately implying a 70 percent probability of it not being necessary. The composite NPV is then:

$$NPV = .7NPV_A + .3NPV_{A+B.}$$

Investment decisions obviously can become rather complex. Here, the intent is only to provide some of the flavor of where this topic could lead without attempting to pursue it further. If nothing else, this brief review touches on one important point: In many investment decisions a choice arises between more investment outlay, so as to have more flexibility among options in the future, and less investment, at the risk of fewer options later. The latter option means lower near-term outlays but higher costs of capital.

CHAPTER 10

Understanding Customer Relationships

A NEXUS OF RELATIONSHIPS

A business enterprise is essentially a nexus of a variety of different types of economic and noneconomic relationships. Managing a business is therefore in substantial part a process of coordinating relationships with customers, employees, outside suppliers, and investors. Corporate managers must align those relationships in a manner that promotes the corporate objectives, particularly the objective of maximizing shareholder values. Strategies to promote those objectives normally begin by focusing on customer relationships, addressing the issues of *what* and *for whom*. Upon identifying what the enterprise hopes to accomplish, managers can turn to the issues of *how* and *when*.

Before turning more directly to market and other economic relationships, however, briefly consider that an enterprise may also encompass various other types of relationships. In particular, social and even personal relationships, whose purpose is not economic, may have intended or unintended effects. To the extent they impact on an enterprise's efforts to achieve its strategic objectives, corporate managers must at least be aware of them, and perhaps to some degree direct or control them. Internal social and personal relationships may contribute value to the enterprise, perhaps by reinforcing a corporate culture that is important to its competitive success.

Such relationships also can undermine achieving corporate objectives. Internal social relationships in Japanese companies, emphasizing decision making by consensus, often seem to retard decision making. Old-boy networks in Japan and elsewhere perhaps also give rise to social structures that deter originality, creativity, and entrepreneurship. Looking toward the future, will Japan, and indeed the United States, be able to compete successfully with the spirit of entrepreneurship that seems common in much of the rest of Asia?

Having suggested a possible significance of noneconomic relationships to a business, this and the following chapter focus on external and internal economic relationships, and particularly on market relationships.

Responding to Market Opportunities

At least as measured by the amount of real capital they represent, customer relationships are much the most important category of economic relationships. They are also the primary focus of two of the three main strategic issues—*what* and *for whom*? Thus, as a logical starting point, this chapter probes more deeply into the value characteristics of customer relationships from a seller's perspective, considering the types of investment opportunities they represent. Chapter 11 continues this discussion by gradually moving backward from the marketplace where a business enterprise sells its products and services into the enterprise itself.

Decisions on relationship investment begin to develop with the recognition that a gap has developed between market opportunities, as they arise from actual and potential customers, and what the enterprise currently offers. The most immediate forms of potential response are likely to be to adjust prices and advertising. Some changes in product and service offerings may also be possible within a relatively short time. Near-term changes are more feasible if they employ familiar technologies and require no major alterations in production or distribution facilities or sources of supply.

Whatever the nature of the required decisions, begin by organizing them into separate sets so that the alternatives within each set are mutually exclusive. This means that the selection of any one set automatically precludes the selection of any other. Perhaps, as the previous chapter suggested, they lie along a continuum representing different levels of outlay. Indeed, these continua may extend into several or more dimensions, each representing a different type or pattern of outlay. Remember that:

- With correct specification and inclusion of all mutually exclusive alternatives within each set, the selection of one from any set is, by definition, independent of the choices in all other such sets.
- Separately identifiable combinations or programs should contain combinations of outlays only if their outcomes interact.
- Each option, however short term, should recognize any long-term effects such as precluding ultimately more attractive long-term opportunities.

The final point is a reminder that sequences of short-term responses are unlikely to promote long-term objectives. It also is a reminder of the *when* dimension of business strategies.

In the restaurant chain example of the previous chapter, the selection of the form of entry into one community was essentially independent of entry decisions elsewhere, perhaps because of the remoteness of the other opportunities. However, the company could not consider the alternative facility configurations within the particular market to be independent. The level of outlay for each facility affected the cash flows from the other facility. Evaluating investments in an additional one therefore could only be in conjunction with evaluating the investment in the first one. With this sort of interaction, the appropriate course required considering the investments in the different facilities in various combinations.

A decision to do nothing, implicit if not explicit, is normally one of the alternatives in each set. Indeed, it may be a more attractive alternative than very modest levels of investment. For example, a single mini-facility requiring little outlay may attract little notice, and thus too few customers ever to break even. The viable choices may therefore leap from nothing to a rather substantial outlay, with no intermediate options. In other cases, doing nothing might itself be unrealistic. It could mean ceasing all investment in customer replacement. In both situations, the more realistic alternatives are often easy to identify and may fall within in a narrow range, allowing a decision maker to focus only on that range.

Fortunately, decisions often become easier because they virtually must be incremental—only relatively modest changes in existing programs are feasible. A relationship marketplace normally requires on-going investment programs for customer replacement, as customer attrition is typically a continuous process. Relationship investment decisions therefore may be simply how much more to invest in those same programs in order to expand the relationship base, either by increasing market penetration or by market extension.

Even when the alternatives involve major shifts in enterprise strategies and direction, the changes may be gradual and tentative. The amount of total spending on soliciting customers may therefore not represent a relevant decision as such. Rather, the relevant question is more likely to be whether to invest a little bit more or a little bit less than the current investment rate. The current level of outlay and the results obtained thus normally have special significance as a base against which to measure other alternatives.

Of course, important exceptions to this incremental view do arise. A major acquisition may substantially transform an enterprise. De novo entries into new geographic or product markets also may require substantial commitments. In retailing, for example, the ability to compete in one local market may depend on the retailer's presence in surrounding markets. One therefore notices that supermarket and drugstore chains tend to be geographically concentrated. Apart from logistical considerations (delivery, servicing, and the like), toehold entries into remote new markets may lack sufficient cost economies in local advertising and promotion. A competitor with extensive market coverage will get far more return from its advertising budget than a small newcomer. More generally, the density of a retailer's market presence usually determines its level of recognition by prospective customers.

It is these sorts of major commitments, in particular, that require looking at some alternatives as sequences of response. It may not be possible to seize an opportunity for entry into a major new market all at once. Because of resource constraints, including on capital, perhaps entry into a new region must take place stepwise, one local market at a time. If undertaken too quickly, the entrant may come under financial strain and perhaps encounter management problems as well. If undertaken too slowly, it may fail to develop the critical mass necessary for effective marketing.

Relationship Pricing and Cost Allocation

Following identification of the relevant range of program alternatives, the next step is to identify their cash flow characteristics. To the extent those cash flows extend into the future, this requires calculating their present values. As already suggested, the cash flow patterns associated with relationship investment can be complex, with further investment in developing and expanding relationships extending through time well beyond their initiation. Following the procedures outlined in the previous chapter, one can then sort and discount present and future cash flows to obtain their net present values.

These procedures assume, of course, that projections of how various levels of investment will attract or enrich different relationships are already in place. They further assume extension of those projections to projections of the different cash flows associated with each investment alternative. Here, corporate managers must appreciate the enormous importance of developing market information that focuses on customer relationships and relationship values. Market research and information technologies assume added importance in transforming from an industrial to a relationship environment.

Projections of revenues and outlays require analyzing pricing alternatives and costs. Whatever the manner of expressing prices, they represent the source of revenue available to sellers for recovering cost and investment outlays. Because of the need for recovery of investment outlays, the costs of producing and delivering a product or service to a customer often have only partial relevance to its pricing. If prices are only in terms of those direct costs, how can a seller expect to recover its investments in developing customer relationships? The issues raised by relationship pricing are, in part, an extension of the earlier discussion of profits.

A classic example of how costs factor into pricing decisions is the pricing of prescription pharmaceutical products. For years, controversies have raged over whether prescription drug manufacturers gouge the public through excessive prices. Drugs costing perhaps pennies to manufacture may sell at enormous multiples of their direct costs. The explanation lies in the research and development necessary to produce new drugs—investment in intangible assets and capital. Hundreds of chemical compounds are likely to be under study in the laboratories, but very few typically prove worthwhile even for animal testing. Fewer yet qualify for human testing, where they must prove to be both effective and to have few, if any, dangerous side effects before they can be brought to market.

Consider the problem: How can one allocate the research and development outlays among those very few therapies that actually make it all the way from the test tube to the marketplace? Unsuccessful experiments and tests absorbed most of those outlays. The result is that prescription drug manufacturers can only recover their investment outlays by setting prices well above their direct costs. By how much should prices exceed the direct costs? The answer is a complicated one involving the characteristics of the demands for different drugs. Generally, the pricing scheme that works best for both the companies and customers is to set prices relatively higher the less the relative reduction in sales revenue from higher prices.[1] Some may see the similarity here with the problem that airlines commonly face, namely, how to price tickets so as best to recover the fixed costs of aircraft and crews.

The pharmaceutical problem involves spreading unallocable costs among different product lines and even different classes of customers. At least as much of an issue with relationship investment is how best to spread recovery of fixed investment over time. Relationship pricing raises two additional and intriguing aspects:

- Generally, some customer relationships, especially those with longer lives, contribute more to investment recovery than others; indeed, those with relatively short lives often do not provide full recovery.
- Relationship pricing often has several dimensions; a seller must consider simultaneously the effects of different price combinations among these dimensions.

On the first point, suppose customer relationships are basically similar except for their different lives. Specifically, each requires the same amount of investment outlay to attract it, and each generates the same cash flows until it terminates. Assuming only normal investment returns (that is, no true profits), roughly half of an initial base of customer relationships will provide less than full investment recovery, while the others will provide more. Analyzing customer relationship lives thus often becomes an exercise in projecting averages for large pools of relationships. To the extent possible, of course, it also means trying to identify types of relationships with longer potential lives.

A previous example of the observation about multidimensional pricing was the multidimensional nature of credit cards. Cardholders tend to have different sensitivities to the different terms. Responding effectively to those sensitivities requires some degree of customization through market segmentation. Some cardholders, for example,

---

[1] In economists' terms, prices should be higher the lower the price-elasticities of demand.

may pay no annual fees, yet pay higher finance charges than fee-paying cardholders.

This analysis of pricing issues suggests a decision model well removed from old-fashioned cost-plus pricing, with essentially arbitrary allocations of fixed expenses, or overhead.[2] The cost-plus model goes back to the early days of industrialization, when even product lines were relatively simple and uniform. The general idea was to determine profitability by identifying the direct labor and materials costs per unit, then allocating overhead in direct proportion to those costs. Thus, common practice was to assign twice the overhead to a unit of output representing twice the direct cost of some other unit. This type of cost allocation can lead to bad decisions even within a relatively simple manufacturing environment. For example, meaningless allocations will arise if a higher-cost laborsaving machine is side by side with a lower-cost machine using more labor.

The deficiencies of the cost-plus approach have been rather obvious for many years, leading to the development of other cost allocation approaches. Activity-based costing divides production processes into many activities, then allocates overhead according to the numbers of activities used for different outputs. Target costing begins with a product design and price determined from marketing studies, works back through costs to produce the item, then revises the design or abandons it depending on the results. Time-based costing allocates plant and equipment according to the amount of production time different products require.

Notice that all of these allocation techniques essentially reflect an industrial setting. All, moreover, reflect the traditional preoccupation with profits within time periods rather than the value-based decision making that a relationship environment requires. They basically derive from financial reporting requirements rather than from internal decision needs. Indeed, as perhaps became clear from the discussion of capital budgeting in the previous chapter, a value-based model could effectively replace all of them for management decision making even within a manufacturing context.

Product and Service Offerings

The basic principles that should guide product decisions are essentially identical to those applicable to promotional and pricing deci-

---

[2]For more discussion of this topic, see Kenneth Preiss, Steven L. Goldman, and Roger N. Nagel, *Cooperate to Compete* (New York: Van Nostrand Reinhold, 1996), ch. 19.

sions. It is important at an early stage to identify, realistically, the expected contribution to relationship values that would result from a new offering or a modification in a current offering. What does a prospective new service add to the existing array? New services may complement existing ones either by adding value to customer relationships or by contributing to their development. Those are likely to be the simpler cases. Alternatively, new products may be substitutes for existing ones. Product decisions therefore include discontinuing current offerings as well as introducing new ones.

Substitute products may have net positive effects on relationship development and values, even after accounting for the displacement of other products. In a competitive environment, substitution of higher for lower quality is often essential for survival. Consequently, the value benefit of offering a new service line may simply be avoidance of the losses in value from not offering it.

Meanwhile, the relationship concept in marketing is of growing importance both to product and to pricing decisions, which are becoming less separable. Newer technologies enable offering wider arrays of services and products and growing opportunities for tailoring their attributes to different customer needs and preferences. Recall, too, that quality may itself have many dimensions. Customers continue to expand the ranges of services that they use and, indeed, have come to expect. The trend toward relationship marketing is gathering momentum, however slowly. A limiting factor, of course, is that the necessary information bases and skills in analyzing that information have been slow to develop.

The niche concept of marketing is a response to the growing array of services and needs arising from new technological possibilities. It is increasingly difficult for individual sellers, particularly smaller ones, to be all things to all prospective customers, even in their traditional markets. Even with outsourcing, there remains the problem of putting together all the combinations required by the relationship concept. For example, some customers demand and are willing to pay for more personalized attention in conjunction with their purchases. Others seek instead the lowest possible prices even if it means turning to remote and impersonal providers. Thus, growing importance attaches to decisions on what ranges of products or services an enterprise will seek to provide.

The Importance of Relationship Lives

Chapter 7 briefly discussed customer retention analysis, which involves the idea that outlays to retain existing customers may be more profitable than using those same outlays to attract new customers. While demonstrating some recognition of the continuing nature of customer relationships, retention analysis falls short by focusing only on near-term earnings. This myopic concept of retention may initially have the desired results, but often at the cost of longer-term value deterioration.

From a value standpoint, retention clearly has an additional dimension. Retaining a customer for, say, five more years contributes much more relationship value, and thus much more enterprise value, than retaining that customer for only one more year. In the first instance, at least, retention analysis would not recognize the distinction. More effective allocation of marketing budgets means more outlay on customers contributing more value. With other factors essentially the same, more value attaches to retaining relationships with longer remaining lives, just as more value attaches to attracting longer-lived relationships. The longer the life of the income stream, or cash flows, resulting from an investment, the greater its value.

Understanding the longevity characteristics of customer relationships represents an enormous new and essential frontier in market research. Different types of customers tend to have different longevity patterns. Various statistical techniques enable analyzing and projecting those patterns. Notice, meanwhile, that the significant issue at any time is the future remaining life of a customer relationship. The historical duration of existing relationships is significant to decision making only to the extent of providing information enabling projections of the remaining relationship lives.

While making this point, a full technical discussion of approaches to identifying and projecting customer longevity patterns is the stuff of specialists and thus beyond the scope of this book. A few observations nevertheless do seem appropriate:

- A natural tendency is to assume customer attrition at some constant percentage per year of the customers remaining at the end of the prior year. For example, suppose x percent of the customers at the beginning of a year sever their relationships during that year. A common temptation is to project the same percentage runoff for each successive year. Actually, the percentage runoff measured in this manner increases with the age of the customer base. The runoff rate thus increases until it finally reaches 100 percent with the departure of the last customer. A constant-percentage attrition therefore tends to be too slow as a customer base ages.

- A straight-line attrition pattern, as is common for plant and equipment depreciation accounting, means a constant amount of runoff each year (which is also a constant percentage of the initial base rather than the prior year's remaining base). Thus, if X customers depart in one year, it implies that X customers will depart each year thereafter. It is typically too slow for a newly developed customer base, but then quickly becomes much too fast as that base ages.

The result is that customer attrition tends to be something between these two extremes. Assume, for example, an initial base of 1,000 customers, and suppose that 100, or 10 percent, depart during the following year. A straight-line runoff pattern suggests that all will be gone in ten years. For many types of services with a similar initial runoff, however, some customers remain for much longer periods. Should one assume that the runoff in any year is 10 percent of the prior year's remaining customer base? In the above example, 900 customers would remain at the end of the first year. Should one therefore assume that 10 percent (now 90 customers) will depart in the second year? At that constant percentage rate, more than 5 percent of the initial base would still remain after 28 years, whereas 15 to 20 years would be more typical. At that rate, too, the last customer would still remain after 65 years—not impossible, but also not typical.

The basic issue in cases of valuing customer bases purchased in mergers and acquisitions has always been the future attrition pattern of customers already in place. Some of those customers may be new while others may be long-standing. Thus, within any one year, attrition rates are likely to differ according to when the relationships originated. In this respect, marketing decisions may be a bit simpler. The basic issue may then be attrition patterns solely for entirely new customers. Curiously, though, the percentage attrition patterns are often fairly similar in both instances.

Projecting an entire attrition pattern over future time is often not really even necessary for applying value-based decision criteria. Instead, one can obtain approximate present value estimates by looking at the average life of a customer base. Consider a simplified diagrammatic example:

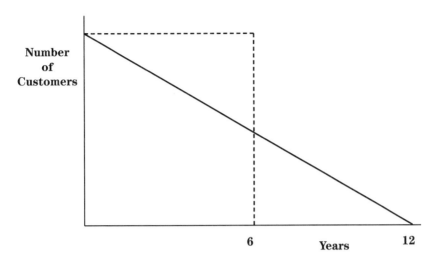

Attrition and Average Life of a Customer Base.

A calculation of a present value might be according to the down-ward sloping line over the full 12-year horizon (which in reality would usually be a longer period). Instead, it could assume the same, constant annual amount of cash flows over the 6-year average life, as depicted by the dotted line. Actually, average lives of 6 to 7 years are rather typical for many types of customer relationships.

Enriching Customer Relationships

An obvious objective of marketing is to attract new customers who will contribute to net enterprise values. Often less obvious, but often as important, is the potential for marketing to enhance those values further. This objective may involve:

- Inducing existing customers to purchase more value-con-tributing products and services than they do already.
- Extending the lives, or durations, of existing customer rela-tionships further into the future.

Diagrammatically, one may depict the cash flows representing enrich-ment of an individual customer relationship as:

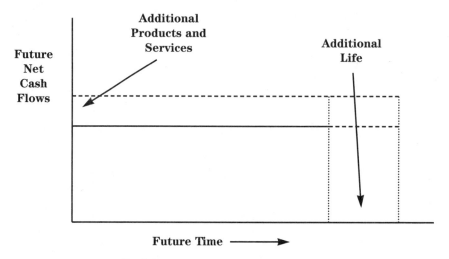

Enrichment of a Relationship Value.

For an entire base of customer relationships, the combined effects of enrichment strategies might appear roughly as:

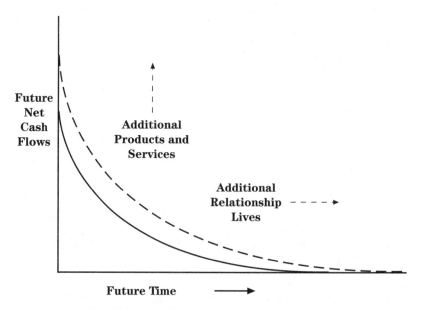

Enriching the Value of a Relationship Base.

These two value-enhancement strategies—adding more products and services, and extending relationship lives—often complement one another. The more products and services a customer buys from a particular vendor, the more inconvenient it may be to terminate the buyer-seller relationship. Nevertheless, to the extent that extending relationship lives requires rather different forms of investment than does expanding their scope, capital constraints may cause these objectives to become substitutes at the margin.

Of course, expanding the scope of customer relationships also provides more opportunities for customer dissatisfaction that will jeopardize those relationships. Customers who believe Prudential Securities misled them into partnership deals that went sour seem unlikely to become Prudential Insurance Company policyholders. Similarly, life insurance policyholders who believe Prudential misled them into borrowing on existing policies to buy additional insurance may be unlikely Prudential Securities clients. Then again, what has become of those customers who read in the press how they had been cheated by Bankers Trust's derivatives traders?

Notice that some of the most extreme cases of souring relationships arise when commission sales personnel are responsible for selling and servicing relationships. Indeed, brokerages and insurance companies may pressure young newcomers into overselling their products. Rather different explanations nevertheless are necessary for cases such as American automobile manufacturing, which let quality decline until Japanese competition necessitated major overhaul to survive. The American companies apparently are still having difficulty convincing much of the public that they have closed the quality gap.

The analysis of alternative programs for enriching existing relationship values is the same as that for attracting new relationships. The program alternatives probably are not the same, however. Information on existing customers should enable more efficient and carefully targeted programs. In fact, existing customers can be a gold mine of market information that many businesses tend to overlook. By enhancing marketing efficiency and effectiveness with better targeting, a particular relationship enrichment program may be warranted even if the additional income flows are less per customer than for new customers.

Relationships in Multiproduct Environments

Establishing a relationship for selling any one product or service often provides opportunities to cross-sell others. Indeed, a common perception of relationship marketing is as consisting of relationship managers whose functions include cross-selling different products and services to current customers. In these circumstances, it becomes important to distinguish their potential functions.

A common characteristic of a multiproduct environment is that different products and services have different functions in developing customer values. Moreover, any one product or service may perform a variety of roles, depending on the situation. Relationship marketing therefore requires understanding and taking advantage of the relationship functions of different products and services. From the standpoint of customer relationship development and retention, they fall into three categories:

- Products and services whose stand-alone projected cash flows represent positive net present values of the investments in the associated customer relationships. In other words, these customer relationships would have positive NPVs if limited to these products and services. These value-contributing services are the sources of the premium (franchise) values in many corporate acquisitions.
- Services and products that directly contribute no NPVs but which help to attract and develop some of the above value-contributing relationships. At least some of the outlays on providing these products and services may properly represent investment outlays on relationship development, retention, and enrichment rather than representing current expense.
- Products and services that have no relationship content. Sales typically represent one-time transactions with no particular expectation that the seller has any advantage in attracting the same customer in a subsequent transaction. Examples might include real estate brokerage, sales of big-ticket consumer durables, corporate financing deals, and commodities trading.

The second of the above situations is essentially a loss-leader situation. For example, public accounting firms sometimes offer free consulting services to attract new audit clients. In other words, one service—consulting—is part of the investment in developing a long-term audit relationship. The basic idea is that because it is inconvenient and costly to change auditors, an audit relationship, once obtained, will remain in place for a number of years. The expectation, of course, is that fees for audit services will eventually provide recovery of the costs the accountants incur for consulting services.

Except perhaps for one-time transactions, the third, simplest case fits the common economics textbook concept of a market. In this commodities model, transactions are impersonal, products are homogeneous, and sales volumes are highly price sensitive. All cash flows and values are essentially immediate, customers are mere transitory events, and sales volume depends solely on prices. The optimal combination of prices and sales volume occurs when the additional (marginal) revenue from a price reduction is no more than the added cost of the additional sales volume. Beyond that point, the additional costs exceed the additional revenues, reducing profit. Even adjustments to incorporate advertising assume that its effects are immediate. Anyone unconvinced of the remoteness of this model from reality should consider the difficulty of identifying examples other than commodities.

The essence of relationships in competitive markets is that they require investment outlays for their development and therefore require some means of recovering that investment with at least an adequate return. Consequently, market relationships must include some value-contributing goods and services. Those value contributions represent the prospect of future investment recovery. In the above accounting firm example, the audit services provide that value.

Sellers thus can make informed market decisions only if they distinguish carefully whether their offerings are relationship-attracting or value-contributing, or perhaps even both. Some individual goods and services can have multiple functions, depending on different customer characteristics. Thus, the accounting firm in the foregoing example might underprice its audit services to some other client who represents a major opportunity for data processing consulting services.

Indeed, the economic roles of different products and services may change over time as well. While accounting firms have previously offered free consulting services as a means of attracting audit clients, a reverse situation may have developed. Because of substantial pressure on audit fees arising from fierce competition, internalization of many accounting and audit functions, and client perceptions of declining value, audit services seem increasingly to be a mechanism for selling consulting services.

Bank credit cards provide another illustration. Historically, banks issued credit cards primarily to their own deposit customers. Indeed, until about 1980 a patchwork of state usury laws and other restrictions severely limited credit card finance charges and fees, and, hence, the value potential of credit card issuance. They nevertheless often served to strengthen and retain depositor relationships. However, during the 1980s, following the removal of most of those legal restrictions, they developed substantial relationship values of their own. As that occurred and cost economies associated with new information technologies favored very large issuers, credit cards became increasingly removed from other bank services. Much of the business moved outside banking altogether. Today, still newer technologies allowing smaller issuers access to more cost economies enable many smaller issuers to remain competitive.

An ideal circumstance, from a seller's standpoint, is when each and every customer contributes something to the value of the enterprise. As a practical matter, of course, sellers often cannot identify in advance those customers who will or will not do so. Moreover, even if they could make these distinctions, it may be difficult to prevent access by noncontributors. Sellers must therefore think in terms of average outcomes for large numbers of customers. The more selectively they target their products and marketing, the more their opportunities to improve those averages.

Value-Contributing Services

Repeating a fundamental proposition, market relationships increase market efficiency by reducing costs and risks. Indeed, it should be apparent by now how difficult it is to conceive of a marketplace that has no foundation whatever of customer relationships. If they contribute to efficiency, even if they are not otherwise inherently essential, competitive survival requires success in attracting and developing customer relationships. Virtually all businesses in a modern economy, including those in the manufacturing sector, are unavoidably relationship businesses to at least some degree. The traditional economics model is difficult to envision other than for commodities and securities markets.

Because some form of investment is necessary to attract customer relationships, those relationships must contribute value sufficient to recover that investment. Previous chapters have indicated that the investment decision process is essentially an exercise in marginal value analysis. Thus, the critical issue in product and marketing decisions is whether a little more outlay will contribute a more than equivalent amount of additional value.

As for other types of capital budgeting decisions, the analysis is fairly simple if marketing is single-dimensional—the enterprise uses only one basic type of approach to attracting new customers. Suppose the selected marketing approach is advertising, thus requiring a decision on an advertising budget. Each new relationship, once it is in place, represents an expected stream of net cash flows extending over the expected relationship life, representing the projected future income, expenses, and any further investment outlays. As in the restaurant chain examples, additional outlays are appropriate to the extent that each increment in value exceeds the marginal outlay. Up to that level of investment, but not beyond it, each outlay increment contributes additional net enterprise value.

The following table provides a simplified numerical illustration of some hypothetical relationship values contributed by different levels of advertising outlay. The nature of the product or service is irrelevant. Suppose that previous marketing analysis has projected both the cash flow contributions of new customers and the effects of different levels of advertising outlay on generating new customers. The result of that analysis is a schedule of the amounts of expected future net cash flows and present values that will result from each level of advertising outlay, as shown in the first two columns of the table. The total and marginal value contributions are present values of future cash inflows, or income. Meanwhile, if the outlays are to extend significantly into the future, they also require conversion to current present values. The dollar amounts might be in thousands or even millions:

Total Outlay	Total Value Contribution	Marginal Outlay	Marginal Value Contribution	Total Net Value	Marginal Net Value
$ 10	$ 20	$10	$20	$10	$10
20	39	10	19	19	9
30	57	10	18	27	8
40	74	10	17	34	7
50	90	10	16	40	6
60	105	10	15	45	5
70	119	10	14	49	4
80	132	10	13	52	3
90	144	10	12	54	2
100	155	10	11	55	1
*110	165	10	10	*55	*0
120	174	10	9	54	−1
130	182	10	8	52	−2
140	189	10	7	49	−3
150	189	10	6	45	−4

The total values depend on the advertising outlays. The third column in the table is simply the increments (at $10) in the first column; correspondingly, the fourth column is the increments in the second column. The fifth column shows the NPVs, deducting the present values of the outlays in the first column from the corresponding present values of the cash inflows in the second column. The last column consists of the increments in the preceding column.

Each additional amount of advertising outlay attracts less additional relationship value, as represented by the declining pattern of additional values. Observe that up to a total outlay of $110, each increment of outlay adds more value than the amount of the additional outlay. Beyond that amount, the additional value contributed is less than the outlay. The point at which the additional value and additional outlay are equal is the point of maximum total net present value, as indicated in the next-to-last column (marked with an asterisk). As the last column indicates, it is also the point where the marginal NPV turns from positive to negative. Further outlays beyond that point erode the net investment value, detracting from enterprise value.

This numerical illustration is much the same as the earlier diagrammatic illustrations. In the following diagram, the horizontal axis represents the total advertising outlays and the vertical axis represents the marginal outlays (constant at $10) and the marginal value contributions. The difference between the two downward sloping lines is simply the marginal outlay ($10).

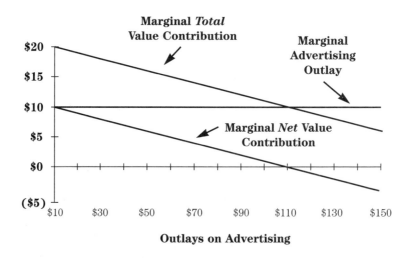

Marginal Value Contributions from Marginal Advertising Outlays.

Again, the value contribution of the advertising reaches a maximum where the marginal total value contribution is equal to the marginal advertising outlay, at total advertising outlays of $110. This same level is where the marginal net value contribution declines to zero.

If different types of marketing programs attract different customer groups, this type of analysis can either be separate for each group and program or it can be conducted as a composite exercise. The former, market segmentation approach probably provides better assurance of precision, and new technologies and data bases are constantly expanding its feasibility. Nevertheless, customer groups and programs still are often not easily broken down according to characteristics and preferences.

Consider a common circumstance in retailing. Perhaps the most important factor for the majority of customers is the convenience of the locations of retail outlets. A retailer may therefore invest heavily in establishing many locations. Yet, customers may also be sensitive to the ranges and types of products available at any one location. For some, this consideration may be sufficiently important that they will sacrifice some locational convenience. Other customers may have less concern with locational convenience but be highly responsive to advertising. The decision problem facing the retailer is how to balance all these factors. Should it seek to compete for all these customer preferences or should it narrow its focus to those it can serve most effectively? The answer probably will depend in significant part on rivals' market strategies.

Many customers respond to combinations of marketing devices that reinforce one another. While these situations can become rather complicated because of large numbers of combinations, the basic principles remain the same. Consider an expansion of the previous example to include two types of marketing to attract new customers—advertising and, say, a gift or premium. The premium could be any of a variety of things, such as a chance in a drawing, free first-year checking at a bank, or merchandise. If it involves providing goods or services in the future, the outlays should be expressed as present values.

There are now two alternative marketing programs to consider—advertising with the premium and advertising without it. The analysis might rely on two schedules similar to the one above, one for each alternative. Each schedule will have its own outlay and value contribution schedules. Which combination provides the highest total net value? The following table summarizes three hypothetical cases, including two different sets of possible outcomes of the premium promotion:

Total Outlay	Total Value with No Premium	Total Values with Premium	
		Outcome A	Outcome B
$ 10	$ 20	$ 18	$ 21
20	39	35	41
30	57	51	60
40	74	66	78
50	90	80	95
60	105	93	111
70	119	105	126
80	132	116	140
*90	144	*126	153
100	155	135	165
*110	*165	143	176
*120	174	150	*186
130	182	156	195
140	189	161	203
150	195	165	210

The outlays and the first set of values, which represent advertising alone, are the same as in the preceding table. The second set of values, A, represents one set of possibilities with the premium added to advertising. The highest total net value obtained in that case is with an outlay of $90, including both advertising and premiums. It results in a total value of $126 (marking the maximum value for each case with an asterisk). The net amount is therefore $126 − $90 = $36, which is a good deal less than the maximum of $155 − $100 = $55 obtained without the premium. In this case, the premium giveaway is simply costing more than the additional value it attracts. The last column of values, B, represents a different set of outcomes in which the giveaway does substantially enhance the advertising. The maximum NPV results from an outlay of $120, generating a total value of $186 for a net value of $186 − $120 = $66. Again, notice that in each case the maximum NPV occurs at the point where the incremental value contribution is equal to the incremental outlay ($10).

Relationship Development Products and Services

Some products and services—those that are primarily for purposes of relationship development—may reduce enterprise values if offered on a stand-alone basis. The free premium in the preceding example clearly is in this category, but such cases are not always so obvious. Notice that the nature of the premium as such is not necessarily as important as is the nature of the marketing. A common example is department store credit cards. Many department stores offer their own private-label credit cards not because they contribute much value, which they normally do not, but to attract merchandise trade. Otherwise, in retailing, the competitive pressures to provide one-stop convenience or full product lines undoubtedly give rise to many similar examples.

Although many products and services in a multiproduct enterprise serve relationship development functions, generalizing with respect to any particular category may be difficult. Analyzing strategies for using relationship development products and services thus requires identifying with precision the revenues and outlays they represent. Basically, the investment outlays are the discounts from the prices that would be appropriate if the services were neither relationship developing nor value contributing. Those stand-alone prices would normally reflect the (marginal) direct costs of providing those products or services. The relevant price against which to measure the discount, in other words, is no different from what applies to any good or service that does not involve customer relationships.

Investments in relationship development services obviously include the fully allocated cash outlays necessary to provide them. The cash outlays nevertheless may not reflect the full costs. In certain types of cases, the presence or absence of these services may also affect the risks associated with market relationships. For example, much of the risk in banking arises from lending, which often contributes nothing more than attracting and retaining depositor relationships. A depositor relationship requiring loans to attract and retain it therefore entails additional cost in the form of more risk. That additional cost, in turn, takes the form of higher discount factors in determining the value contributions of those higher-risk relationships. Thus, depositor relationships requiring loans to attract and secure them often have less value than pure depositor relationships that are otherwise identical, even if a bank otherwise breaks even on the loans.

A Nexus of Market Relationships

A special type of market relationship problem arises when the product attributes a seller can offer in one market depend on what it offers in some other, otherwise separate, market. The seller, in other words, becomes a nexus of two very different types of customer relationships. A daily newspaper provides an illustration. Its ability to attract advertising depends on its circulation and thus on its base of subscriber relationships. Its ability to attract subscribers depends both on its investment in promoting subscriptions and on the quality and extent of its news and editorial content. The quality content in turn depends at least partly on its advertising revenues. The newspaper publisher must therefore decide simultaneously how much to invest in developing advertiser relationships and how much to invest in developing subscriber relationships.

Analyzing this decision problem involves a simple extension of the earlier models. It can be set up in either of two ways, both of which should result in exactly the same composite investment decision. Each schedule in the following diagram shows the composite marginal NPVs associated with various levels of investment in developing subscriber relationships, with the amount of investment in advertiser relationships remaining constant. Each schedule represents a different (constant) level of investment in advertiser relationships. While the number of possible schedules could be enormous, a decision maker would typically focus on a very narrow range of relevant options. Just a few such schedules are sufficient for this illustration.

First, consider Schedule *A*. It assumes some constant level of investment in advertiser relationships, so total relationship value—advertiser and subscriber—would increase only with more investment in subscriber relationships. At that given level of investment in advertiser relationships, the maximum obtainable composite NPV is where the marginal NPV shown by *A* is zero, where *A* crosses the horizontal axis above point *a*.

Suppose, next, that the newspaper publisher increases the investment in advertiser relationships to some new (constant) level represented by Schedule *B*. The result in this case is to increase relationship values. Notice that for every level of investment in subscriber relationships, the marginal NPV represented by *B* is higher than that represented by *A*, indicating more additional NPV and thus a higher total NPV.

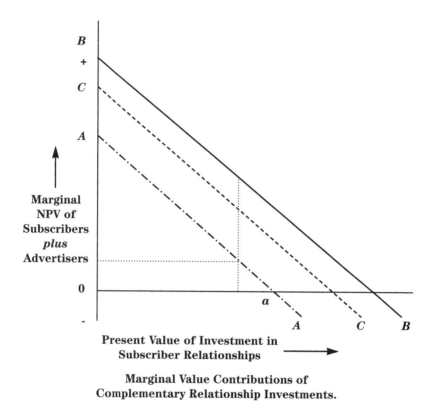

**Marginal Value Contributions of
Complementary Relationship Investments.**

To complete the illustration, suppose Schedule *C* represents an even higher level of investment in advertisers than does *B*. That it lies below *B* suggests one or, more likely, both of two factors:

- Investment in attracting additional advertiser relationships has encountered substantially diminishing returns: At some point in extending investment in those relationships from *B* to *C*, each additional dollar of outlay began to yield less than a dollar in present values of additional advertising revenues.
- Extending the investment in advertisers from *B* to *C* required sufficient additional capital to raise the publisher's cost of capital, reducing the NPV of each amount of additional net cash flow.

The consequence is that as the investment in advertisers moves toward *C*, the marginal NPV of outlays on advertiser relationships at some point becomes negative—additional investment produces less than an equivalent amount of additional relationship value. The objective, then, is to increase investment in advertiser relationships to the extent that it shifts the NPV schedules upward and to the right, but no further.

An absolutely equivalent formulation of this investment decision is with each NPV schedule representing a constant level of investment in subscriber relationships, varying the investment in advertiser relationships along the horizontal axis. The schedules would look very similar, and the optimal investment amount and allocation would be identical. Fundamentally, each of the two approaches is a two-dimensional depiction of a three-dimensional decision problem. Expansion to additional dimensions would follow the same principles, although with escalating complexity. One might consider, for example, that developing an editorial staff is yet another form of relationship investment that affects the newspaper's ability to attract subscribers and advertisers. To include this possibility would follow the same principles, but now in four dimensions.

11

Toward Relationship Management

A RECAPITULATION

Whether investment is in tangible or intangible assets, the fundamental rule is *always* to extend that investment to the point at which the net present values (NPVs) all reach zero. Beyond that point, the (negative) values of any further investment outlays will exceed the values created, reducing total value contributions. A variety of procedures for calculating the NPVs will lead to identical results—identical total outlays and capital allocations.

Nevertheless, the scarce resource in any investment program is the amount of available capital. With different programs and projects drawing on the same capital pool, keeping track of the amount of capital commitment each represents is essential. The passage of time gives rise continuously to new opportunities requiring new investment decisions. It is also likely to shift the terms on which capital is available. As an enterprise grows and demonstrates effective use of the capital it has already obtained, it is likely to develop access to additional capital, perhaps from sources that were previously unavailable. Evidence of wasting capital correspondingly reduces its availability.

Meanwhile, another basic rule of investment in any form is never to look back. The success or failure of past investment should never factor directly into new investment decisions. A previous investment program may have turned out badly, for example, but some additional investment in that same program might be worthwhile by reducing the loss by more than the investment outlay. Past successes and failures are important mainly for their informative value concerning new opportunities.

The competition for scarce capital arises not simply for investment in market opportunities and customer relationships; rather, it extends to the entire array of external and internal forms of relationship capital as well as to investment in other intangibles and, of course, in tangible capital.

Supplier Relationships

As a nexus of market relationships, many of the roles of a business enterprise are as a buyer, often with continuing relationships with sellers. Supplier, or seller, relationships are essentially customer relationships viewed from the other side of the marketplace. Every customer relationship also represents a supplier relationship, and vice versa. The normal situation is for sellers to take the main initiative in seeking out and developing customer relationships. Competition to develop market relationships is normally much stronger among sellers than among buyers. Correspondingly, because of competition, control over relationships resides with buyers, while the larger part of the investment in their development is by sellers. This general pattern applies especially to retail markets, but it is also much the most common one in others as well.

Situations nevertheless do arise when, instead, buyers have particularly strong incentives to initiate market relationships and possibly even to compete for them. These situations perhaps have become particularly noticeable with trends toward outsourcing procurements of parts and services. The concept of initiating a relationship introduces an additional dimension to market relationships. In Japan, for example, a common practice has been for large manufacturers to initiate close, sometimes almost tyrannical, relationships with parts suppliers. Sellers often have had to compete vigorously to establish those supplier relationships. The prospective reward for sellers has been that once these relationships were in place, they enjoyed sheltered markets. More recently, however, the practice has begun to break down, with growing pressures on Japanese manufacturers to seek out lower-priced, more competitive supply sources.

The following diagram illustrates possible configurations of relationships between buyers and sellers:

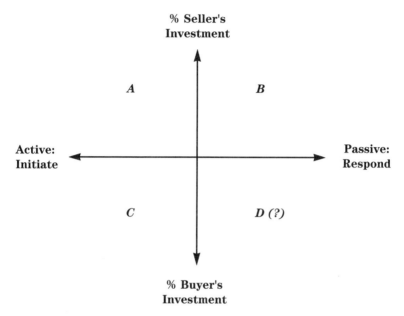

Configurations of Buyer-Seller Relationships.

In moving from the top to the bottom of the diagram, the proportion of the total investment in relationship development attributable to the seller falls from 100 percent to zero, where 100 percent is attributable to buyers. Moving from left to right means assuming an increasingly passive role in developing a market relationship. Point A might represent a typical retail market situation, where a seller is the primary initiator and bears most of the investment burden. Buyers nevertheless exercise some initiative (such as by narrowing their choices). Point A also suggests that they represent some of the relationship investment (as in time and effort to investigate alternatives). Point B could be a major manufacturer seeking out suppliers capable of meeting its particular specifications. Perhaps sellers must invest heavily in developing proposals, altering their production processes, or adding facilities in order to respond.

Point C in the diagram might be a situation in which a buyer actually provides financial assistance to certain sellers in order to assure reliable sources of supply or to support research and development. This situation essentially represents buyer-initiated collaboration, rather in the nature of a partnership. Obviously, buyers would take this course only with expectations of obtaining significant value once the relationships are in place. Some familiar examples in the United States probably involve development of new technologies in military and aerospace manufacturing. Large retailing enterprises sometimes adopt this approach, particularly when they want a role in product design or assurances of quality.

Finally, point D is inserted for completeness, but may be uncommon. It implies buyer passivity, yet also buyer willingness to undertake the larger part of the relationship investment after a seller has initiated it. Perhaps a seller brings an idea to a buyer's attention but leaves it to the buyer to pursue it. Some cases of buyers soliciting proposals requiring a substantial investment in preparation provide examples that at least lean toward this model.

Cases A and B therefore are simply common variants of the conventional customer relationship model, whereas C is somewhat different. In a competitive marketplace where buyers usually have many options, why would a buyer initiate relationships with sellers to the point of bearing most of the investment in their development? A few possibilities are:

- An enterprise may want to assure a reliable source of supply but cannot achieve as extensive cost economies of large scale as those available to a specialized supplier.
- Diseconomies of scale have set in—the business has reached a size and complexity exceeding the capacity of its current management and organization to manage it effectively, so it turns increasingly to outsourcing.
- Opportunities otherwise existing for internalizing production exceed the ability of the enterprise to obtain the necessary capital, at least in the near term, so it seeks outside suppliers with better access to capital.
- An enterprise is able to exercise more market power externally than internally, as might be the case when its own employees are strongly unionized.

While one commonly thinks of cost economies from larger size (scale) in a manufacturing context, it is more likely today to involve technology, as in managing large databases or undertaking research and development programs. Thus, many types of organizations offer credit card programs without themselves having the capacity to be issuers. The American Automobile Association's card program is an example of a case of a buyer having substantial leverage over suppliers. The American Association of Retired Persons exercises similar leverage as an intermediary in the sale of insurance and prescription drugs to its members. For the same sorts of reasons, research and development arrangements take a variety of forms, including coventures and partnerships as well as buyer-seller relationships. Such arrangements have become commonplace for aerospace development projects.

The trend toward emphasizing core competencies may reflect similar pressures, particularly when accompanied by reduced vertical integration in production and distribution. Perhaps those pressures emanate from management limitations or constraints on capital availability. One might think of a corporation encountering these circumstances due to its growth, but they may arise as well from inability to adapt sufficiently to changing markets and technologies. Some enterprises may narrow their focus, downsize, and outsource mainly because they encounter more severe capital limitations and they see the financial community applauding such measures. Such cases may result from strategic shortcomings, hardly deserving of investor approbation.

Meanwhile, to what extent are commercial and industrial buyer-seller relationships likely to blossom into partnership, strategic alliance, and joint venture relationships? They probably risk instability if they are not secured by formal contracts. Once such arrangements are in place, their participants may become concerned about whether they are obtaining their fair shares of the benefits. Economists observed many years ago that industrial cartels often had difficulty holding together even when the benefits clearly extended to all their members. Changes in the market environments in which they variously operate, by causing departures from the premises that were the basis for those arrangements, exacerbate concerns with the distribution of those benefits. A modern version of instability in cooperative arrangements is persistent squabbling between the accounting and consulting components of the leading public accounting firms.

The difficulty with any form of cooperative arrangement is that it is not an arm's-length relationship. Thus, unlike normal buyer-seller relationships, the distribution of the benefits arises from other than purely market forces. Cooperative arrangements of this sort are likely to be sustainable for longer periods the more obvious the economic benefits compared to other alternatives. For the most part, they seem to work most effectively when formed for discrete, well-defined projects that extend over limited periods of time.

Whatever the incentives from which supplier relationships arise, the appropriate method of analyzing these situations is identical to the analysis of customer relationships. The nature of the investment, of course, is likely to be quite different. Instead of involving marketing, advertising, and pricing issues, it may be in the forms of management time, research and development outlays, and provision of capital.

Employer-Employee Relationships

However important, issues of labor relations, industrial psychology, and the like must lie for the most part outside the scope of this discussion. The capital nature of much of a workforce nevertheless needs some consideration. A vestige of the industrial age is a tendency to view employees as representing current cost rather than accumulated investment. For present purposes, consider employees to include everyone receiving wages or salaries and thus to include all levels of management and administration. Theoretically, at least, even chief executives belong in this category.

Many management consultants and employers talk about "knowledge workers" and "employee empowerment," but not necessarily with a full understanding of some basic issues:

- What are the attributes that make some employees more effective than others? In precisely what ways do employees (including managers) contribute value to the enterprise?
- How can an enterprise recruit and develop an employee base most effectively? How can it obtain the most value from those employees?
- How should it determine how much to invest in recruitment and in increasing employee effectiveness?

Obviously, much of the human capital that an employee brings to an enterprise resides in that employee. Moreover, some of an employer's investment in an employee—additions to that human capital—also becomes embedded in that employee. It is, in other words, portable, and thus lost to the employer should the employee terminate the relationship. Thirdly, while general knowledge and work skills compose much of the human capital, other attributes—leadership qualities, imagination and creativity, attitudes toward seeking security or taking risks, adaptability to change, and cooperativeness, to name but a few—can assume varying degrees of importance.

Just how much an employer can enhance the nonskill qualities of managers and employees is an open question. Recall, for example, the discussion in chapter 7 about the methods some management gurus employ to encourage out-of-the-box thinking. Turning more specifically to knowledge capital, one might distinguish among:

- General knowledge and skills that accumulate outside any employment context from schools, family, and community. This category extends to specific job skills from training programs not specifically sponsored by actual or prospective employers.
- Industry-specific knowledge and skills that result from prior and current employment and that are transferable among employers.
- Enterprise-specific knowledge, which might include highly specialized skills as well as understanding of the inner workings of the business.

A general presumption is that to the extent investment is necessary for the first category, it is the responsibility of the individual and the public sector rather than of employers. Perhaps the same applies to the second category as well, although cases have arisen when members of an industry have a collective interest in developing certain skills. At least much of the value arising from the third category presumably resides with the employer. Even here, however, perhaps one can distinguish:

- Value that is claimable by an employer only as long as the employment relationship continues.
- Value that an employee contributes that can provide continuing benefits to an employer even after employment termination.

The second of these categories might include:

- Benefits of skill and experience transferred to other employees.
- Contributions to the development of a corporate culture.

- Creative ideas contributing to innovation.
- Diagnoses of internal problems and inefficiencies.
- Diagnoses of problems with products and services.
- Diagnoses of problems with inputs and suppliers.
- Facilitation of communication with customers and suppliers.

Remember that employees in a relationship marketplace are on the front line in dealings with actual and prospective customers to a degree that was unimaginable in the traditional industrial environment.

At least some of the foregoing distinctions are probably too facile, however. Immobility and imperfect information in employment tend to shift them. For example, an employer seeking to grow while confronting a deficient supply of qualified workers might very well invest in educating and training local workers, including in skills that would be portable in other circumstances. This approach may make sense for an employer in a remote, low-wage location.

Upon identifying the potential value contributions and investment opportunities, the analysis follows the same format as do other types of relationship investment. Whether employers commonly think in these terms is an altogether different matter. Consider some of the evidence:

- Decisions on downsizing and other forms of restructuring typically rely more on how they affect current costs than on the amount of embedded capital to be lost.
- Selecting candidates for termination due to restructurings is often delegated to lower management levels or outside consultants, including to "change managers" specializing in downsizing terminations.
- Terminations focus particularly on older workers who, while possibly representing higher costs, may also represent more value due to enterprise-specific knowledge, more experience in adapting to change, and other forms of human capital.
- Responsibilities for recruitment and reviewing applicant qualifications, even for relatively senior management and professional positions, often fall to low-level employees, temporaries, or outside clerical workers.
- Screening of employment applicants is commonly designed to eliminate all overqualified candidates—those whose qualifications exceed designated, often quite restrictive, boundaries.
- Common practice is to define qualifications of current and

prospective employees very narrowly in terms of only their current responsibilities rather than total experience, skills, or potential.

In other words, current cost considerations rather than investment principles tend to drive human resource management. Employee attributes that exceed the experience and understanding of human resource administrators are likely to receive little weight, whether in restructuring programs or hiring decisions. Restructuring programs that result in employee layoffs and premature retirements therefore often overlook the human capital being thrown away. More curiously, according to some human resource professionals, corporations seem to be much more sensitive to the costs of hiring people than to the costs of forced terminations, even though the latter are often substantially higher. Also, a frequent consequence of terminating higher-paid employees with a view to cutting costs is an elevation of lower-level workers to higher-paid positions.

Normally missing is a recognition that identifying and fully developing the value potential embedded in human capital itself requires a certain amount of investment. In other words, if human resource professionals seem to be doing a poor job of employee recruitment and development, it is likely due to insufficient resources being available for this function. Senior managers tend to look on human resource functions as representing overhead costs, and thus an unavoidable drag on earnings.

Setting value objectives brings into focus the fact that a corporate enterprise, while an instrument of its shareholders, is fundamentally a human organization. It is a social as well as a microcosmic economic system. To dehumanize that system is to render it dysfunctional. Certainly, some recent corporate trends have had this consequence, in part because of attaching excessive significance to shorter-term earnings goals.

True employee empowerment is not so much assigning decision making responsibilities as devising systems for identifying and using human resources to their maximum capabilities and aspirations. Information technologies that increasingly segment actual and potential customers according to their characteristics suggest possibilities for significantly more targeted methods of human resource management.

Employment Flexibility

Today's workplace reality often seems a substantial departure from management theories about employee empowerment or knowledge workers. A former business school dean and now president of a major university recently advised his children to disconnect from their employers—advice that he never dreamed of giving a few years ago. The message getting through to many younger employees is to protect themselves by focusing on their individual self-interests. Certainly, the modern work environment too often exhibits an expanding gulf between the potential rewards of relationship-directed management and myopic oversight.

A "Manager's Journal" column in the *Wall Street Journal* offered an interesting perspective on management disconnection not too long ago.[1] It asked why corporate executives commonly engage high-priced consultants to address problems to which employees already know the answers. Whatever its deeper roots, this practice seems to arise from communications breakdowns that begin at the highest management levels. Many senior executives know rather little about their employees; perhaps some are fearful of their employees knowing too much about them. The message emanating from the executive suite is likely to be one of a lack of confidence and trust. In many cases the message from employees is that the problems originate in the executive suite.

From the employees' perspective, why extend loyalty and trust to an employer who reciprocates neither? Why venture imagination and creativity when it is likely to go unrewarded? Why network within the enterprise when one's best options may lie outside? Obviously, the mutuality that relationships imply is in jeopardy. Employees in this sort of environment focus more on avoiding mistakes than promoting new ideas.

Where it does exist, many of today's workplace problems arise from the difficulties many corporate enterprises are having in adjusting to changing markets and technologies, both in the short and the long term. Employer-employee disconnection may seem to be a mechanism by which management can obtain more flexibility in adjusting outputs and costs. Loyalty is unreciprocated because it is potentially costly. A common tendency is to regard many employees as merely temporary, to one degree or another. Why, then, invest in all those

---

[1]Craig J. Cantoni, "The Consulting Mystique," *Wall Street Journal,* 10 March, 1997.

things that engender employee loyalty, even if they significantly enhance employee performance, when you may soon be laying off those employees?

Chapter 10 observed that the various means of obtaining more flexibility normally require more investment outlay. The economists' conventional model views employees as variable inputs, the amount of employment changing with output requirements. Plant and equipment are fixed inputs that are much less adaptable. Nevertheless, with additional investment, a producer may obtain built-in flexibility whereby it can adjust the plant and equipment to different output configurations. The more employees represent invested capital, the more important it is to view them in the same manner. Thus, employees with more and broader experience are likely to be more adaptable to new circumstances even while they require more compensation.

The cheapest way of producing a particular output is sometimes to use low-cost plant and equipment that is not adaptable to other uses. The consequence is that when output configurations change, plant and equipment can either result in much higher production costs or require replacement altogether. In the same manner, internal disconnection may reduce both operating costs and investment outlays in the short run. It nevertheless tends to reduce the adaptability of the enterprise when market circumstances change in ways for which management is unprepared, thereby entailing much higher costs in the longer run.

With employee disconnection, moreover, employees are likely to contribute less value to the enterprise even without market changes. Employee turnover will be higher, perhaps substantially, and such capital and enterprise value contributions as employee terminations represent may be recoverable, if at all, only with much higher outlays than retaining them would have required. In the same manner as a customer base, the most effective investments for the long run are often in enriching relationships already in place. Either employers will find ways to reconnect with employees or they will face a persistent capital drain.

Investing in broader experience and skills and in professional development is not necessarily the best course in all cases. For example, some information technology companies seem to thrive on a constant inflow of recent technical graduates, who import some of the newest technologies, and high turnover. About all that can be said about these cases is that employees should understand the character of their environment.

Corporate Culture

Corporate culture at least encompasses the knowledge and experience that seems to be specific to an individual enterprise. It deserves separate mention because of the significance often attached to it. Chapter 2 defined it rather loosely as a shared sense within the enterprise of its direction and of how to do things. Perhaps an appropriate definition is even broader, including the ephemeral qualities that sometimes distinguish athletic teams from one another—leadership qualities, intensity, focus, confidence, and sense of momentum, to name a few. Whatever it is, corporate culture may be an important factor in differentiating an enterprise from its rivals. Particularly among service enterprises, whether or not in conjunction with product sales, it may even be the determining factor in developing and maintaining some customer relationships.

Two questions arise, neither of which is likely to have easy answers:

- In exactly what ways does a corporate culture create enterprise value?
- How can an enterprise create value in the form of a corporate culture?

Some of the value presumably arises from higher productivity of managers and employees. A shared sense of direction and procedures should facilitate communication and decision making, imparting more agility in adjusting to market changes. It may also add to productivity by providing employees with a sense of accomplishment, of being appreciated, and even of esprit de corps. It may furthermore promote a climate that encourages imagination and creativity. Indeed, where an enterprise sits on the spectrum of responsiveness to change may reflect its corporate culture, which can either encourage or impede adapting to new economic circumstances.

A corporate culture can represent either positive or negative elements of enterprise value. Indeed, negative values may be more typical, particularly abroad, as is arguably the case in Japan, but also in the United States. What is a corporate culture if it is not somewhat institutionalized? How can one maintain it upon departing from a status quo? When does a shared sense of direction and procedures open or close doors to unconventional new ideas, including to criticism of current ideas and practices? A corporate culture, in other words, may simply be the sand in which a corporate ostrich hides its head.

Alternatively, a corporate culture can serve to impart a competitive edge to an enterprise. It will do so only if senior management assures that it encourages communication and creativity rather than reactiveness, and progressiveness rather the regressiveness. While meeting that challenge first depends on the attitudes and leadership of senior management, middle management probably also plays a major role in determining its shape, direction, and endurance.

The Varying Roles of Middle Management

Many recent cases of corporate restructuring have resulted in eliminating layers of middle management. In theory, perhaps middle management can become redundant with sufficient empowerment of knowledge workers. If so, the traditional corporate pyramid would collapse into a mostly horizontal structure under a senior executive suite. Shifting from theory to reality, however, a growing number of observers are now suggesting that such summary dispositions of middle management have been shortsighted.

Does middle management have particular value attributes that chief executives fail to recognize and appreciate? The question is an important one insofar as middle managers often represent a major component of a corporation's employment costs. Furthermore, as reengineering advocates seem to suggest, middle management may impede rather than facilitate work flows and processes. If so, costs may escalate even further. On the other hand, if important elements of value are lost through this sort of restructuring, they may never be recoverable. An organization cannot simply turn around and summarily replace what it had just summarily abolished.

Some of the issues concerning middle management seem at least in part to reflect confusion about definitions of *manage* and *manager*. *Managing* implies some degree of supervisory authority—responsibility for decisions on actions to be taken by others within an organization. In that sense, bank customers, for example, would likely regard efforts by a bank relationship manager actually to manage their relationships as offensive.

One also might usefully distinguish between management and administration. Administrative decisions are generally nonsupervisory. Thus, for example, deciding whether or not a customer should receive a requested amount of credit represents an administrative rather than a management decision. Many of the tasks that process reengineering seeks to eliminate seem primarily to be administrative rather than managerial. At least some discussions of employee empowerment similarly concern decisions that are not really supervisory or managerial. Does the authority to halt an assembly line because of a production flaw truly represent management?

That said, a corporate enterprise should take special care to understand the distinctive ways in which middle management can be a significant source of shareholder value. Consider the possibility that the roles of middle management have changed significantly as the business environment has changed, but not necessarily so as to diminish its value. Consider that:

- Middle management presumably will continue to be the training and testing ground for replacements for senior management. Outside recruitment of top management replacements may not be a full substitute for internal upward mobility, particularly without more investment in recruitment.
- Particularly if a shortage of middle management candidates compels reliance on outside recruitment to fill top management positions, the distinguishing characteristics arising from a corporate culture may be difficult or impossible to develop and sustain.
- Middle managers may be the primary sources of new ideas and innovation; they should also be conduits, and perhaps the primary conduits, for transmitting useful information from the marketplace and employees to senior management.
- If many production employees do not want empowerment, employee at higher levels—middle managers—must exercise more decision-making responsibility.

Advocates of the horizontal corporation seem at odds with the fact that, with rare exceptions, decisions themselves are unavoidably hierarchical. Decisions obviously vary in levels of detail and responsibility. Most significantly from the standpoint of erecting a decision-making framework, they vary in terms of their impact on enterprise value. A management organizational structure that departs from the hierarchical nature of value-based decisions is difficult even to imagine. In this respect, consider that:

- Above all else, the linkages of decision-making responsibility to the consequences for enterprise (shareholder) values are themselves hierarchical as measured by their value consequences.

- Decision making is at least a two-way process. On one hand are decisions to take actions. On the other are decisions on what information to pass up to higher management levels for their decision making.
- Understanding how to make effective decisions comes only from experience, presumably with successively higher levels of responsibility.

In reality, how many managers avoid decision making? How commonly do they absorb themselves in administrative detail and aimless meetings? How often do they delegate major decisions to committees? Why is it that many chief executives and senior managers have little time to think strategically? Does management attach value to contemplation and reflection, or dismiss them as wastes of time? To what extent does it judge employee performance by the numbers of extra hours expended? Is restructuring management the same thing as restructuring administrative functions?

Assessing Management Performance

Each level of management presumably has responsibility for supervising the performance of one or more lower managerial levels. The ultimate test of effective decision making, particularly in a relationship environment, is whether decisions add to or detract from the value of an enterprise.

Consider this point at the highest level of management. One can begin by cataloguing the market values of all of the underlying assets and liabilities from which the enterprise derives its value—resources that the shareholders have made available. From those values, determine the net asset value of the enterprise, including all identifiable intangible assets except any value directly representing senior management. Next, compare the resulting net asset value with the aggregate values of the enterprise determined by other techniques, such as:

- Its total market capitalization value—the total market value of its stock—perhaps with adjustment for inactive trading or controlling interests.
- Its discounted cash flow value as a going concern, perhaps employing a dividend valuation concept adjusting for growth or earnings, and adjusted for noncash expenses (by adding depreciation back to earnings, for example).

- An earnings value employing ratios of share prices or acquisition prices to earnings.

Compare these values with the net asset value representing the underlying assets and liabilities. A net asset value significantly higher than the other values may mean that senior management is not making effective use of the resources at its disposal. Why should the value of the whole be less than the sum of the values of its parts unless something unidentified is reducing that whole? Some qualification of the significance of this type of result is necessary, however. The value measures may contain too many imperfections to attach significance to any but major discrepancies.

Even then, an immediate objection to this approach is likely to be the difficulty, or even the impossibility, of attaching values to the underlying assets, particularly to the intangibles. That sort of objection raises a challenge to management that it may wish to avoid. How can senior management meet its responsibilities, making decisions in a manner promotive of shareholder values, unless it fully understands those underlying sources of enterprise value? Is suggesting that senior management has a responsibility at least to try to understand those value elements unreasonable? Is corporate management to be simply a crapshoot in the dark?

A net asset value somewhat higher than the other values may occur for one of at least three reasons. All three suggest that the directors should look more closely at management policies and practices:

- Perhaps some of the assets have more value if put to uses other than the business of this particular enterprise. The enterprise should either redirect its business to more value-producing activities or consider divesting assets.
- The discrepancy may arise because of management deficiencies—the enterprise simply is failing to make effective use its available assets, even though more productive opportunities exist within it.
- Whether because of directors' inattentiveness or collusion between directors and the chief executive, senior management may simply be grossly overcompensated.

The enterprise valuations normally would be net of executive compensation. Strictly speaking, that compensation should be in terms of present values of current and future compensation, including golden parachutes and other contingent and deferred forms of compensation. Meanwhile, some possibility exists that the enterprise values significantly exceed the net asset value, perhaps suggesting a net positive value of senior management. Negative management values seem to be particularly characteristic of established enterprises that have begun to stagnate or even to decline, while positive values are more likely for rapidly growing entrepreneurial enterprises. In the latter case, much of the expected compensation may be from rising values of the shares held by the principals.

An important feature of this approach is its potential applicability to different business units within the enterprise. More specifically, begin by summing the underlying values of assets within a business unit. Collectively, they should generate total cash flows with a net present value that at least equals the sum of the underlying values. Again, any substantial discrepancy suggests a need for a closer look.

What does a value perspective imply about compensation? In a frictionless world, present (DCF) values of executive compensation would gravitate toward the DCF values of their net value contributions to the enterprise. In other words, as before, the business would invest in its executives to the point at which their net present values are zero. Excess value would disappear with competition. Thus, if a chief executive contributes more value than the compensation value, some other enterprise should be willing to offer more. If the value contribution is less, the directors should reduce the compensation.

The real world, of course, does even not approach adherence to this model. As a rule, substantial discrepancies must exist before the forces of competition begin to work. One obvious reason, assuming responsible corporate governance, is that an executive who has been in place for some length of time should represent more value than a newcomer who otherwise has identical qualifications. An incumbent presumably understands the organization and its culture. Another reason is that institutionally, if not logically, actually reducing compensation is unacceptable. An executive typically would terminate association with the enterprise rather then accept lower compensation, even if it meant accepting still less compensation somewhere else.

Corporate Directors

The foregoing discussion suggests that corporate directors have substantial oversight responsibility for corporate direction and management. Indeed, it suggests a directorship model somewhat different from those common among today's corporate enterprises. Who actually would, or even could, take on the responsibility for reviewing the compensation of senior executives by examining their value contributions? Is this task something that a compensation committee of a board can realistically perform? To suggest as much is laughable, considering that board committees typically meet only for a few minutes prior to full board meetings. It is also laughable when a chairman who is also the corporate CEO sets a board's agenda. As a matter of pure logic, senior management cannot properly represent both its own self interests and those of shareholders unless its compensation depends substantially on *long-term* shareholder returns. Often, even when senior managers have significant equity interests, their ability to cause short-term deviations of share prices from underlying values can give rise to conflicts of interest.

The corporation of the future, even if more distant than immediate, will maintain its competitiveness by functioning rather differently. One approach would be to require directors to devote far more time to meeting their responsibilities, with appropriate compensation. Directorships would thus be part- or full-time employment. The days of simply spending a few hours reviewing materials forwarded by the CEO before attending a quarterly board meeting are probably numbered in any event. So, too, are the days when the primary or only measure of attentiveness of directors to their responsibilities is attendance at board meetings.

A rather different approach might be an audit model. All but very small corporations today typically have internal auditors who report to an audit committee of the board of directors. As costs of outside, independent audits have escalated, corporations have internalized more audit functions. An enterprise could apply the same concept to value audits. Indeed, the modern corporation risks substantially more impairment of underlying value components due to mismanagement than from the types of malfeasance traditional audit functions might detect. Value auditing probably would require trained professionals, much as conventional audit functions do.

Corporate Relations with the Financial Community

The final links, working back through the relationship chain, are those extending from the enterprise to the financial community, which includes:

- Current shareholders.
- Potential future shareholders.
- Current and potential creditors.
- Financial professionals—analysts, investment bankers, etc.
- The financial media.

In theory, of course, the enterprise and its current shareholders are one and the same. Their mutual objectives are to maintain the best terms on which current shareholders can sell their shares, should they wish to do so. To that end, they are also to maintain the best terms on which the enterprise can issue debt. Meeting those objectives obviously depends on the quality of management and direction. It is also depends on the quality and quantity of information that the enterprise provides to the financial community.

Unfavorable information does not remain hidden indefinitely, whereas attempts to conceal it create uncertainty. The marketplace generally discounts share prices according to the associated degree of uncertainty. Generally, less rather than more information ultimately penalizes the current shareholders. Possible exceptions are instances when a corporation can slip through a new stock or debt issue before unfavorable information becomes public. As chapter 5 indicated, required public disclosures can be misleading and uninformative. Such practices may be self-defeating in the long run as investors learn to become more skeptical.

The availability of information also bears on the issue of the confidence that the financial community has in enterprise direction and management, focusing in the first instance on corporate governance. What is one to make of corporate CEOs who schedule shareholder meetings in remote locations or who severely restrict shareholder inquiries? What, too, is one to make of a chairman-CEO of a major corporation whose "independent" directors include his personal attorney, his children's former elementary school principal, and three former company executives?[2] How much confidence can investors have that such hand-picked directors will exercise the independent oversight they owe to the shareholders? In such cases, can they truly have confidence that the directors have the experience and knowledge to exercise that oversight? In the instant case, at least, several major retirement funds, including the California Public Employees'

---

[2] Bruce Orwell and Joann Lublin, "The Plutocracy: If a Company Prospers, Should Its Directors Behave by the Book?" *Wall Street Journal,* 24 February, 1997, A1.

Retirement System, the Wisconsin State Board of Investments, and TIAA-CREF, stepped forward and registered their objections (apparently to no immediate avail) by withholding votes for some or all of the directors.

Actual and Potential Shareholders

Acting on behalf of current shareholders does not necessarily mean adjusting to their specific preferences regarding risks and dividend policies. An enterprise should always entertain the possibility that some other set of shareholders would value it more highly than the current shareholders if it were to adopt different policies. If so, the current shareholders would benefit from higher share prices than would ever prevail otherwise.

For illustration of this point, consider the appropriate amount of long-term debt financing. Some shareholders like to leverage the returns on their equity more than others. Financial leveraging (*gearing* to the British) means financing an investment with relatively more debt and correspondingly less equity. Because the direct costs of borrowing are somewhat less than the costs of equity capital, particularly as interest expense is tax deductible, leveraging results in higher expected rates of return on the equity. The cost of leveraging is that it results in higher risks for both equity-holders and creditors, raising costs of both debt and equity. The higher cost of equity reflecting that additional risk is an additional, indirect cost of more debt.

The amount of leverage appropriate for an enterprise thus depends on the risk preferences of its shareholders. Many shareholders can create their own leverage through personal borrowing to purchase stocks. However, because of transaction costs, tax treatment, and risk factors, they usually cannot borrow on as favorable terms as the corporations whose shares they hold. Thus, if the equity markets are shifting toward more willingness to assume risks, the effect is much the same as if equity investors perceived less investment risk. In this situation, some corporations should find it advantageous to shift toward higher leverage, attracting new shareholders at higher prices.

Somewhat the same ideas apply to dividend payout policies. Corporations are perhaps more sensitive today than in the past to the double taxation of dividends paid to personal investors. They therefore tend to defer dividends by reinvesting more earnings. Nevertheless, no such tax penalty arises for dividends paid to retirement funds, which may therefore have different sets of preferences.

These observations suggest possibilities for a substantial amount of fine-tuning of corporate financial policies. They nevertheless are the stuff of theory. To the extent that corporations actually are sensitive to these issues, it is likely to be unconscious. In time, however, competition for funding should gradually increase those financial sensitivities and bring these issues into sharper focus.

The Private Sector and Government

Corporations spend enormous sums on government lobbying and political contributions. One must therefore conclude that they receive at least equivalent value in return. Much of that value, it seems, is in preserving an established status quo—it is essentially defensive. Thus, independent insurance agents and institutional investors fought for years to prevent incursions into their business by banks, which face stagnation in much of their traditional business. Tobacco companies continue to fight vigorously to prevent further government restrictions on sales of their products. The potential rewards from such efforts are often no more than reducing and postponing losses.

In some cases, entry into some new activity requires government approval. Usually the rewards, if any, will be temporary—economic profit that will erode with competition. Longer-term profits may occasionally arise from natural monopolies, which are situations where cost economies of scale preclude competitors. For example, restrictions on bank branching that were common for many years surely reduced competition in financial services in many remote rural communities. For the most part in the United States, however, government regulation prevents market exploitation by natural monopolies.

Government collaboration in maintaining monopolies is, indeed, normally the only means by which a corporation can continue to exercise substantial market power. One way or another, it is sustainable only by preventing entry into a business by rivals. In the United States, at least, monopolies are for the most part politically unacceptable. Many cases of remaining government involvement tend to arise from agreements with other countries, an example being ocean freight cartels. Looking abroad, the days of the great monopoly trading companies, such as the East India Company, are long gone, although many less developed countries tend to be lenient toward monopoly practices.

Price supports, subsidies, and special tax benefits do not have the same effect as restrictions on market entry. Without such restrictions, competition will erode the direct benefits. The public at large continues, of course, to bear the ultimate costs, whether as higher prices or taxes or as reductions in government services.

Management at a Crossroads

To describe the present business climate as primarily a relationship economy obviously does not mean full understanding or effective management of economic relationships. As long as any divergence exists between shareholder objectives and management incentives, corporate decision criteria will diverge, often haphazardly, from value principles. The consequence must be that even with a general, essentially qualitative, appreciation of the idea that internal and external economic relationships are important, the basis for rigorously seeking to maximize relationship values will be lacking. As corporations make inefficient and ineffective uses of their resources, so also does society at large. For society as a whole, the sharp contrast between national prosperity before and after 1940 should illustrate how far an economy can slip behind its true potential.

Today, however, the resulting condition is not a status quo representing suboptimal satisficing. Gradually, a few enterprises are taking a closer look at applying value principles to economic relationships. They are slowly learning to manage those relationships more effectively. As that process gathers momentum, a few will break out ahead of their rivals and join forces with the world's emerging entrepreneurs. Laggards will join the debris littering the corporate landscape. Many of today's corporate directors and chief executives are running out of time to decide which way they will turn.

One might be tempted to suggest that this seemingly dismal view is at odds with an economy that seems again to have become the world's most powerful engine of prosperity. That characteristic in itself should be a major cause of concern. One lesson of the past generation is that in the United States, at least, individual corporations, including their directors and managements, are altogether expendable. In an openly competitive economic society where capital is highly mobile, ample replacements are always at hand to shove the corporate sluggards aside.

PART 4

Modern Foundations for Strategies and Decisions

Though economic analysis and general reasoning are of wide application, yet every age and every country has its own problems; and every change in social conditions is likely to require a new development of economic doctrines.

Alfred Marshall, *Principles of Economics* (1890)

CHAPTER 12

Value Elements in Financial Decisions

RECOGNIZING UNDERLYING VALUE ELEMENTS

Recognition of intangible sources of value, and particularly of the significance of relationship assets and capital, initially emerged from analyzing deals—mergers, acquisitions, and major purchases and divestitures of assets. Relationship assets initially attracted attention because of the possibilities for amortizing them for tax purposes. Value nevertheless is not something that sits in a vacuum defined by tax law. What quickly became obvious was that values of relationship assets explained much, if not all, of the purchase premiums in acquisitions of service and publishing enterprises.

Thus, a useful transition from managing underlying components of enterprise value to developing value-based corporate strategies is to examine transaction values, particularly as they arise in business combinations. To engage in a business combination should be an expression of a corporation's overall strategy. If it is not entirely consistent with existing strategy, that strategy requires reconsideration. Moreover, a business combination should represent strategic considerations driven by shareholder interests and thus by value criteria.

Business combinations tend to be of interest if only because of the large amount of current merger and acquisition activity. They have become a popular method of at least appearing to cope with economic change. Perhaps they sometimes serve as substitutes for, rather than expressions of, corporate strategies. In any event, widespread fascination with mergers and acquisitions may attract more attention to the relationships and other intangibles they involve.

Acquisition and divestiture analysis should begin with the same value concepts as those forming the foundation for management decision making and strategy development. It nevertheless involves some special considerations in a relationship environment. As adapted to evaluating business combinations, this analysis applies as well to valuing corporate stocks.

Any acquisition, merger, or divestiture represents an exchange of assets, and perhaps liabilities as well. An acquirer may make payment by issuing liabilities to a seller, whereby they become assets of the seller. Also, an acquirer may assume liabilities of the seller, for which it would receive additional assets as compensation. Cash, as in a sale, or an equity position in the other party to a transaction, are therefore only two of a number of possible forms of consideration.

The assets in a sale may be an entire enterprise. Alternatively, in the case of a divestiture by a surviving enterprise, the sale may include only selected assets, perhaps as sales of some business units. Common examples of the latter are selected publications, retail outlets, and business divisions.

The relevant issue should always be the value received relative to the value conveyed, regardless of the form of the transaction. Value considerations nevertheless often seem to enter into acquisitions and divestitures only rather haphazardly. Very rarely do either acquirers or sellers actually try to analyze the underlying sources of value directly.

Chapter 6 briefly described various approaches to enterprise valuation. The most direct method, and the most meaningful in many cases, is to analyze the prices at which a corporation's stock has traded. Those prices nevertheless tend to be distorted simply because the market is reacting to imperfect and inadequate information. On average, stocks trade at prices lower than would prevail if investors had access to more accurate information. Stocks that trade infrequently tend especially to have lower prices because of buyer concerns about being able to sell them later and because they attract less attention from stock analysts.

Otherwise, the most common method of analysis, and the starting point for most acquisition analyses, is to rely on earnings and price multiples of those earnings. An earnings analysis is usually the first step even for asset transactions involving business units as well as entire corporations. Indeed, discounted cash flow valuations of going concerns rely primarily on conventional earnings measures. The distortions in conventional financial reporting due to the omission of most intangible assets thus carry over into merger and acquisition analysis. Because of both their relative importance and their invisibility, the problems arising from neglecting underlying value components are likely to be particularly acute in a relationship environment.

Valuing businesses on the basis of their net asset value becomes especially useful when either observable earnings performance clearly is unrepresentative of potential performance or when meaningful earnings measures simply are unavailable. Apart from being distorted measures of value, current earnings may also be distorted measures of longer-term earnings. Sales of individual assets or selected business units are common examples of cases in which meaningful earnings measures are often unavailable. Attempts to conform these situations to conventional earnings analysis can yield bizarre results when earnings data, however meaningful otherwise, simply have no predictive value.

Impulses for Doing Deals

An enterprise seeking some form of restructuring of its business may do so relatively gradually by de novo means—investing directly in means of production and distribution. Examples include opening new outlets or closing old ones, changing product mix, or shifting marketing focus. Acquisitions and divestitures often provide more dramatic examples. Expansion by acquisition is often more advantageous than de novo expansion. With an acquisition, the acquirer normally obtains information about the markets it is entering. Moreover, expanding de novo injects more competitors into a market, whereas the number of competitors remains the same or declines with an acquisition.

Acquisitions generally avoid the initial losses that often occur with de novo market entry. Particularly in cases of geographic expansion, but sometimes also with new products and services, attracting a critical mass of customers is necessary to break even. Acquisition premiums are simply substitutes for these initial losses to the extent they represent investment in building relationships for the longer term. Contraction by sales of assets or by seeking acquisition similarly tends to be preferable to simply withdrawing from a market. Asset sales often provide opportunities to recover at least some of the relationship values that market withdrawal would otherwise abandon.

At least in theory, an enterprise on a path to decline should consider either major restructuring, possibly by divestiture or even liquidation, or looking for an acquirer. The issue confronting it is how to salvage the greatest possible value from its assets, including its relationship assets. Often, however, floundering businesses waste or trash much of their underlying value before their directors and senior executives fully comprehend its circumstances. One challenge for potential acquirers is to identify how to salvage value from situations already in advanced stages of deterioration.

Most businesses can expect eventually, in order to confront opportunities or needs, to be a party to some sort of business combination. Possibilities include:

- Acquiring other enterprises, perhaps as part of a deliberate expansion strategy, or possibly because acquisitions become available as bargains. Prospective acquisition targets may not really understand the values of what they are selling or how to realize those values in the marketplace.
- Purchasing assets, for essentially the same reasons as acquiring other corporations. This category of possibilities can include every type of acquisition short of acquiring an entire enterprise. Opportunities may arise as others divest assets to emphasize their core competencies.
- Combinations among equals. Businesses sometimes perceive a future in combining with other enterprises of similar size. The concept often seems appealing because no party to the transaction is a buyer or seller. In reality, one party is likely to assume dominance. An ostensible objective of many recent combinations of this type has been to achieve cost economies.
- Divesting assets by sale to others. For enterprises confronting declining markets, asset sales may be the most effective method of downsizing and refocusing their businesses.
- Absorption by acquisition or merger. This situation occurs with the absorption of an enterprise into a significantly larger one, essentially losing its identity. This route may be the only available escape for enterprises in advanced stages of deterioration.

Individual corporations may pursue two or even more of these possibilities simultaneously. Nevertheless, they typically focus either on an expansion or on a contraction path, but not both. Although they might sometimes make sense as a means of strategic repositioning, simultaneous programs of acquisition in some markets divestiture in others seem uncommon. Whatever the program or the reasoning behind it, its success will depend on its strategic relevance. Even a bargain purchase can be a mistake in the absence of a strategic fit. A particular problem in acquisitions of declining enterprises is that realizing their potential often absorbs unexpectedly high levels of management attention.

The incentives that give rise to these activities differ considerably, which helps to explain the wide variations in how transactions occur and in transaction terms. Reasons such activities take place include, but surely are not limited to:

- Strategic responses to opportunities or needs to reconfigure market positions by acquisition or divestiture. They imply the formulation of a program prior to seeking out specific transaction possibilities.
- Unplanned opportunities, such as unsolicited acquisition offers or acquisition targets offered unexpectedly for sale on attractive terms.
- Personal circumstances and contacts, in which chief executives of different corporations perceive benefits, whether to shareholders or to themselves, from combinations.
- Approaching retirements of chief executives, particularly in the absence of arrangements for succession.
- Capital deficiencies, perhaps resulting from growth opportunities outstripping the willingness of the financial markets to provide the necessary funding.
- Opportunities to reduce competition. Although antitrust laws normally severely restrict these opportunities, enforcement of those restrictions tends to be less in declining industries.

Many business combinations in recent years have sought to achieve cost economies from larger size or by eliminating redundant facilities or activities. Opportunities to consolidate branch facilities, for example, have driven much of the wave of consolidation in banking. Unplanned opportunities and opportunities arising from personal contacts may or may not fall into place in some previously developed strategy. When they do not, the risks that the benefits of a transaction will ultimately be disappointing are much higher. Many transactions fall into this category, and many clearly fail to work out as expected.

Although personalities may play significant roles in giving rise to transactions, they can also scuttle otherwise mutually beneficial ones. Situations occasionally arise when there is agreement on transaction terms and virtually everything else except who is to be the chief executive. Here, too, shareholder interests may sometimes be constraints on how far chief executives can promote their individual best interests.

Once the possibility of a transaction begins to develop, and occasionally even before, a variety of different players may get into the act:

- Senior executives who are prospective parties to a transaction. In addition to exercising their management responsibilities, some executives may believe themselves capable of acting as their own financial advisors.
- Investment bankers and other financial advisors. Investment bankers at least give the appearance of promoting the best price for their clients, however much they want to complete a transaction, and they provide a useful buffer in negotiating transaction terms.
- Public accountants acting as financial advisors, particularly as they seek new ways to broaden their range of services and to obtain new flexibility in fee structures.

Form sometimes competes with substance for priority. Virtually all of these players rely on the same types of financial analysis and market data. Also rather standardized is the manner of providing information to prospective acquirers and conducting purchase investigations. Similarly, as captives of conventional accounting standards, most share the same deficiencies in understanding relationship values and how they contribute to enterprise values. They nevertheless obtain comfort in following conventional procedures. Indeed, fairness opinions, or comfort letters, themselves rely substantially on form, the supporting analysis often being rather superficial. Financial advice may also exploit disparities between management and shareholder interests. Advisors may furthermore tend to favor clients that will continue as going concerns over those that will not. Each assignment offers opportunities to extend contacts for the future on the other side of the market.

Pretense aside, no adequate substitute exists for a corporate management's own understanding of the value characteristics of its business, including the underlying components of that value. Apart from any conflicting interests, outside experts do not generally have access to the information necessary to value a relationship business. For the present, at least, if management provided them with that information, it would probably also need to provide assistance in interpreting it. In general, a seller that fails to understand fully the underlying value components of its business will encounter more difficulty obtaining a fair price. A buyer without a thorough understanding of both its own and the seller's value components will surely encounter difficulty in trying to integrate them.

Most financial advisors today have little or no expertise in valuing relationship capital. On the other hand, value-based management—the development of value-based strategies and the adoption of value criteria for decision making—assumes management understanding of those value elements. Again, how can one truly manage a business otherwise?

Acquisitions and Purchases

The most widespread deficiency in analyzing prospective acquisitions and purchases is giving insufficient attention to relationship values. To be sure, the information that sellers and their financial advisors provide is typically deficient, but prospective acquirers certainly can and should do much more analysis of these assets than is now common. Failure to do so is to forfeit a useful and potentially important technique of financial analysis—net asset valuation—and to impart a superficial quality to many purchase, or due diligence, investigations. Indeed, preacquisition analysis of prospective acquisitions is often little more than a review of conventional accounting information, often undertaken by outside public accountants.

Actually, the purpose of a due diligence investigation has two rather different interpretations. One is that the investigation is primarily an audit to ensure the integrity of the financial reports. To that extent it may have little direct relevance to the values involved in the proposed combination. A more enlightened view is that the purpose of due diligence is to identify directly those value elements.

Adopting the second interpretation, a due diligence investigation in a relationship marketplace should most certainly seek, within reason, to acquire information about the value attributes of the intangible as well as tangible assets. A few cases have arisen of inducing sellers to provide sufficient information to analyze their customer relationships, including data for customer longevity projections. Instances of so much as requesting that sort of information are nevertheless rare. Even when it is not obtainable as such, acquirers are surely remiss to the extent they fail to seek other information of a more qualitative nature. For example:

- What products and services contribute directly to the value of the enterprise, and which ones serve only to attract other value-contributing customer relationships?
- What are the scope and quality of customer information that will be transferred to the acquiring enterprise? How useful will that information be for later decision making? Can it distinguish value-contributing customers from others? Is it useful in identifying opportunities to reinforce value-contributing relationships? How much investment will be necessary to upgrade customer information to the acquirer's standards?
- How has the seller made decisions on service offerings and pricing? Has it targeted particular types of customers? How has it used such information as is available?
- How did the seller attract its existing base of customer relationships? What does that indicate about the strength and durability of those relationships? How sensitive are those relationships to competition? Has the seller attempted to enrich those relationships with more services or other means of extending relationship lives?
- What information can the seller provide by which to assess and project customer relationship attrition characteristics? Is it possible to sample customer longevity data by which to make such assessments?
- What are the opportunities for enhancing the values of these customer relationships, as by extending their lives and by sale of more value-contributing products and services? How much investment would enrichment programs require?
- What special sources of value exist internally? Do the managers and employees of the seller have special skills that would be of value to the buyer? Does the enterprise have a corporate culture that enables it to do things more efficiently and effectively? Would these various value attributes actually transfer to the buyer?
- Is the particular buyer in the best position among competing buyers to realize the values of the sellers' intangibles? If some

other, competing buyer is better positioned in this respect, should others drop out of the bidding?

Interviews of marketing executives are often particularly useful in pursuing lines of inquiry pertaining to customer relationships. In cases of commercial and industrial customers, interviews with some of those customers would be appropriate. For retail customers, the availability of customer and market information is especially important to a prospective acquirer, as it sets the limits on the range of alternatives available after acquisition.

Focusing on an acquirer's concerns should not detract from the significance to a seller, or target, of essentially these same issues. A management seeking the best possible terms on behalf of its shareholders should normally try to direct prospective buyers' attention to the underlying value elements. One reason, even if the value attributes are weak, is that opening them up to inspection serves to dispel buyer uncertainty. Typically, with all else remaining the same, buyers will pay more the greater the available amount of relevant information. Instances actually have occurred when buyers have paid unusually high prices when sellers have highlighted their hidden value components representing relationship intangibles.

Combinations for Stock

Many business combinations take place through exchanges of stock, often but not necessarily as poolings of interest. Transactions of this type are especially popular when the prices of the shares of the acquirer are relatively high. In some cases, an active acquisition program tends itself to boost acquirers' share prices, adding more momentum to the program. Acquisitions for stock also are popular as a means of deferring taxes on capital gains of the acquired corporation's shareholders.

Poolings of interest are of particular interest here because of the manner in which they take account (or, more accurately, fail to take account) of the intangible capital. In contrast to a purchase, all assets and liabilities in a pooling retain their pretransaction book values for financial reporting. To the extent that intangible assets are invisible prior to a pooling, they remain so throughout the process. Poolings are popular with acquirers because they avoid the necessity of amortizing the goodwill and other intangible assets they acquire, with the consequent reduction in reported earnings. As poolings of interest are subject to strict and complicated rules, many acquisitions for stock do not qualify for this accounting treatment.

The primary method of analyzing combinations through exchanges of stock is to focus on dilutions in the earnings and net worth of the respective parties. The more stock an acquirer pays for an acquisition, the larger the claim of the seller's shareholders on the acquirer's earnings, assets, and net worth. The effect on the seller's shareholders is a corresponding dilution (reduction) in their claim on earnings and net worth. Thus, for example, financial advisors might regard a reduction in the earnings per share—the earnings dilution—of the acquirer as acceptable if expected earnings growth will restore that dilution within some specified period of time. A common rule of thumb is that dilution effects should dissipate within two or three years.

A frequent problem with focusing on the dilution effects of a merger is that it is difficult to formulate meaningful standards of what should or should not be acceptable. Comparisons of earnings and, better yet, cash flows are likely to be much more meaningful than balance sheet comparisons. Even they can be substantially misleading, however, particularly if the respective partners have significantly different customer characteristics. A focus on net asset values, including intangibles, provides a much more precise as well as more meaningful way to analyze values in acquisitions for stock. In particular, dilution may simply reflect real elements of value conveying in a combination. If dilution does not do so, something may be awry with the transaction terms.

Bank mergers are perhaps especially appropriate for illustrating the application of value principles to combinations for stock. Horizontal mergers—combinations of relatively similar enterprises—have probably been more common in banking than any other type of business. Understand, however, that analyses of relationship intangibles have typically not been any more a part of the merger drill in banking than elsewhere.

If two banks, A and B, are exactly alike in every respect including size, neither should experience any dilution whatever in their earnings or net worth if they decide to merge. Suppose, however, that they are exactly alike except that A is nine times larger than B. In a competitive market for business combinations, the owners of B should end up with 10 percent of the combined enterprise, including a 10 percent stake in its net worth and earnings. A correspondingly should end up with a 90 percent stake. Again, neither party should experience any dilution. Of course, A's larger size could mean other differences that the transaction terms might take into account, such as ability to achieve greater cost economies.

Analyzing these sorts of business combinations in terms of net asset values, including relationship capital, becomes potentially much more important when the respective parties are quite dissimilar beyond differences in size. This analysis is essentially the same as analyzing an acquisition by purchase except that it extends to both partners. Thus, suppose that *A* proposes to merge with *B,* and that all the intangible assets in both cases resulted from internal investment and are therefore hidden—they are unrecorded assets and thus do not actually appear in net worth. Assume the following characteristics, with the intangible assets in brackets to emphasize that they would not appear on either partner's balance sheet:

	A	*B*
Assets		
Tangible	$20,000	$5,000
[*Intangible*	*1,000*	*500*]
Liabilities	$8,500	$4,625
Net Worth		
Tangible (Book)	$1,500	$ 375
[*Intangible*	*1,000*	*500*]
Net Asset Value	$2,500	$ 875
Number of shares	100	
Net income	$200	$60
Net income per share	$2.00/share	
Share price	$20/share	
Ratio of earnings to:		
Tangible assets	1.0%	1.2%
Book net worth	13.33%	16.00%
Net asset value	8.00%	6.86%

For present purposes, the significant difference is not *A*'s larger size; rather, it lies in *B*'s much higher ratio of intangible to total assets and capital, presumably representing a richer base of customer relationships. *B* therefore has a slightly higher ratio of earnings to tangible assets and book net worth. Yet, because of larger size and higher efficiency, *A* has a higher ratio of earnings to net asset value.

If *A* offers *B* 35 shares of *A* (newly issued for the merger), the combined corporation will have 135 outstanding shares. At *A*'s current share price, the offer is equivalent to $700, representing a premium of $325. B's shareholders would receive 35 ÷ 135 = 25.93 percent of the combined entity, in which case their stake in the combined net asset value would be $875, which is exactly what they contributed. From this perspective, the terms of the transaction seem entirely fair and reasonable.

Nevertheless, offering conventional advice, A's investment bankers might raise some doubts by observing that:

- A's earnings per share fall to ($200 + $60) ÷ 135 = $1.93 rather than the prior $2.00.
- B's earnings per share rise to 35 × $1.93 = $67.55 rather than the prior $60.00.
- A's tangible net worth per share falls to ($1,500 + $375) ÷ 135 = $13.89 rather than its prior $15.00.
- B's share of the tangible net worth rises to 35 × $13.89 = $486.15 rather than $375.00.

The conventional conclusion would be that A's shareholders would have significant earnings and book net worth dilution as a result of a combination on these terms. Perhaps, then, the investment bankers would advise A to accept the deal only if it expects sufficient improvement in earnings over the ensuing two to three years, either from growth or from additional economies due to the merger. Such advice would be wrong. In value terms, the transaction is an entirely equitable one—neither party loses any value if nothing further happens. Cost economies of larger scale nevertheless hold forth the prospect of increasing cash flows from the richer relationship base of the smaller partner, to the subsequent benefit of both.

The common concept of dilution is that it affects the larger partner to a merger unless the partners are of similar size. If, as suggested, earnings and net worth dilution occur from mismatches in the underlying relationship or other intangible values, might a much smaller partner experience the dilution instead? The answer is that if the merger terms are competitive and reflect the actual net enterprise values in the exchange, smaller partners to altogether equitable and reasonable combinations indeed can experience dilution in earnings and book net worth.

Why is this pattern seldom evident in the real world? One reason may be that the conventional wisdom of the marketplace is that smaller partners should expect premiums upon merging. Significant premiums obviously are routine in purchases of relationship businesses, so surely exchanges of stock similarly should include premiums. In the latter case, however, a premium is invisible. The investment community has therefore adopted dilution measures, which are observable, as proxies for premiums.

Here is a demonstration of the widespread lack of understanding of the value elements underlying acquisition premiums. Because of that lack of understanding, some absorptions must be detrimental to the shareholders of the larger partners to stock transactions. Management incentives to expand may induce payments of hidden premiums without their shareholders receiving commensurate value in return. A problem for shareholders is that no one, including senior executives and their directors, is likely ever to be the wiser.

Another possible reason why premiums may sometimes be skewed the wrong way is suspicion among acquisition targets that acquirers inflate near-term earnings to boost share prices, thereby seeking to reduce the dilutions they incur. Targets who are aware of this perhaps transparent strategy should respond by demanding more shares. If they do, the apparent earnings dilution of acquirers would appear to be larger than otherwise. The artificially inflated share prices could thus give the appearance of premiums that do not really exist.

Special Tax Treatment of Purchased Intangibles

Purchases of intangible assets may be eligible for special tax treatment that gives rise to additional value. Although these opportunities are peculiar to U.S. tax law, they may otherwise be instructive. Beginning with the 1992 U.S. tax revisions, taxpayers can write off as amortization expenses all purchased intangibles regardless of type and including goodwill. The only allowable tax amortization is on a straight-line basis over a period of 15 years. The amortization deductions reduce taxable income and thus tax liabilities. By increasing the net cash flows the intangibles generate, tax amortization results in somewhat higher values than would prevail otherwise. In the case of DCF valuations of intangibles such as customer relationships, the effect on value is obtainable by calculating a tax shield factor that, for 15 years, is:

$$\text{Tax Shield} = \frac{15}{15 - [(\text{Tax Rate})(\text{Annuity Factor})]}$$

To illustrate, suppose the net cash flows from some purchased customer relationships have a net present value of $100. Following their purchase, the buyer will amortize them for tax purposes. The buyer's marginal effective tax rate—the tax rate applicable to any additional income—is 34 percent, and the appropriate discount factor (cost of capital) is 12 percent. A cash flow of $1 per year for 15 years (received at the midpoint of each year) has an annuity (present) value of $7.21, or an annuity factor of 7.21. The tax shield is therefore:

$$\text{Tax Shield} = \frac{15}{15 - [(.34)(7.21)]} = \frac{15}{12.55} = 1.195$$

The value of this intangible, while only $100 to the seller, becomes 1.195 × $100 = $119.50, or nearly 20 percent higher, to a buyer.

Does it really make sense that an asset can increase significantly in value simply by its sale? Does the prospect of higher value suggest that some enterprises might develop customer relationships for the express purpose of selling them to others? Might cross-sales of customer relationships be a method of building up their values? In concept, these possibilities do indeed exist, but they probably require a more efficient marketplace than now prevails to ever become entirely realistic.

Securities Analysis in a Relationship Environment

The problems confronting a potential acquirer in obtaining value information are typically even more severe for securities analysts. Furthermore, the task confronting securities analysts and investors is different insofar as it normally requires judgments about enterprise direction and management capabilities. An acquirer, on the other hand, may look toward changing management and direction, and assess the target's value potential in those terms.

A general principle of financial analysis when information is imperfect is to use as many approaches as are available. In addition to the more conventional analytical techniques reviewed in chapter 6, an analyst might consider two supplementary approaches:

- Probing various qualitative issues that shed light on the direction and management of the enterprise.
- Examining the enterprise in light of the potential customer relationship values in the markets where it competes.

The feasibility of the second of these approaches varies widely according to the nature of the marketplace, although it need not imply actual valuation of market potential. For example, an analyst might be able to determine that the lives of subscriber relationships for some publication are unusually short, suggesting lower value. A next step might be to investigate why customer loyalty is relatively low or high. In other cases, an analyst might observe that the types of services customers are buying tend to contribute less or more value than is typical of the industry. Generalization on this point is obviously impossible, as its application depends so heavily on the nature of the particular business. The main point is that an understanding of relationship value characteristics opens up new dimensions of inquiry.

More general principles apply to assessments of management and direction. Earlier discussion suggests such topics as the following for analysts and, to the extent possible, for all investors to explore:

- Does management have a clear understanding of the limitations of GAAP financial data as a basis for decisions?
- How well does management understand the sources of value of its business? In particular, does it have a firm grasp of the nature and significance of its relationship and other intangible assets?
- Does the enterprise have information systems that enable value-based decisions, including with respect to investment in relationship and other intangible assets?
- Does the enterprise appear to have a well-defined sense of strategic direction? To what extent does it reflect shareholder value objectives?
- How does the enterprise respond to change? Is it essentially reactive or does it anticipate change?
- How forthcoming and forthright are the enterprise's communications with the financial community?
- How independent is the board of directors of the enterprise? Are the directors both able and willing to exercise their oversight responsibilities?
- What are the incentives that guide the behavior of the enterprise's senior executives, and how consistent are they with shareholders' objectives?
- What are the general strength and durability of the enterprise's relationships with customers? How does it go about enriching those relationships?
- To what extent do the enterprise's internal relationships and culture add to its competitive vitality?

- How do the employees of the enterprise view its leadership and sense of strategic direction?
- Defining leadership to include inspiring others to want to follow, what is the quality of the leadership of the enterprise?
- How does the enterprise regard creativity and criticism? Is it trapped in the box, or does it encourage out-of-the-box thinking?
- If the enterprise has engaged, or is about to engage, in a major restructuring, why, and what does it imply about direction and management?

Many of these issues seem to be what financial professionals have in mind, if only implicitly, when they talk about the quality of earnings. The very idea of earnings quality is itself an open admission that the reported numbers themselves are inadequate measures of financial performance.

A Qualitative Dimension to Capital?

Why not, then, correspondingly consider capital in terms of its qualitative dimensions? *Capital* has two rather different, but both legitimate, definitions:

- Real capital as those factors of production that result from saving and real investment.
- Capital as a financial cushion that protects an enterprise's creditors.

The first economic definition refers to any asset that adds to future output, and should require no further comment.

The second definition requires clarification. One interpretation is that capital is what would remain if a business failed with retirement of all its debt. The greater the amount of capital in this sense, the more assurance creditors have of repayment. This interpretation, while fairly common, is usually not very useful. Once a business approaches insolvency, the likelihood of full debt repayment is probably remote. A more meaningful view in most instances is within the context of a going concern: Capital represents the capacity of the enterprise to generate cash inflows after operating expenses, or net receipts, over and above what is necessary to service debt. It is in this sense that an excess of income-producing assets over liabilities is most important. Notice that whether as a liquidation value or as income capacity, capital in the second definition is unrelated to any particular set or type of assets.

Obviously, both definitions of capital are somewhat removed from the net worth appearing on a corporate balance sheet. Both, moreover, must include relationship assets and other intangibles to the extent they represent capacity for generating income. In other words, the inclusion of intangibles in the second definition follows directly from their inclusion in the first, as both pertain to their capacity for generating future income.

13

Confronting the Relationship Environment

DEVELOPING STRATEGIC OBJECTIVES

The economists' concept of a short run implies fixed production capacity and product offerings. In the corresponding long run, however, every aspect of the production and distribution process—*what* to produce, *how* to produce it, and *for whom* to produce it—can vary. The long run allows for investment in new capacity, products, and services by redirecting facilities, equipment, and personnel to entirely different uses, or perhaps simply by reducing capacity. The purpose of developing a business strategy is to anticipate and, to the extent possible, to control that economic long run. Strategic decisions therefore are those decisions pertaining to realignments of capacity and products to respond to changing market opportunities. A strategic horizon thus extends at least as far into the future as the outcomes of today's decisions.

Essentially the same significance attaches to focusing on the long run with what may be a more familiar strategic formulation. While it leads to the same issues as the foregoing formulation, it defines a strategy as addressing the following issues:

- Where do we want to go, and why?
- Where can we realistically go, and when?
- How can we best get there?

An enterprise lacking a firm concept of its ultimate destination can easily stray in a wrong direction, perhaps forfeiting any chance of ever reaching it. It will have drifted out of control, like a ship with a damaged rudder.

However formulated, developing a business strategy must be a continuing as well as an incremental process. It is in part a constant process of responding to unanticipated as well as anticipated changes in the economic environment. Consider an enterprise embarking on a major reinvention of itself, perhaps because it has adjusted inadequately in the past. However urgent the restructuring, it probably should not try jumping all at once from one configuration to an altogether different one, regardless of reengineering theories. At least one reason is that it probably cannot fully determine what its new configuration ought to be in a single step. It simply is unlikely to have all the necessary resources, including enough information, to identify and assess any configuration that is very different from its current one.

Developing a business strategy first requires defining objectives. To reemphasize, that means accepting above all the proposition that the paramount corporate objective must be to maximize the value of the shareholders' investment in the enterprise. Of course, setting that objective means uniformly pursuing it, undeterred by the likely reality that it will elude full achievement.

With proper care in setting priorities and assuring consistency among them, setting additional objectives may promote the primary one. Setting aside notions of other stakeholder claims, other objectives might usefully focus on developing value elements that contribute to the total enterprise value. In other words, defining additional objectives can impart additional precision to pursuit of the ultimate objective. Implicitly, if not otherwise, such secondary objectives represent or require underlying investment decisions. Simply to convey the gist of this point, a few among many possibilities are:

- Achieving a better public image of the enterprise by involvement in community, cultural, and charitable activities, commitment to environmental programs, and use of institutional advertising.
- Upgrading the education and training of employees, perhaps including programs to assist them in assuming decision-making responsibilities and dealing more effectively with customers.
- Achieving a better image in the investment community by in-

creasing and improving the information available to shareholders and financial analysts.

- Committing to adopting a more anticipatory posture in dealing with economic change, implying a commitment to developing more effective business strategies.

Secondary objectives are likely to represent implementation of prior decisions. The phrasing of the above possibilities suggests recognition of deficiencies requiring remedy by investing more heavily in certain areas or activities. Perfectly legitimate objectives might be simply to maintain or even to reduce certain commitments. One might, for example, set as a secondary objective maintaining employee turnover at current levels. Another might be orderly withdrawal from certain markets whose potential has declined. Meeting that objective without undue loss of value could require a number of decisions stretching well into the future.

An additional point to notice in considering these possibilities is the extent to which they reflect relationship issues. Indeed, this characteristic seems to apply to many corporate statements of objectives and mission, however unconsciously. Normally, of course, they reflect little or no recognition of the investment and capital characteristics of economic relationships.

Corporate Commitments to Developing Strategies

An immediate concern among financial analysts should be whether or not a corporation truly has a well-defined business strategy. An enterprise lacking a firm sense of direction and destination will surely waste resources and squander shareholder capital. The mere existence of a strategic planning process is insufficient for comfort, however. Some common shortcomings are:

- Even with a current strategy, earlier inattention to strategic issues may have caused the enterprise to fall substantially out of alignment with the current external technological and market environment. Corporate reinvention may not even be a positive step relative to other remaining alternatives, such as dismemberment or acquisition.
- Even the best-intentioned strategy development programs will flounder if they lack the full commitment, involvement, and leadership of a corporation's directors and top management.

Internal strategic planners may facilitate the process at a staff level, but they cannot have ultimate responsibility for implementing it effectively.

- Confidence in outside strategy consultants is too frequently misplaced. They can in no case substitute for an internal strategic planning program. Many have little or no true strategic vision. Few consultants look beyond earnings to enterprise values, recognize the investment nature of market relationships, or fully understand the shortcomings of conventional accounting measures.

- The level of investment in the process of developing and implementing a strategy may fall short of what is necessary to keep pace with the growing complexity of the marketplace, including the increasing heterogeneity of competing products and services.

Particularly for enterprises that are faltering, reducing investment in strategy development is a tempting way to cut reported expenses.

A corporate strategy is not something that is ready-made for near-term delivery. Strategic planning has a long history of falling along the wayside and into disrepute because of insufficient management involvement. One common problem has been misunderstanding of the purpose of the process. Another has been reluctance to invest in developing the information and analysis necessary to implement meaningful strategies. Without the necessary commitments, a strategy can have no operative significance.

Effective strategic planning may not require that senior management itself has an initial sense of strategic direction. Conceptually, chief executives can develop strategic visions by drawing on the ideas of subordinates and outsiders. To be effective, however, strategy development does require that chief executives recognize its importance, even if it means coming to terms with their own deficiencies. It furthermore requires those chief executives to exercise leadership in developing and executing strategies. Recall that the supreme Allied command of the Normandy invasion was intimately involved from beginning to end both in developing the strategy and in implementing it.

Strategy development is essentially a process of defining the enterprise—what it is and where it is going. As such, it is both decision making of the highest order and investment in improving decision making at all levels. The payoffs, or rewards, from investing in strategy development ultimately are measurable directly in terms of additional enterprise values. In other words, the criteria for determining how and how much to invest in developing a business strategy are the same as for any other form of real investment.

Defining the Enterprise

From the outset, part of an ongoing strategic planning process must be defining, with ever-increasing precision, the external and internal circumstances of the enterprise relative to its environment. Its strategic options are essentially a process of gradually pushing out from its current position to something else. Diagrammatically, suppose the innermost (solid) circle, A, represents a composite of the current characteristics of the business, including the various resources it currently has in place.

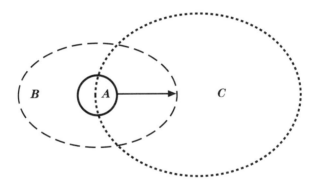

Developing New Opportunity Frontiers.

The larger area depicted by B (the broken line) represents a current opportunity frontier. It encompasses the range of characteristics that the enterprise could assume over some defined period of time, such as the next year. It derives from a variety of strategic directions that the enterprise could adopt today. The further the enterprise moves out beyond A into B, the more its resources and business are reconfigured.

By definition, the enterprise cannot take on any characteristics lying beyond B within that time period. B, for example, would include the amount of capital obtainable within that period, and thus the limits on the size of the enterprise. Those characteristics might in turn limit the cost economies achievable in that period. This opportunity frontier B reflects the fact that *how* to produce tends to be subject to substantial constraints in the short run.

The scope of B, or the size of the circle, depends on the relevant time period. More time simply means more options. Developing a strategy therefore might include considering an array of opportunity frontiers similar to B, each representing a different time horizon. The main point, however, is that whatever the time horizon, the range of possible options—the opportunity frontier—is constantly changing. Indeed, it will change virtually regardless of any course of action or inaction the enterprise adopts. New configurations of B continually emerge.

Many of the options in B will be inconsistent with one another, and capital constraints will in turn limit the number of options the enterprise can select. It must therefore select some at the exclusion of others. Suppose, then, that one option for the next year is to adopt the strategic direction indicated by the arrow in the diagram. For example, the enterprise might decide to give more emphasis to some core competency, and thus dispose of certain noncore activities. This course would open up the range of possibilities outlined by the dotted line, C. Notice that the first set of options, moving out from A to B, contains all of the characteristics in A. However, upon selecting a strategic direction, the enterprise may simply dispose of some of the characteristics in A. Thus, upon divesting noncore activities, it disposes of the capabilities and markets associated with those activities. To illustrate this possibility, C does not entirely overlap with A. Meanwhile, moving out of A into B and thus to C gets increasingly to the issues of *what* and *for whom* to produce.

Any number of different directions may be available today, each represented by an arrow similar to the one in the diagram, and each with its own set of subsequent composite characteristics of the sort depicted by C. Of course, C contains its own set of strategic options, any one of which would open up a more distant frontier of possibilities, D.

Alternatively, one of the current options is to do nothing—the arrow simply collapses inside A. In that case, C not only would collapse toward B but, with extension of the time horizon, probably would collapse to inside of B:

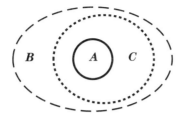

Lost Opportunities from Nonresponse.

The reason for this collapse is that in a rapidly changing economic environment, doing nothing today probably means fewer available options in the future. Certainly over the longer term, inaction becomes untenable. Eventually, inaction will cause all three of these opportunity frontiers to collapse inward with dissipation even of the resources currently in hand.

At least in the near term, however, deferring or avoiding adopting a strategic direction does not necessarily have adverse consequences. Remember that the diagrams represent current and future circumstances only as they appear today. It may be that a year from now a whole new and currently unexpected set of opportunity frontiers will develop. For the most part, they will represent unexpected changes in the external environment.

Consider the position of the enterprise relative to that external environment. What is the current configuration of its customer base, geographic representation, and product offerings? Are these current characteristics already in a process of change as a consequence of prior decisions? Recalling that quality has many dimensions, what are the directions of the business in terms of strategic options such as:

Product specialization	versus	Product diversification
Customer specialization	versus	Customer diversification
Local delivery	versus	Remote distribution
Lower costs and prices	versus	Higher quality

Internally, what resources are currently available to the business? How effective is the utilization of those resources relative to its current configuration in the marketplace? What constraints do those resources impose on its ability to reposition itself? What changes in those resources are necessary and feasible if the enterprise is to reinvent or reengineer itself? How does it define itself with respect to:

Reactivity	versus	Anticipation
Hierarchy	versus	Horizontal structure
Growth	versus	Decline
Earnings	versus	Values
Conglomeration	versus	Core focus

These sorts of contrasts are, of course, meant only to be examples. What is actually relevant will vary from case to case. Indeed, an essential part of the exercise is to determine what really is relevant.

Within any particular industry, most enterprises are likely to be rather similarly positioned. Nevertheless, as new horizons of possibilities open up with new technologies, competing successfully means constant effort to differentiate oneself from rivals. As customers demand and expect differences in goods and services that are more responsive to their expanding array of wants and needs, each customer will require more reasons for selecting individual vendors over others.

The development of business strategies is likely to be more difficult the greater the similarities among rivals, which is more likely the more homogeneous their products and services. In particular, identifying those specific strengths that give any one seller a competitive advantage is more challenging. Yet, just as customers expect and seek more variety in offerings of goods and services, new technologies continue to provide ever more opportunities for vendor innovation and differentiation.

Traditionally, a safe course in many lines of business has been simply to emulate rivals rather than to attempt being a leader in innovation. Innovations may have been easy to follow, with products and services little more than commodities. Now, with the opening of vast new technological possibilities, reassessment of this go-slow strategy may be in order. The success of a rival in setting forth on a particular course may alone be good reason for others not to follow suit. To the extent that is so, it is also an argument for setting one's own separate course. As rivals stake out their claims in increasingly differentiated markets, delay in selecting and pursuing one's own future direction may mean forfeiting the most attractive strategic alternatives. Focusing on traditional core activities may bring short-term comfort to noninnovators but be perilously retrogressive over the longer run.

A recurrent theme is the need to innovate simply as a matter of maintaining one's competitive position in a highly dynamic market environment. This characteristic of today's marketplace overlaps with and certainly extends beyond the significance of market relationships.

Competition commonly means differentiating oneself as well as, if often as a means of, attracting long-term customer relationships. To a growing degree, the rewards of innovation are not so much economic profit as the avoidance of economic loss due to being left behind.

Internal Resources for Strategy Development

Focusing on the long run means the flexibility to add and subtract internal resources, recognizing that shifts in direction cannot be instantaneous. A threshold issue is the resources required and available to make such decisions. Developing business strategies itself requires at least the following:

- Value-based systems for measuring and projecting the financial performance of the enterprise.
- A cost allocation system that properly ascribes costs to functions, products and services, and ultimately to customers, thereby:
  - Distinguishing investment outlays from current expenses.
  - Assigning outlays to outputs instead of costs to inputs.
- Customer data for identifying the value determinants and attributes of existing customer relationships.
- Market data for both current and prospective new markets to identify the value potential of customer relationships in those markets.
- Personnel with the skills necessary to analyze the foregoing financial performance, cost, customer, and market data and to identify strategic options for consideration by top management and the directors.
- Management with an understanding of strategic vision, the dedication to pursue enterprise value objectives, and the ability to identify future directions and to manage change.
- Directors who share that sense of strategic vision, who respect their fiduciary responsibility for shareholder value objectives, and who understand and hold managers accountable for achieving those objectives.

If they were to take inventory of their internal resources today, many corporations would surely find themselves short in at least some of these respects. Notice, in particular, the demands that this process imposes on the skills and experience of middle management and employees as well as on the leadership of top management.

Assessing Market Potential

What and *for whom* should the enterprise produce and distribute? Within the constraints of available technology, the marketplace ultimately drives a business strategy. The objective is a continuing process of positioning an enterprise within the changing marketplace to its best advantage as measured by net asset values and thus by shareholder value. Understanding, and indeed anticipating, the market environment therefore becomes at least as important as understanding emerging technological possibilities.

A market environment consists of many individual markets. One concept of a market is a group of similar customers, potential as well as actual. It is often useful to aggregate groups of customers in this sense by somewhat broader characteristics, as represented by product or geographic markets. This view is consistent with the economists' definition of a market simply as the existence of a price.

Assessing the value potential of markets is necessary for identifying alternatives for entry or expansion, whether de novo or by acquisition, or for contraction or withdrawal, whether by divestiture or abandonment. Chapter 12 suggested that contraction and withdrawal may be important alternatives. Repositioning may mean pulling back from some markets even while expanding in others. Withdrawal ideally would be by selling assets at their full values, but this is unlikely to be achievable if the enterprise overlooks its potential or resists it while values deteriorate.

Market research is an indispensable predicate for decision making and strategy development. Many businesses have been perilously remiss in developing and analyzing market information, perhaps again due to viewing the necessary outlays as expense instead of investment. The more customization of products and services the marketplace demands and expects, the more the required investment in compiling and analyzing such information. Evaluating market potential in a relationship environment obviously requires using such techniques as are available for valuing customer relationships, although the same level of detail available to evaluate one's current customers may not be possible.

Performance Assessment

How should the enterprise go about producing and distributing its wares? Developing business strategies also means assessing the internal capabilities and current performance of the enterprise. Indeed, how can it expect to succeed in developing and implementing new strategies unless it is properly managing its existing business? Self-assessment may result in improving the performance of some elements of the business while indicating abandonment of others.

A value-based performance assessment should begin with an assessment of management effectiveness, as outlined in Chapter 11. An extension of that concept involves three steps:

1. A threshold question is the attractiveness of the various markets in which the enterprise already competes from the perspective of possible expansion or contraction. The objective is to assess the value characteristics of the relationship base of each market and how they may be changing.
2. Secondly, assess the market shares of the enterprise as measured in relationship value terms. Is it succeeding in attracting at least a proportionate share of the new customer relationships in each market? If not, what does that suggest about the approach being taken by management to that marketplace?
3. Thirdly, compare the net asset value that the enterprise draws from these markets with the enterprise value implied by current earnings and cash flows. If the net asset value, representing the accumulated investment, is significantly higher than that implied by other valuation approaches, the enterprise probably is not obtaining value commensurate with its resources.

This sort of performance assessment can highlight good performance and opportunities that otherwise may be overlooked. Commonly used profit measures of performance tend to penalize business units that are investing heavily in developing customer relationships by treating those investments as current expenses. The penalty thus imposed is more severe the higher the growth in the customer base of these units. Growth can be misleading, however. It is truly meaningful only in the context of the growth in market potential. A rapidly growing unit may be an underperformer in the sense of lagging behind its market. The same may be true for an entire corporation.

Growth in market share itself may be misleading as well, as the true objective should be in terms of growth in values. Thus, at least in some cases, the recent emphasis of the corporate community on revenue growth may be misplaced. One unit may be growing at a modest rate but developing more relationship premium value than another unit that is growing more rapidly. For example, the slower-growing unit may be attracting longer-lasting customer relationships.

Units or activities with shrinking markets may correspondingly convey false impressions of superior performance. As seems too often to happen with downsizing, allowing markets to shrink by underinvesting in new customer relationships is one way to disguise poor performance, if only for a while.

Current levels of customer relationship values do not really matter when looking ahead except to diagnose performance shortcomings. Outcomes of past investment are otherwise essentially irrelevant; rather, what is relevant is what to do next. The objective remains the maximization of the net value contributions of relationships, comparing the values of new or expanded relationships with the investment in developing them with current programs. Suppose that two stores seem to be in similar markets and that both have the same marketing outlays, yet one is developing less relationship value than the other. The performance of the former may warrant investigation, but the implication may simply be to direct more marketing investment to the market generating more value.

Market Entry, Expansion, Contraction, and Exit

Implicitly, if not explicitly, strategies involve a continuous process of assessing opportunities for varying degrees of market entry or expansion or, conversely, market contraction or exit. These decisions may involve geographic markets or different products and services. Analytically, the underlying principles are the same, although the scale of investment may differ. In either case, entry may require a certain critical mass to be viable. That critical mass may require some time to develop after entry has occurred.

Exit from a market may involve abandonment of relationships that still retain significant value. Perhaps a sale of customer relationships, and perhaps of other assets as well, can salvage some value upon exiting a market. At some point in a declining market, however, the loss of value from abandonment may become less than the loss from remaining in that market. Market exit decisions also should encompass the opportunities for otherwise using capital those withdrawals make available.

Consider aligning retail enterprises along a continuum according to the degrees of local presence required for marketing and customer convenience. A high degree of local presence often involves personalized marketing and delivery as well. Retail banking, property insurance, securities brokerage, and tax preparation services as well as consumer goods are common examples. Many business services are also in this category. Obviously, market entry decisions for providers of these services usually involve geographic markets.

At the other end of the continuum are services such as telecommunications that have traditionally required little or no local representation. Furthermore, many services have been shifting from the localized end of the spectrum toward more remote marketing and service provision. Credit cards are an example of a retail service that have undergone this shift, and even deposit banking has begun to move in that direction. Credit information is an example of a business service that has exhibited the same pattern, shifting from local credit bureaus to national information centers. Market entry decisions for vendors of these services tend to focus primarily on products and customer characteristics. Factors underlying this trend at the retail level include:

- Modern communications and information technologies enable quasipersonalized substitutes for direct, face-to-face communication. The marketing and provision of mutual fund and other securities brokerage services often take this form.
- In some cases technologies enable a partial shift whereby some other enterprise acts as a local sales agent while the production is centralized (an example being the Levi Strauss "Personal Pair" jeans program).
- Costs of maintaining a traditional local market presence have often risen more rapidly than costs of marketing and service provision from remote, centralized locations. Thus, First Direct banking provides traditional retail banking services throughout the United Kingdom, but only by mail and telephone from a single location.
- Customer characteristics other than geographic location have grown in significance as modern technologies enable more targeted marketing and service specialization. Location, for example, has little association with the characteristics that differentiate different types of credit card customers.

Targeted marketing and specialized or customized service offerings often require extended geographic markets to achieve the scale economies necessary to be cost competitive. A common pattern is that the products and services that new technologies make available to large businesses today eventually become available to consumers.

Following identification of the strategic alternatives, the decision process is similar to other types of marketing decisions in relying on value contribution criteria. It, too, requires identifying the various levels of additional relationship value obtainable from different levels of relationship investment. The start-up costs that make up the first step in relationship development are likely to become a major component of the investment. A new retail facility or product may be unprofitable until the customer base builds up to some break-even level.

As a practical matter, most de novo market entry tends to be into adjacent geographic markets or into products and services similar to previous offerings. Exceptions are most common when new markets grow rather rapidly. The entrant may already be familiar to prospective customers in adjacent markets; indeed, entry of this sort sometimes represents following one's own customers, as in cases of suburban expansion. Rapid growth, like rapid customer turnover in a market, often means more prospective new customers with no established loyalties, making it easier for a new entrant to attract customers.

Because of lags in entry, rapidly growing markets may have few competitors relative to the prospective customer base. Lower levels of competition enable near-term recovery of the entry costs, including as a result of the lower levels of other types of investment required to develop customer relationships. Rapidly growing markets are not always attractive from this standpoint, however. The prospect of market growth sometimes attracts so many entrants as to assure more than ample competition for years to come. Retailers staking out good sites sometimes anticipate more rapid real estate development than actually materializes. This pattern was common throughout much of Florida during the construction slump of the mid-1970s.

Strategies may involve combinations of expansion and contraction within geographic and product markets as the relationship marketplace becomes more customer focused and differentiated. The following diagram depicts what is likely to be a common type of situation:

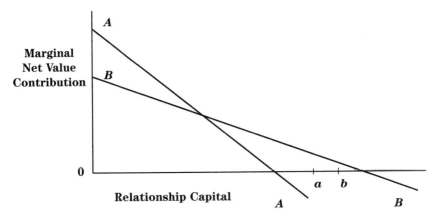

Increasing Values by Reallocating Investment.

In this case the diagram represents the amounts of capital, *a* and *b*, already invested in markets *A* and *B*. These markets need only represent customers with different characteristics; they may or may not otherwise coincide geographically or in terms of product design or service characteristics. Currently, at least, the amount of capital in *A* is excessive, whereas too little is invested in *B*. The obvious solution is a shift in strategy to direct more investment toward *B*. The diagram also suggests the potential for further raising the net enterprise value by simultaneously disinvesting in *A*. This reconfiguration may mean divesting some of the customer relationships represented by *A*, or it may even mean abandoning them by market withdrawal.

Business Combinations as Market Entry

An important incentive in many recent business combinations has been the prospect of achieving substantial cost economies from larger scale marketing and production; thus, many mergers and acquisitions involve partners who have been rivals in the same markets. Even these cases nevertheless involve some element of market entry. The fact is that the customers of each of the respective parties, in selecting among products and vendors, previously selected one rather than any other. The differences in preferences may or may not be important in reconfiguring the combined institution.

Regardless of geographic or product overlap, consider analyzing an acquisition candidate as if it represents a new market, although usually with the availability of much more information. This approach can involve essentially the same three steps as suggested earlier for assessing market potential:

1. Determine whether or not the market occupied by the acquisition prospect is a promising one for entry. Market growth probably is less important in the success of an acquisition than for de novo entry, but serious difficulties can arise in trying to extricate assets and capital from a declining market.
2. Assess the market share of the acquisition prospect when measured in relationship value terms. In particular, has it attracted at least a proportionate share of the new customer relationships in that market? If not, what does this suggest about the approach to its marketplace being taken by the prospect's management?
3. Compare the net asset value of the prospective acquisition, including the premium values of its customer relationships and other intangibles, with the enterprise value implied by current earnings and cash flows. A significantly higher net asset value may indicate that the prospect's management is not obtaining maximum financial performance from its assets.

Deficiencies identified in the first step need not deter an acquisition, but they certainly deserve consideration when determining its terms. Meanwhile, growing markets do not necessarily represent the most significant values. Customer relationships may be more stable and predictable in more established markets.

Deficiencies uncovered in the second and third steps may have either or both of two implications. One is that the prospect's management essentially has negative value, suggesting turnaround potential. The acquirer subsequently may have to dedicate significant additional managerial and other resources should the acquisition be completed. That additional investment suggests a compensating adjustment in acquisition terms. The second possible implication is that other potential acquirers may have overlooked the discrepancy between net asset value and observed financial performance. Perhaps there is an opportunity for a bargain even after accounting for any necessary turnaround investment.

Prospective acquirers typically review market potential in some fashion, but rarely from a value perspective of the sort recommended here. Nevertheless, a few exceptionally astute investors do seem have a demonstrated ability to identify turnaround potential and to use that information to obtain bargain acquisitions. They may not have access to the most appropriate valuation concepts, but perhaps they have an acute sense of what franchise values and premiums really represent.

Discount Factors, Costs of Capital, and Risks

One of the more arcane topics of financial theory and valuation is the determination of the appropriate discount factors for discounting future cash flows to present values. A few basic principles should suffice for most purposes. Perhaps the most important one is that for all the abstract theorizing this topic seems to attract, even the most sophisticated analysts ultimately fall back on a good deal of intuitive judgment. Some understanding of the underlying issues is helpful, but precise formulas and measures actually are unlikely to be nearly as meaningful as they sometimes appear.

That much said, a discount factor consists of four basic components:

- A pure interest rate representing the time value of money—the compensation that an economic society requires to forego current consumption in favor of saving and investing. It is essentially the cost of postponing the enjoyment of current income to some future time.
- An offset to expected future inflation. Those elements of future income that simply reflect higher prices of goods and services, and thus no additional purchasing power, have no value. If income doubles but prices also double, there is no gain or benefit. Inflation itself represents no value whatever.
- The expected (actuarial) value of loss that an investment may incur, representing a recognition that investment involves risks. One may view this component as representing an amount in excess of a risk-free rate of return whereby with many repeated investments of the same type the expected average return would tend toward that risk-free rate.
- Compensation for assuming risk with an investment. As a rule, investors are risk averse and must receive compensation over and above the actuarial value of loss if they are to be willing to take on risk. To illustrate, most people would pay something less than $5,000 for a 50-50 chance of winning $10,000.

Among the risks requiring compensation is the risk that inflation expectations will turn out to be incorrect.

Care is necessary in discounting future cash flows to assure that the inflation elements in the discount factor match those in the cash flows. Market rates of interest, which typically provide the initial reference for determining discount factors, automatically include an inflation factor—an offset to expected future inflation plus compensation for inflation risks. Thus, either the cash flow projections should incorporate those same inflation projections or an adjustment in the discount factor is necessary to conform to the cash flows. While overlooked with dismaying frequency, this point is particularly important when valuing some types of relationships. It is common and often convenient to project relationship cash flows in constant, or real, amounts, such as numbers of customers or accounts, representing constant purchasing power. In those cases the discount factors should similarly be in real terms, excluding inflation.

Some analysts treat the third and fourth components as constituting a single, more broadly defined, risk component. As chapter 2 observed, the fourth component, compensation for assuming risks, should reflect the fact that most investors seem to be strict risk averters—as risk increases, the compensation investors require increases at an accelerating rate. Thus, obtaining more investment capital ultimately means that costs of capital must rise at an increasing rate.

A pure interest rate that reflects no inflation probably does not exist in the real world, notwithstanding recent efforts to develop government bonds with this feature. Inflation defies accurate, objective measurement. Also as a practical matter, inflation itself is uncertain. The inflation component of market interest rates simply represents a current market consensus—a subjective consensus expectation that very likely is something other than just the current inflation rate. Every financial instrument, including money, entails some risk if only because of inflation. Correspondingly, a long-term interest rate, as on a conventional Treasury bond, reflects a market consensus about inflation patterns from the present to the bond maturity.

Earlier chapters referred to the concept of a cost of equity capital as the discount factor shareholders apply to the returns they receive on their investment. Chapter 9 then introduced the concept of a weighted-average cost of capital as the average return that a corporation must receive from investing in real capital, including intangibles. It reflects the fact that a significant portion of the funding for those investments will be from issuing long-term debt. The value of the equity to shareholders is the net cash flows the shareholders expect to receive discounted at the cost of equity capital. Similarly, the total market value of the enterprise, including its long-term debt plus its equity, is the expected cash flows to the shareholders and long-term creditors discounted at the weighted-average cost of capital.

Costs of debt capital are observable market variables. Costs of equity are more difficult to identify. One approach, which has been in use for many years, is a derivative of the dividend valuation concept. Suppose that P is today's share price and D is the current annual dividend, both expressed in dollars. Suppose, too, that investors expect those dividends to grow indefinitely at a constant annual rate g, and define r to be the cost of equity capital. The value (price) per share should then be:

$$\frac{D}{r-g} = P.$$

Notice the similarity of this expression to that for dividend values in chapter 6. Here, however, it allows for dividend growth at a constant annual rate g and the formulation is in terms of price per share instead of the total equity value. Thus, for example, if the current annual dividend is $5 per share, expected to grow indefinitely at 5 percent per year, and the cost of equity capital is 15 percent, the share price should be (expressing percentages as decimals):

$$\frac{\$5}{.15 - .05} = \$50.$$

As the share price is normally observable, whereas the cost of equity capital is not, a useful transposition of the first expression is:

$$\frac{D}{P} + g = r.$$

Notice that the cost of equity is therefore simply the current dividend yield ($5 ÷ $50 = 10 percent in the example) plus the expected dividend growth rate (5 percent in the example), for a cost of equity capital of 15 percent.

An alternative approach that has become fashionable is the capital asset pricing model, or CAPM. It posits that a cost of equity consists of a risk-free rate of return (such as a long-term Treasury bond rate) plus a risk premium reflecting the overall stock market, but adjusted for the particular industry to which the enterprise belongs. Thus:

$$r_E = i + ß[E(r_M) - i].$$

Here, r_E is the enterprise cost of equity, i is the risk-free long-term interest rate, $E(r_M)$ is the expected overall rate of return on stocks (generally an historical average), and $ß$ (beta) is a risk factor calculated from the statistical correlation of the industry's stock returns with the overall market. The expression *industry beta* is part of the everyday language of many financial professionals. A positive $ß$ less than 1.0 means that the industry's stocks move in the same direction as the overall market, but fluctuate less. The lower $ß$, the more stable the industry's share prices and the lower the risks. If the $ß$ is negative, it means that stock prices for that industry tend to move in directions opposite to the overall market. Such stocks provide good opportunities for portfolio diversification, but are very rare.

The most valid element of this construction is that it expresses a cost of capital as a risk-free rate (time value of money) plus a risk premium. That it otherwise may seem rather hocus pocus should not cause concern. CAPM simply is not very reliable. While in widespread use among financial professionals, concerns have been growing that the historical data on which it relies actually are poor predictors of future market behavior. In particular, historical volatility in the prices of an industry's stocks—the source of data for estimating $ß$—seems not to be a good predictor of future volatility. Estimates of costs of equity therefore must rely at least as much on judgment as on number-crunching.

Meanwhile, much the same concept as underlies the weighted-average cost of capital comes into play in analyzing internal investment opportunities. Different forms of capital are likely to entail different levels of risk. If so, logic suggests that the discount factors, or costs of capital, should vary according to those different risks. Suppose that an enterprise has two different lines of business, A and B. If they were totally separate corporations, their respective weighted-average costs of capital would be r_A and r_B. If A and B each represents half of the enterprise capital, one might suppose that its overall weighted-average cost of capital, r^*, would be:

$$r^* = .5r_A + .5r_B$$

If this were correct, the r_A and r_B would be the discount factors to apply to investments in those respective activities. To assume as much, however, is the most conservative approach. If the two activities reflected different sets of business conditions, and hence their respective cash flows fluctuated differently, they would effectively represent some degree of diversification. If so, the composite risk would be less, reducing the respective costs of capital. The effect is essentially having an internal ß less than 1.0. Actual practice, however, is often to focus on a single discount factor—an estimate of r^* or some higher hurdle rate, and apply it in assessing all for all capital budgeting decisions.

One can, of course, break the foregoing construction down into any number of business units and activities. Furthermore, it applies to different types of investment within what seem to be the same lines of business. For example, investing in developing altogether new customer relationships by entering new markets probably entails more risks than replacing customer attrition in an existing market. Furthermore, investing in customer replacement may represent greater risk than investing in extending relationship lives among existing customers. Whatever the case, higher risks call for higher discount factors.

Two points conclude discussion of this topic. One is that an enterprise cost of capital typically pertains only to an incremental change in the scale of the enterprise. Any change in its business mix, even without seeking additional capital funding, will likely change its risk characteristics and costs of capital. Also, simply because more rapid expansion suggests more risk, more than an incremental change in scale is likely to change its costs of capital even if the business mix stays the same.

Secondly, some businesses have developed complex formulas for directly allocating capital to different business units. Typically they incorporate, at least implicitly, the same considerations as enter into estimating the costs of capital applicable to activities representing different risks. Indeed, they appear in many cases simply to involve an unnecessary additional step that mostly succeeds in complicating matters. Why not just directly apply the costs of capital as adjusted for different risks?

The Value Basis of Business Strategy

The subject of business strategies keeps coming back to issues of value and valuation. Strategies and value are inseparable. A strategy lacking a basis in value principles cannot be a viable strategy, particularly in a relationship environment. A business strategy is therefore a framework for managing values, recognizing the future dimensions and risks that different decision alternatives entail. Risk management is therefore part of value management. To be meaningful, in other words, a business strategy must in the first instance be a value-based strategy. In today's environment, it must be value-based with a relationship focus.

With the requisite fundamental principles in place, at least in broad form, perhaps some consideration of how to implement a value-based strategy will be useful. The next chapter concludes the discussion of strategies in a purely business context by suggesting some practical steps toward strategy development and implementation. Of course, any program would require adaptation to the particular circumstances of a business.

14

The Future Is Now!

CONFRONTING THE FUTURE

Given its solid foundation in economic and financial principles, the general concept of value-based strategies and performance measures is irrefutable. Thus, rather than attempting to question its logic, much of the business community will probably just ignore it. It may seem too difficult to adopt. After all, few seem to be giving it much attention anyway. Alternatively, it may simply seem too far off the beaten track. Perhaps above all else, however, it confronts a bewilderingly complex environment from which much of society would rather escape.

Some earlier comments on internal enterprise relationships referred to a process of disengagement. At least some senior executives, having detached themselves from lower levels of management and employees, now see the same process at work in the opposite direction. Perhaps society at large, confronting problems for which it sees no solutions, is undergoing a process of disengagement. Of course, this solves nothing, nor can it continue indefinitely. Escapism is no way to win a competitive race. It is simply a forfeiture of relationship capital and opportunity.

Dismissing the importance of value-based strategic principles would be a mistake, for a number of compelling reasons:

- Some corporations have already quietly begun to develop value-based decision programs in at least some business units.
- More generally, notwithstanding persistent stakeholder theories of corporate governance, shareholders are demanding and receiving more attention to their concerns and interests.
- Institutional investors, in particular, are adopting increasingly aggressive programs to promote shareholder claims, suggesting that issues of corporate governance will continue to attract more attention.
- Whatever the true state of affairs, the public at large perceives significant problems with corporate accountability.
- Some corporations are at least beginning to focus more on the importance of securing and extending customer loyalties.
- Perhaps having learned some lessons about the perils of downsizing, more corporate attention is focusing on the investment nature of a corporate workforce.
- Recognition is growing that corporations must develop and articulate business strategies, although not of the mechanical sort fashionable during the 1970s.
- Unlike the quick fixes peddled by many management theorists and consultants, a full value-based decision framework is likely to require at least a couple of years to develop and implement.

These trends mean that some enterprises will become more competitive both in attracting customer relationships and in developing and retaining human capital. The sooner an enterprise adopts value-based decision principles, the more likely it will be among the survivors and eventually dominate its markets. These enterprises will be smarter, more agile, and more anticipatory than their rivals. They will target customers more effectively, attracting and developing those customer relationships that contribute more value. They also will manage their internal resources more effectively, providing higher quality with more efficiency. They will tend to be more innovative, and to innovate more effectively, because they listen respectfully to both their customers and employees. They will be the enterprises with the most favored access to the capital markets. Ultimately, they will be the enterprises that will have asserted control over their destinies rather than allowing themselves to be capsized by events.

By definition, others will fall behind—laggards and sluggards left to flounder and sink. Of those, probably most never will fully recover. Recall the enormous effort required of IBM to overcome its excessive commitment to mainframe computers and catch up in the personal computer market. Few corporations have IBM's resources with which to achieve similar recoveries.

This shift to a value focus is, to be sure, still in its infancy. The important point is that it is happening and it is attracting more attention. That attention, moreover, is from a variety of perspectives. It only needs a unifying framework to take hold and gather momentum.

Decision Thresholds

An enterprise considering developing a value-based decision framework must begin with a firm commitment to cross each and every one of a series of decision thresholds. It must cross the first two before it can even begin to develop an effective and responsive value-based relationship strategy.

- *Why* change?

A trivial answer, which would miss the entire point of the exercise, is that change is necessary to keep up with the marketplace. Chief executives proceeding only this far may be content to drift with industry trends, at best simply accepting rather than initiating change. A changing marketplace represents pitfalls as well as opportunities. Drifting with the tide may convey the false illusion of being the safest course, but not for long. A dynamically competitive marketplace is intolerant of drifters.

Complacency in the face of economic revolution systematically subverts shareholder values. Without the value contribution decision framework that a relationship environment requires, management decision making has become haphazard, biased against relationship investment and toward less productive investment alternatives. Consequences include higher business and investment risks, capital wastage, declining competitiveness, and eventual corporate evisceration.

- *When* to change?

The answer to *why* it is so important to change contains much of the answer to *when* to change. The costs of failure to change are too substantial to warrant postponing adoption of more effective management decision frameworks. Practicality nevertheless imposes some major constraints. Corporate reinvention requires a significant amount of internal infrastructure investment before strategy development can move very far. There are no shortcuts. The answer to when to change is therefore to begin the process yesterday, but to do so in an orderly fashion supported by a commitment to keep the process moving forward. Unrealistic expectations of quick results will meet disappointment and perhaps undermine the entire process.

- *What* to change?

The purpose of strategy development is to identify *what* to change. Addressing this issue fully may indicate that an enterprise must reinvent itself, both internally and by repositioning itself in the marketplace. Whatever else may change as new corporate strategies unfold, a change in management decision criteria is mandatory. The process of developing a value-based decision framework, which will require significant time and investment, should begin at the very outset of a strategy development program.

Directors and management may constitute an initial, potentially insurmountable threshold. The higher their resistance, the more likely the answers to what to change begin with them, but admissions by either of inability to cope with the prevailing business environment are unlikely. Initiation of decisive remedial action by shareholders may be the only remedy if these cases are not to become terminal.

- *How* to change?

Developing a new decision framework requires new skills and techniques. Cost and revenue allocations need more careful and precise identification and classification, both to distinguish current expenses from investment outlays and to assign them to different services and customer relationships. Customer data require statistical analysis, first to identify and then to predict customer value attributes. Those value attributes require further analysis to determine how to manage them in a manner that maximizes customer value contributions to enterprise values. The value contributions of relationships with employees, suppliers, and the financial markets similarly require analysis, perhaps leading to overhaul of many of those relationships.

- *Whom* to change?

Whom to change should fall into place in addressing what and how to change. Above all, a change in senior management will be necessary if current management fails to provide leadership in developing a strategic vision and a convincing sense of direction for the enterprise. Lower levels of management may also require restructuring—process reengineering, employee empowerment, total quality management, and similar ideas contain merit, even if none provides a full set of strategic solutions. Apart from the effects of streamlining business processes, adapting to a relationship environment both requires more emphasis on market research and customer analysis and the development of value-oriented management information systems.

One should not simply assume that recent management initiation of decisive corporate restructuring programs indicates that management is on the front edge of change. A lingering question might be why the enterprise drifted so long that only major upheaval could realign it with current realities. Have matters slipped beyond any likelihood of remedy? Even if not, is the follow-up to substantial restructuring to be another period of drift? How much confidence can one have in directors and management that allowed that slippage in the first place?

Reach for the Opportunity Frontiers!

According to an article in the *Economist* not long ago, management theorists have begun to shift the focus of their debates from abstract definitions of business strategy to more practical issues of how to develop business strategies.[1] Assume, then, management recognition of a need for true strategic planning programs, keeping in mind that a business inevitably pursues *some* strategy, consciously or otherwise. Assume, too, that this recognition occurs in an atmosphere of incipient but not irremediable business stagnation. In other words, management suddenly realizes that it must do something differently. What should it do next?

However embarrassingly simplistic, return both to the idea of an opportunity frontier in the previous chapter and to the box concept presented in the introduction. By now, a convincing case has emerged that to at least some extent, most corporate enterprises remain trapped in a box of conventional assumptions and practices. Being

---

[1]"Making Strategy," *The Economist,* 1 March 1997.

caught in a box of retrogressive convention essentially means failure to reach out and explore the full range of current possibilities that external and internal circumstances afford.

Case *1* of the following diagram shows the box as situated well inside the current opportunity frontier. Here, the circles marked *A* are the innermost circles in the opportunity frontier diagrams in Chapter 13.

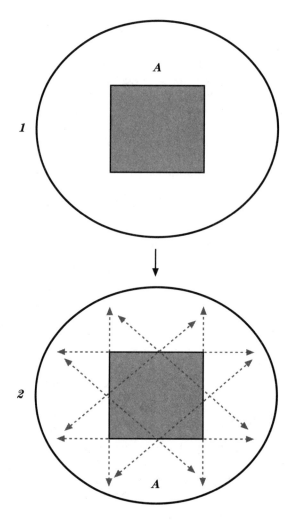

Breaking Out of the Box.

The first step therefore is to extend strategic thinking out to the limits of that frontier, moving from *1* to *2*. The dotted-line arrows emphasize the point by tracing out the solutions to the out-of-the-box puzzle in the introduction. Only upon exploring the limits of the current opportunity frontier does it make sense to begin extending the strategic horizons to future possibilities, as depicted by *B* and *C* in the chapter 13 diagrams.

How does an organization reach out to its opportunity frontiers? Doing so requires management leadership in developing a strategic vision: Where is the enterprise headed and how should it get there? In some cases the chief executive may have the requisite vision as well as the leadership qualities to implement it. In others the vision must develop by assembling inputs from other senior managers, middle management, employees, consultants, and even outside suppliers and customers. Attentiveness to customer and employee suggestions and criticism can be major sources of new ideas, but only if a mechanism is in place to consider them and put them to use.

Here, the importance of a commitment to looking beyond the boundaries of convention is impossible to overemphasize.[2] The consequence otherwise is likely to be reinforcement of an outdated status quo. Obviously, no one can generalize about the sources of good ideas. The main points are to solicit those ideas from every available source without being too quick to judge their usefulness. Then, once a strategy begins to emerge, instill an organizationwide dedication to—indeed, enthusiasm for—its constant improvement and implementation.

Develop a Value-Based Decision Process

Understanding the various thresholds to cross, and further understanding that it may ultimately entail reinventing the enterprise, how should management, as a practical matter, proceed to develop value-based strategies for a relationship environment? Strategically, simply restructuring a corporate organization overnight is out of the question, however much the process reengineers or other consultants may promote it. Fortunately, many businesses can begin to incorporate essential elements of a value-based framework in a stepwise fashion before that framework is fully in place. Because some investment is

---

[2]An extended treatment of this point is found in Wayne C. Burkan, *Wide Angle Vision* (New York: John Wiley & Sons, 1996).

necessary for this purpose, doing so can nevertheless give rise to all sorts of excuses for backing away from the entire concept.

Set forth below are some relatively modest, practical steps by which an enterprise can begin to incorporate value principles in its corporate direction and management decisions. As each step is taken, a value-based framework gradually takes shape. Recognizing the need for a long-term commitment at the outset, and that survival requires investing in the organization itself, some suggested steps are as follows:

Discard subversive measures of enterprise performance as management information and decision tools. An essential early step is to develop a decision framework appropriate for a relationship-driven economic environment. That requires coming to terms with the deficiencies of public financial reporting conventions for internal decision making. Instead, formulate decisions with reference to market values, as set forth in chapter 9. Try measuring enterprise performance in terms of changes in net asset values and shareholder dividends. Share prices assuredly will not track these net asset values with any degree of consistency, but the different value measures must tend to converge over time. To repeat, pursuing shareholder value objectives requires a focus on the long run.

Compile the information necessary to apply value principles to economic relationships. Begin by taking an inventory of the enterprise's assets, including its internal as well as external economic relationships. What are the enterprise's resources that define its current circumstances and opportunity frontiers? Include among its assets the base of customer information that is available. Corporate management in a relationship marketplace normally requires at least three general categories of information to determine *what* and *for whom* to produce and distribute its wares:

- *Information on current customer relationships* for use in:
    Identifying the value attributes of different types of relationships, providing a basis for projecting value contributions of future investment alternatives.

    Identifying opportunities for expanding and enriching existing customer relationships through sale of more products and services and extending relationship lives.

- *Market information* for identifying the characteristics of prospective customers, both in existing geographic and product markets and in markets that are realistic candidates for entry.
- *Information on income and expense allocations* by which to:
  Properly distinguish investment outlays from current expenses.

Assign receipts and outlays to outputs of goods and services, and ultimately to customer relationships.

Promote public understanding of the value characteristics of the enterprise. One way to approach this step is to develop a market value balance sheet similar to the example in chapter 8. This requires developing techniques for valuing at least the major categories of customer relationship intangibles. Financial or marketing analysts within the organization should be able to learn the necessary valuation techniques without much difficulty. Outside consultants may be helpful at the outset, but the necessary understanding of the characteristics of the business, including supporting data, must come primarily from internal sources. An objective of this step is in any event to internalize the process so as to be able to redirect it to strategic analysis and decision making.

The primary purpose at this stage is to learn to identify and understand these assets. Some corporations, such as service and communications enterprises, might also consider disclosing them in their financial reports as experience with these valuations develops. Disclosure has the potential for opening up entirely new dimensions of communication with the financial community. Here are some aspects of this exercise to consider:

- Disclosure conveys the message to investors that the underlying values of many types of corporations are significantly above book net worth. It further provides a measure of enterprise value that is an alternative to, and often more meaningful than, measures developed by securities analysts and investment bankers.
- The exclusion of customer relationships and other intangible

assets from independent audits should not mean that corporate directors and management are not accountable for them. Disclosure is a step toward recognizing that accountability.

- Disclosure also provides a basis for management to communicate its sense of long-term direction to investors. In the years ahead, simply having a coherent sense of future direction will set some enterprises apart from their rivals.

- Developing these relationship valuations requires identification of the customer information and of the income and expense allocations that they require. An adjunct to the valuation program itself is therefore a program for identifying information needs and for developing and continually improving the necessary information bases.

- Disclosure essentially forces senior executives and directors to buy into value principles and relationship concepts. How else are they to explain and make the most effective use of the information they provide? How else are directors to exercise the fiduciary responsibilities entrusted to them?

- An enterprise nevertheless should consider that, once commenced, disclosure may imply a commitment to its continuation.

- At least in the near term, much of the financial community may not fully understand relationship value disclosures. For the most part, a corporate management can rely only on itself to explain relationship value concepts. It can facilitate this process by seeking out those analysts and other members of the financial and consulting communities who do understand it.

Of course, it is possible to obtain many of the benefits of relationship valuation without actual disclosure. Perhaps the most important near-term benefit of disclosure is imparting discipline to the valuation process and to interpreting and using the results. As value information accumulates, a corporation may actually have a fiduciary as well as public responsibility to disclose it to the investing public. Stated another way, to what extent can it be appropriate to withhold material information bearing on enterprise value?

Developing an understanding of relationship investment and values among corporate directors and executives is insufficient, however. If corporations are to avoid pressures to pander to a misinformed financial community, they must educate the investing public on the true nature of their enterprise values. Correspondingly, they must regard investor communications opportunistically rather than as a burden. The most effective means of communicating the significance of economic relationships to enterprise values is to demonstrate their significance to corporate strategies and decisions. Otherwise, they will encounter continuing skepticism as well as misunderstanding in the financial marketplace.

Adopt a performance assessment program applying value principles. Net asset value comparisons for performance assessment should begin at the enterprise level and work downward. An objective is to identify clearly whether or not value contributions to the enterprise, direct or indirect, are consistent with the available opportunities. Some reasons to begin this process at an early stage include:

- Establishing credibility. Criteria for use in decision making have no legitimacy unless they rely on performance measures that are actually in use. Value principles gain added credibility if used promptly to redress obvious deficiencies.
- Demonstrating commitment. Use of relationship value concepts for performance measurement is yet another means of tying senior management and directors into the concept.
- Strategic inputs. Value-based strategies and decisions require self-assessment programs as predicates to identifying realistic strategic alternatives.
- External perceptions. A few analysts, investors, and consultants have begun to perceive some of the specific relationship factors that contribute value. The financial community will not continue indefinitely to overlook value shortcomings in an enterprise.
- Selling the value story. Probably the most effective way to convince the investing public of the significance of relationship values is to communicate their use as decision tools.

Some instructive ways to introduce a value-based performance assessment program into the mainstream of management decisions are:

- Compare the enterprise's net asset value to other value measures. Identify the reasons for significant discrepancies.
- Retrace the ground covered by previous cost-cutting and other

restructuring programs. What changes might value principles suggest?

- More specifically, apply value criteria in assessing the performance of business units within the enterprise.
- If the enterprise has recently engaged in any acquisitions, review the results of those acquisitions in light of relationship value concepts.

A net asset approach to performance assessment should, of course, be in addition to other types of performance measures such as peer comparisons of income and expense ratios. As in medicine, a variety of different diagnostic tests is often necessary to determine the condition of a patient and to prescribe the proper course of treatment. New approaches to performance assessment will be necessary in any event as growing heterogeneity among corporate enterprises reduces the relevance of intercorporate comparisons.

Discard and avoid perverse management incentives. Obviously, if the paramount objective of the corporation is to maximize shareholder values, management compensation schemes should promote that objective. Correspondingly, tying executive and employee compensation to inconsistent objectives such as earnings and costs is inappropriate. Equally inappropriate is engaging outside consultants on the basis of expected cost reductions or earnings improvement, whether or not those expectations are the basis for engagement or affect the consulting fees.

Use the results of the performance assessment to evaluate the internal strengths and weaknesses of the enterprise. This step might logically be part of the asset inventory but nevertheless is likely to require special attention. Begin at the top and work downward:

- What do the directors contribute to the enterprise? To what extent do they exercise their fiduciary responsibilities to shareholders? Do they have the confidence of the investment community?
- How does the financial performance of the enterprise compare with the potential performance that its net asset value suggests? What does this comparison indicate about the perfor-

mance of senior management? Does management have a firm grasp of strategic direction? Does it have a thorough understanding of the underlying value components of the enterprise? Does senior management encourage and value creative ideas? Does it encourage or challenge in-the-box thinking?

- What information is available and used about the competence of middle levels of management? Are these levels good sources of new ideas and, if not, why not? Do managers at each level take full advantage of the abilities of their subordinates? Does the organization of the enterprise facilitate or impede effective and timely decision making? What sorts of criteria apply in recruiting and promoting middle managers and employees?

Taken as a whole, does the enterprise provide an atmosphere that encourages everyone to think strategically? Does it encourage reflection, contemplation, and self-criticism? Does it ceaselessly ask:

- What is your business?
- Who is your customer?
- What does your customer consider value?[3]

Reconnect the various internal components of the enterprise. The responsibilities of a corporate enterprise to its shareholders include making the most effective use of the resources those shareholders have provided. Among those resources is the capital embedded in various levels of management and employment. Disconnection between the executive suites and other levels is a breakdown of communication and an effective severance of internal economic relationships, even without employee terminations. The consequence is at least to waste that value and probably eventually to lose it irretrievably.

Adopt relationship value concepts for acquisition and divestiture analysis. When available, this step is one of the easier and more effective ways to become familiar with the value attributes of relationship assets. The premium values representing economic relationships obviously are important elements in the

---

[3]John Mickelthwait and Adrian Wooldridge, in *The Witch Doctors: Making Sense of the Management Gurus* (New York: Times Business, 1996), attribute these questions to Peter Drucker on page 74.

terms of any acquisition or divestiture, even when a combination is simply by means of an exchange of stock. Disregarding the underlying sources of these values in analyzing a prospective acquisition or divestiture is as irresponsible as it is common. So also is undue reliance on fairness opinions that fail to examine these value components. Some simple steps include:

- Include net asset valuation in any acquisition and divestiture analysis. Its use in conjunction with other valuation techniques will both add value insights and provide support for the validity of net asset valuations as decision-making tools.
- Apply relationship value principles in any purchase (due diligence) investigation. Intangible assets warrant at least as much attention as other assets, even if common practice is to ignore them. Use this process to explore the quality of the economic relationships that are for sale. Obtain additional information, including longevity data, to assist in their valuation.
- To assess the quality (value potential) of customer relationships, investigate the programs that attracted and developed them. Purchase investigations should pay substantial attention to marketing factors even if the acquirer plans to adopt altogether different approaches.
- Avoid being deterred by skepticism among outside financial advisors, consultants, and accountants. Few have any experience with net asset valuations or relationship value concepts.
- Do not take investment banker fairness opinions any more seriously than the quality of the supporting analysis warrants. They may provide some legal protection but are not otherwise guarantees of value received.

Apply relationship value concepts to analyzing market potential. Market assessment in relationship value terms is an aspect of performance analysis as well as significant for evaluating entry and exit alternatives. To facilitate developing this sort of approach to market assessment, apply it first to existing markets, for which there should already be a substantial amount of useful information. This effort alone has an additional diagnostic benefit, as it extends one step further a self-examination of how much the enterprise really knows and understands about its current customers.

Explore alternatives for extending relationship lives. This step, of course, assumes that as a result of prior steps in the program, an enterprise has developed techniques to identify and monitor relationship lives. Once that information is available, a further step is to develop analytical procedures for putting it to use. An enterprise can then begin to analyze what customer characteristics tend to extend relationship lives and thus what variations in service and product characteristics serve to strengthen and extend those relationships.

Explore alternatives for expanding existing customer relationships. Programs to expand or enrich customer relationships by including more value-contributing services presumably would accompany programs to increase relationship lives. Together they constitute programs for relationship value enhancement by means of analytically disciplined approaches to cross-selling products and services. An initial effort might be to develop more creative approaches to pricing and cross-selling, paying closer attention to the roles of different services in developing and retaining customer relationships. A logical next step might be to consider introducing new services and products.

Explore alternatives for eliminating relationships that detract from value. The flip side of enriching existing customer relationships is to seek ways of deterring and eliminating relationships that contribute no value. This exercise similarly has marketing implications for programs seeking new customer relationships. In the meantime, keep in mind that:

- Because the initial focus is on existing customers, the relevant cash flows for identifying value are only those extending from the present into the future. The cash outlays of the past, however mistaken they might have been, have no subsequent relevance other than for the analytical insights they provide.
- Currently unprofitable relationships may represent significant value. Negative near-term cash flows may be part of the investment necessary to develop many value-contributing relationships. Some research is likely to be necessary to distinguish these from others.
- Currently profitable relationships can detract from enterprise value. This situation is unlikely to be common, however, as the

enterprise presumably has already incurred the initial outlays to develop the relationships.

Question the outside advisors. Be skeptical! Remember that the business of outside advisors—consultants, investment bankers, accountants, visionaries, or whatever—is selling what they think they know best, not necessarily what clients need most. Even without their direct involvement in developing business strategies, serious problems can arise if their strategic perspectives and sense of direction differ from those of a client or otherwise lack value content. What is the point of an elaborate management information system that provides irrelevant or misleading information? Why undertake a marketing campaign without a focus on developing customer relationship values? How can a value-oriented enterprise rationally embark on corporate restructuring without attention to the capital embedded in its workforce? To be sure, outside advisors can be informative and useful, and are often necessary. It is important to reject bad advice while recognizing and appreciating good advice.

Redefine the Enterprise

Somewhere along the way, a corporation's directors and chief executives must determine its strategic direction. Otherwise, they are a ship at sea without a compass, perhaps prone to hitting a shoal and losing a rudder. The foregoing implementation steps only provide some of the tools necessary to begin identifying strategic alternatives. They consequently are but a predicate for beginning seriously to develop value-based strategies.

Corporate strategies often assume that an enterprise can at least stay on course and thus that the objective of planning is to develop opportunities for growth. Such assumptions are often unrealistic. Business strategies may instead need to come to terms with shrinking traditional lines of business, downsizing, divestitures, and perhaps absorption. Strategic contraction in today's environment should extend beyond the popular idea of refocusing on core businesses.

Even with contraction rather than expansion, a focus on promoting and preserving relationship values should best achieve enterprise value objectives. Many enterprises, of course, will never reach a point at which they can make informed, value-based strategic choices. These companies will be acquisition opportunities for others.

Perhaps earlier chapters have succeeded in communicating the urgency of recognizing the significance of economic relationships and of adopting value principles. These value principles provide the keys to determining who will be selected in or selected out in a merciless Darwinian struggle for survival. Those who do survive will be those who are most attuned to emerging new realities.

CHAPTER 15

National Wealth and Public Policy in a Relationship Economy

APPLICATIONS TO THE PUBLIC SECTOR

Government is predominantly a service enterprise, and it has been struggling to incorporate modern information and communications technologies. Many of the characteristics of a relationship economy are therefore familiar in a public sector context. As in much of the private sector, efficiency suffers from lapses in competitiveness, which obviously tend to be more severe in the public sector.

Without stretching the point to an overall theory of government, the public sector has much to learn, and in some cases is learning, from private enterprise models. Cities and states are learning that they must be competitive with others to attract and retain sources of income and employment. Some are learning that they must compete for the economic contributions of senior citizens, who increasingly seek out more favorable climates for public services and tax burdens. Nations, too, are competitors in the economic arena.

In the same vein, many of the shortcomings common in private enterprise are also common in the public sector. As in many corporations, problems often begin with breakdowns in accountability. Absent strict enforcement of responsibilities, to shareholders in one case and to the public at large in the other, decision makers have some freedom to pursue their own narrow, and typically near-term, objectives. Thus, much as directors and senior executives may add extra feathers to their nests, politicians cuddle with moneyed elements who can help them pursue their political goals.

These freedoms are, to be sure, subject to severe restrictions, and major abuses seem uncommon. A more significant problem than abuses is substantial inconsistency and shortsightedness in setting and pursuing objectives. Government is for the most part a retrospective strategic wasteland. To the extent political success depends on image and charisma, the political process generates few true leaders. Their emergence often requires a sense of crisis, as has occurred in some major cities. In others, even imminent crises are insufficient to overcome political expediency.

Particularly at the national level, the absence of any sense of strategic direction is not because the issue has not attracted attention. Private-sector think tanks have had concerns with this issue for many years. It also does not seem to be attributable to widespread differences of opinion among the electorate. The inability of Congress and the White House to deal adequately with health care, tax simplification, and gun control is substantially due to political expediency. Politics for many is a career, creating concerns with personal goals. A frequent consequence is general leadership vacuum.

If public policy were to adopt a more strategic orientation, it would need a stronger foundation in economic principles. The problem is not a lack of economists in government—they number in the thousands; rather, economic principles usually have no more than a tangential influence on public policy. In part, too, the problem is with economics as a discipline, which chapter 4 suggested as slow to break loose from industrial-age thinking.

Misdirection in government policy substantially impacts market behavior in the private sector. Perhaps contrary to some impressions, Adam Smith was not a pure laissez-faire theorist. He recognized perfectly well that government can play a major role in promoting national wealth and prosperity. At the same time, however, he also recognized that the government role can also be seriously perverse. His particular concern was the propensity of governments to impede competition in private enterprise.

Matters are not terribly different today than they were in Smith's time. On one hand, governments often promote economic inefficiency by directing resources toward unproductive activities. On the other, they promote more private-sector efficiency by providing an infrastructure that facilitates economic activity and reduces economic risks. Politics and economics tend to converge more than diverge in democratic societies, but when they diverge, politics usually take precedence. Eastern Europe shows how political intrusions in the marketplace can drag national economies into ruin when economic principles become too widely ignored. Even much of Western Europe is struggling to overcome misguided public policies of the past and restore some semblance of economic rationality to the private sector. The current plight of many of those countries demonstrates how misguided policy can develop its own powerfully entrenched constituencies.

On occasion, however, the economists themselves weigh into policy making with untoward consequences. Too many economists seem unable to resist offering policy advice even when it is on thin ice. Some recent instances involve their own misperceptions of the current economic climate. In particular, failure to understand the significance of the emergence of a relationship economy distorts economic policy prescriptions. Consider, very briefly, three types of cases that illustrate the problem:

Is the Stock Market Too High?

In the United States, the monetary policies of the Federal Reserve System are the predominant active policy mechanisms for stabilizing the economy. Monetary authorities in other countries play similar roles. Monetary policy helps to contain inflation by increasing interest rates, thereby reducing spending. It may stimulate an economy in recession by stimulating spending with lower interest rates, but this often occurs too slowly to be very effective. The resulting stimulus may occur only after economic recovery is well underway.

Otherwise, economic stabilization mostly depends on so-called automatic stabilizers. As income and output fall, tax receipts fall and unemployment benefits rise, causing more spending. The opposite occurs with more exuberant economic activity. Even monetary policy is in part automatic, as interest rates tend to rise or fall with spending without any Federal Reserve intervention. Indeed, when the monetary authorities announce a change in their interest rate target, they often are simply following the market.

It probably is just as well that government's ability to intervene further is limited. Except in instances of severe depression, stabilization measures enacted by Congress would undoubtedly come into play so slowly that their effects would likely be perverse. Recall that the measures of output and income on which policy makers rely are distortions of reality. Even the actual rate of inflation defies definition and measurement. It is not always possible to be certain whether it is increasing or declining.

Promoting economic stabilization through use of monetary policy is by no means the Federal Reserve's only role; Congress, over the years, has assigned to it a variety of regulatory responsibilities as well. Even so, however, Federal Reserve officials seem compelled to go beyond their assigned responsibilities. In particular, the chairman pronounced some while back that stock prices had risen to excessive levels. Few financial professionals are likely to believe Federal Reserve officials have any special insights into stock price behavior. The potential problem, rather, is that rightly or wrongly, the Federal Reserve has enormous power to enforce its views. The true concern of the financial markets is that it might put upward pressure on interest rates for no reason other than to contain stock prices.

Without pretending to know where stock prices will or should be at any future time, consider the basis for the chairman's position. It consisted simply of comparing current stock prices with historical price ratios using conventional measures of financial condition and performance. The fact is that the market climate for stocks today is truly different than in the past. Enormous caution is in order in seeking parallels from the past. Of course, no one knows whether or not the market climate is in any sense better than before, nor whether or not it is any more or less immune to major price swings. In any event, risking some repetition, consider some of the differences:

- As previous chapters demonstrated, conventional measures of financial condition and performance—net worth and earnings—tend increasingly to misstate, and often to understate, true corporate financial condition and performance.
- Even by conventional measures, corporations are tending to pay out lower dividends, reinvest more earnings, and to repurchase their outstanding shares, in substantial part due to shareholder exposure to double taxation of dividends.
- The growth in relationship capital and other intangibles, recorded as expense rather than as investment, means that business saving and investment is growing faster than conventional financial measures indicate.
- In ways that no one seems yet to have identified fully, the sta-

bility characteristics of the economy seem to have changed, possibly with more modest swings in total economic activity and less inflationary pressure.

- Government deregulation and budget constraints hold out possibilities for less counterproductive interference with economic activity.
- For all its faults, the U.S. economy is exhibiting more resilience and adapting better to economic change than the rest of the world, probably because it is more open to competition.
- The baby-boom generation is now moving from the household-forming, dissaving life-cycle phase into a saving phase, looking toward retirement.

If these differences seem to portend stronger economic performance and higher growth in stock prices for the future, consider that a number of negative factors remain. Some of them also have failed to attract the full attention they deserve from economists and the business community:

- Those elements of society that should be increasing their saving rates substantially—the baby-boomers—actually have been slow to do so.
- Underemployment, not contained in any official statistics, among both recent college graduates and older workers, including managerial and professional workers, is substantial and growing, reducing tax revenues, draining the Social Security system, reducing private saving rates, and generally wasting national resources.
- Substantial government deficits continue to sustain the current modest levels of economic activity and growth, with much of the funding of government debt and private investment coming from abroad.
- Substantial economic upheaval implies more uncertainty and thus more business and investment risks, and consequently a more treacherous climate for stocks.
- Much of the nation's physical infrastructure—transportation arteries and systems, public buildings, and older inner cities—continues to deteriorate.
- Enormous national problems, including a growing unaffordability of medical care and a potential breakdown in Social Security, continue to escalate as they remain unaddressed.

- No one really knows what has happened to business cycles, and particularly whether or not the economy has somehow become immune to major depression.

The possibilities of more overall economic stability, yet more business and investment risks, may seem inconsistent, but that need not be so. The rise and fall of individual enterprises may, to some degree, tend to cancel out in the aggregate.

The final point deserves additional comment. Neither economists nor anyone else really understands what causes an economic depression—prolonged periods of high unemployment and little or no growth that seem to recur cyclically every forty to sixty years. Depressions defy analysis because each is very different from its predecessors, and their causes include important noneconomic as well as economic factors. Disagreement persists on whether the stagflation of the 1980s constituted a depression.

Perhaps the best way to think about economic depression is as a tsunami of change crashing into a decayed but still intact structure of outmoded economic and social institutions. The availability of government remedies for depression is doubtful. The New Deal did not end the depression of the 1930s; rather, only massive expenditure on war materiel restored national prosperity.

The Threat of Stakeholder Capitalism

A second arena where some economists have had an unfortunate impact concerns corporate governance. Chapter 7 gave brief attention to the idea that corporations have obligations to stakeholders in addition to their shareholders. This stakeholder idea is not simply idle management theory; rather, it has been receiving serious attention as a major initiative of public policy, both within the Clinton Administration and in the Congress. In this view, the general public as well as corporate employees are stakeholders, to some degree, but current policy proposals focus primarily on employees. A leading proponent of an activist approach to recognizing employees as stakeholders has been the first Clinton Administration's secretary of labor, himself an economist.

Generally, the idea is to enact legislation by which government can force companies to limit worker layoffs. In other words, corporations would be subject to substantial constraints on how much and how rapidly they could downsize or otherwise restructure. It is, of course, mostly a reflexive political reaction to the widespread corporate lay-offs that have been characteristic of the 1990s. One senses, too, an undercurrent of opprobrium attaching to the corporate sector as a consequence of mounting concerns with corporate governance and management accountability. Meanwhile, government intervention seems fatuous, considering that the public sector is itself engaged in substantial efforts to downsize.

One approach was a bill introduced in the 104th Congress that would designate some corporations as "most favored" on the basis of meeting certain as yet undefined training and compensation stan-dards. This group would be eligible for special tax and other benefits. Of course, from looking abroad, positive incentives of this sort are not the only approach. A further step could be statutory prohibitions.

As an example of the prohibatory model, German law requires worker representation on the supervisory boards of the larger corpo-rations, while workers' councils can mount legal challenges to layoffs. In France, too, organized labor has substantially stymied efforts to in-crease efficiency and competitiveness. Indeed, one need only observe the high unemployment rates prevailing throughout most of Europe to conclude that those sorts of direct and indirect public policy inter-ference impede national prosperity.

The idea of tax credits and other favors to encourage corporate-sponsored worker training sounds appealing. It is nevertheless dubi-ous both because tax incentives and subsidies typically create inefficiencies on their own merits. To be sure, some worker training conveys benefits to workers that are portable. Employees themselves or society at large therefore might reasonably bear the corresponding costs. Yet, are deficiencies in the availability of worker training truly a problem, or is the real problem the resistance of some elements of so-ciety to seek the education and training that is already available? Moreover, is it just poorly trained or untrained employees that are commonly the victims of layoffs? Consider the large numbers of mid-dle- and senior-level managers and professionals who have been riffed. Financial services and government consulting provide exam-ples of layoffs simply because the jobs evaporated.

In many cases, worker protection against layoffs would be counter-productive. The alternatives to layoffs might be either bankruptcy or government bailout. In the one case, employees lose their jobs any-way. Bailouts, on the other hand, typically do not facilitate adjust-ments to new market conditions; rather, they are more likely to put corporations on the welfare dole indefinitely. Inducements to undertake worker training similarly are unlikely to be effective when corporations are otherwise under financial stress.

None of the foregoing is to suggest that U.S. labor markets function especially well. Information flows on employment opportunities are poor or worse. Many, and perhaps most, employers tend to give recruitment and other human resources functions short shrift, viewing them as cost burdens rather than a form of investment. Age, race, and gender discrimination remain commonplace, in part because they are difficult to demonstrate.

Consumer protection and the public interest at large are traditional public policy concerns quite apart from any stakeholder theories. One such concern is with externalities—primarily costs of production that, absent government intervention, are passed on to society at large rather than being borne by producers. Environmental issues fall into this category. Another concern is that consumers be properly informed about product and service offerings, particularly to the extent they are potentially harmful. Much murkier are concerns with protections that prohibit consumers from purchasing harmful items (narcotics, for example) and require them to purchase protective ones (seat belts, for example). These topics have some association with relationship concepts insofar as corporations causing public harm eventually tarnish their reputations and undermine their relationship capital.

Concerns with competition perhaps also belong in this discussion. Absent restrictions, businesses do occasionally have opportunities to collude with rivals or otherwise restrict competition so as to exploit their customers. These types of opportunities appear to be more likely to arise in a traditional, stable industrial context than in a rapidly changing relationship economy. As suggested earlier, governments are usually responsible for sustained anticompetitiveness, typically as a result of some past policy concern that has lost whatever relevance it might once have had. The main problem with the private sector is competitive failures caused by distorted information and decision making.

To summarize, the emergence of stakeholder capitalism theories adds nothing new to traditional principles of governance. Generally, attentiveness to different forms of relationship capital will address legitimate stakeholder claims. Indeed, this prospect applies broadly to many concerns with business ethics. Stakeholder theories represent a potential source of widespread mischief. A virtual certainty, for example, is that labor markets in the United States will adjust to new economic circumstances sooner and more fully than in countries embracing nonmarket principles.

Public Policies and Income Disparities

A wider debate among economists and others concerns the apparent growth in income disparities between upper-income and lower-income groups. Specifically, real incomes at the top levels seem to have grown much more rapidly than at the low end of the scale, where they may not have grown at all. The debate concerns the reasons for this pattern, on which there seem to be two schools of thought:

- Lower-income groups cannot improve their lot because foreign competition, using cheap labor, has deprived them of many employment opportunities.
- Lower-income groups have been the primary victims of displacement by new laborsaving technologies.

As often happens, the parties to this debate tend to overstate their own cases while disparaging opposing views with excessive zeal. Both views probably contain some validity, but neither adequately explains much of anything.

No resolution of the differences seems likely until the respective parties fully recognize the nature and extent of the revolutionary change that the economic system is undergoing. Economic change inevitably means displacement, perhaps faster at some times than at others. Consider how modern economies developed and where they are heading. Throughout much of history, natural resources—first, land, and much later, minerals—had a major role in determining national wealth. Real capital then accumulated in the forms of land improvements, livestock, and trade inventories, followed by transportation equipment. By the late nineteenth century, plant and equipment for manufacturing began to assume a position of dominance.

An important characteristic of national wealth, as Adam Smith viewed it, was that much of it was not readily transferable across national boundaries. Contrast that situation with today, when Third World countries can easily assemble and operate steel plants, textile mills, and other types of manufacturing facilities. Indeed, they can buy computers and provide data-processing services halfway across the world. Countries like India and Ireland, with education systems that otherwise significantly exceed the ability of their economies to use the resulting skills fully, now can sell many of those skills anywhere.

In the future, then, what will distinguish the national wealth and prosperity of one nation from another if most forms of physical capital can locate anywhere in the world? The obvious answer lies in the intangible forms of capital embedded in the national infrastructure, levels of education and training, and economic relationships. In other words, it lies in the ability to develop and manage new technologies.

Notice that high levels of education are a necessary but hardly a sufficient condition for a nation to become an economic power. The manner of organizing social and economic relationships, both nationally and within and among economic units, also is of critical importance. Developing the necessary attributes requires investment, which in turn requires strategies to be maximally effective. Consider that an absence of any national sense of strategic direction seems to be among the problems afflicting American education, which too often seems less effective the higher the outlays.

The idea that growing income disparities result from changing technologies begs the question: What is the alternative? The idea itself is reminiscent of the Luddites—organized groups of English laborers who, from 1812 to 1818, smashed manufacturing machinery to protest the phasing out of hand labor. Machinery, of course, created the Industrial Revolution, which in turn absorbed vast amounts of labor already displaced by revolutionary changes in agriculture. For the most part, worker displacement was a temporary phenomenon that would have been a good deal less temporary had it not been for the emergence of machine manufacturing. Much of the similarly displaced rural population of Ireland had no choice but to emigrate. Today, of course, much of the manufacturing sector is stagnating in any event, while new technologies are essential to creating employment in a relationship environment.

Some proponents of the technology displacement view disparage the foreign competition argument on the basis that international trade is a very small proportion of U.S. output. While factually correct, it is irrelevant. In an industrial-type economic environment, if international markets are competitive, that competition will force manufacturing toward those locations where production costs are lowest, enabling the lowest prices. If physical capital is mobile, those locations will tend to be where labor costs are lowest. To that extent, at least, the foreign competition argument has a point—the consequence must be to hold down the wages of marginal workers in higher-cost locations.

That view nevertheless overlooks the growing significance of intangible forms of capital, including economic relationships, even in manufacturing. A consequence is to reduce the transferability of much of the capital that is an essential component of the production-distribution process. This potential limitation applies not just to relationship capital but also to physical capital that is complementary to relationship capital in production and distribution.

Both views seem to support dubious policy proposals to encourage more worker training. At least some proponents of both apparently also favor tax policies that would more aggressively redistribute income from the top to bottom income groups. That, too, seems dubious to the extent that it would likely deter saving and investment. The likely result would be inconsistent with the view of both camps that the ultimate solution to such income disparities is to stimulate economic growth. Stimulating consumption while deterring investment is likely to be merely inflationary in the long run. That would upset the capital markets and be self-defeating.

Perhaps higher economic growth would favor those income groups that seem now to be disadvantaged. Indeed, a more robust economy would help to address many social and economic ills. As enticing as the idea of stimulating faster growth might seem, it remains to determine how to achieve it. More government spending and lower taxes are traditional economic stimuli. Nevertheless, they risk inflation and reduced competitiveness in foreign markets. More generally, these sorts of approaches tend to prolong and exacerbate inefficiencies in economic resource utilization. A much better approach, because it would be more enduring, more competitive, and less inflationary, would be to use existing productive resources more efficiently. Opportunities abound for achieving more efficiency. Primarily, they involve adopting more relevant and effective decision criteria and more intelligent and informed management of those resources.

Index